Presidential
Influence and the
Administrative
State

Presidential Influence and the Administrative State

Richard W. Waterman

The University of Tennessee Press
Knoxville

The paper in this book meets the minimum requirements of the
American National Standard for Permanence of Paper for Printed
Library Materials. ⊚   The binding materials have been chosen
for strength and durability.

Library of Congress Cataloging-in-Publication Data

Waterman, Richard W.
  Presidential influence and the administrative state.

  Bibliography: p.
  Includes index.
    1. Presidents—United States. 2. Administrative
agencies—United States. 3. Bureaucracy—United States.
I. Title.
JK518.W384 1989   353.03′23   88–33960
ISBN 0–87049–609–3 (cloth: alk. paper)
ISBN 0–87049–626–3 (pbk.: alk. paper)

*This book is dedicated
to my mother
and to the
memory of my father
and my brother*

Contents

Acknowledgments

This book would not have been possible had it not been for the hard work of a number of talented people. First and foremost among these is Richard Barke. He read the entire manuscript on a number of occasions and provided me with many useful comments. A number of other people were also kind enough to read the entire manuscript and to provide incisive comments. They include James Stimson, Bruce Oppenheimer, and Harrell Rogers. Others also made contributions. James Anderson first got me interested in the subject of trucking deregulation. He and Alan Stone both read earlier versions of chapter 4. Joseph Stewart, David Hedge, Robert Duval, Susan Hunter, Manny Avalos, and B. Dan Wood also offered encouragement when I needed it most.

To the University of Tennessee Press I am particularly grateful for the support I received from Cynthia Maude-Gembler. Her encouragement kept my spirits up when I really needed it. I would also like to thank the reviewers, whose comments helped me to better focus the manuscript: Peri Arnold and Michael Fitzgerald. Finally, Bettie McDavid Mason copyedited the entire manuscript and made a number of changes that will inevitably convince others that I am a better writer than I really am.

I would also like to thank a number of people at the Interstate Commerce Commission, the Environmental Protection Agency, the Nuclear Regulatory Commission, and the Federal Election Commission who were nice enough to allow me to interview them or who provided me with information about their agencies.

Finally, I would like to thank a number of friends who were kind enough to listen to my many rambling comments on the book without telling me that they were bored. These include Michael Spikes, David Romero, Lisa Auerbach, John Bretting, Bruce Doyle, Gail Doyle, and Beverly Elliott. I would also like to thank my family for encouraging me and always standing by me.

Presidential
Influence and the
Administrative
State

Introduction

Presidential scholars agree that presidents must bargain and compromise with the legislative branch of government in order to increase their influence on Capitol Hill,[1] for constitutionally, the president and Congress share power, and neither branch of government (Executive or Legislative) is predominant. There is no such scholarly consensus regarding the question of how presidents can best increase their influence over the administrative state. Here two views prevail. One view is that a president is best served by a non-politicized bureaucracy because it provides the Chief Executive with neutral information about a wide range of policy alternatives. This is the view of the bureaucracy as the purveyor of "neutral competence."[2] An alternative view is that presidents should politicize the bureaucracy in order to increase their influence over it.[3] Only by politicizing the bureaucracy can presidents hope to influence administrative behavior and thus promote their policy objectives. The goal then is not "neutral competence," but rather "responsive competence."[4] To gain greater control, presidents must rely on a variety of techniques — such as their powers of appointment, removal, and reorganization as well as their budgetary authority — to encourage bureaucratic compliance with administration goals. Richard Nathan has characterized this approach as the "administrative presidency strategy."[5]

Both of these approaches to presidential-administrative relations have limitations. The view of the bureaucracy as the purveyor of neutral competence reflects the doctrine of the politics-administration dichotomy which states that politics and administration should be separated. This view was soundly rejected in the 1940s by public administrators who argued that it ignored the inherently political nature of the bureaucratic process.[6] The idea that the bureaucracy is or should be neutral in presidential-administrative relations is susceptible to criticism on the same grounds.

The administrative presidency strategy, in contrast, rightly acknowledges that politics plays a central role in presidential-administrative relations. If presidents are to achieve their goals, they must have greater control over the bureaucracy, and this involves politics (whether bargaining or coercion). But, by relying on a confrontational approach to policy development, this strategy underestimates the risks that are associated with presidential attempts to centralize greater control over the administrative state. These risks emanate from the fact that the president, though head of the executive branch, has neither the constitutional nor the statutory authority to compel subordinates to comply with presidential orders. The various presidential techniques for centralizing control over the bureaucracy (such as the presidential powers of appointment, reorganization, and the budget) are shared with Congress or limited by statute (such as the president's removal authority). As a result, presidential attempts to coerce bureaucratic compliance can involve the president in protracted struggles with Congress. Such attempts can also provoke bureaucratic opposition in the form of resistance to presidential initiatives and leaks to interest groups, the press, or congressional committees as well as possibly involving the president in protracted court challenges, which can potentially reduce presidential influence.

If both strategies have serious limitations, then what is the alternative? It will be the argument of this book that presidents must seek to persuade key elements within their own executive branch that the policies they advocate should be adopted and implemented. In much the same manner as a president must bargain and compromise with Congress, a president should attempt to build support within the executive branch for that particular administration's policies. In so doing, presidents can still usefully employ some of the techniques of the administrative presidency strategy, especially the president's appointment power.

Presidential Leadership and Presidential Power

Although this book is primarily concerned with an analysis of presidential-administrative relations, it also addresses the question of whether the presidency has grown too powerful. Have presidents exceeded their authority in employing the various techniques of the administrative presidency strategy? Should presidential power and influence be constrained? To answer these questions it will first be necessary to examine how perceptions of the presidency have changed over the past fifty years. The administrative presidency strategy has not developed in isolation. Rather, it is part of a pattern that includes the evolution of the presidency and the changing role of public expectations.

Over the last half-century, public expectations regarding the proper role of the presidency in our constitutional system have been radically altered. After a period in which the president was more of an observer than an active participant, the presidency has become the fulcrum of American politics. The evolution of the presidency occurred because Congress was unable to adequately perform the many political and management tasks that were demanded of an emerging international power. Out of the late nineteenth-century period of congressional domination, the presidency evolved to fill the emerging void in American politics.[7]

Although Theodore Roosevelt and Woodrow Wilson opened the door for the powerful twentieth-century presidency, Franklin Roosevelt made the greatest contribution to the growth of presidential power. More than any other president since Abraham Lincoln, Roosevelt provided a clear rationale for the extension of presidential power. Roosevelt's leadership style transformed the office, making it impossible for any of his successors to avoid the new responsibilities and demands of the modern presidency.

Prior to Franklin Roosevelt's presidency, strong, decisive presidents were the exception. After Roosevelt, presidents exerted considerably more influence over the policy process, primarily because Roosevelt had altered public expectations regarding the role of the federal government. With the passing of the days in which the government and the president were perceived by the public more as bystanders than participants, the federal government from the 1930s onward was expected to deal with the myriad problems of the economy, provide security for the elderly, price supports for farmers, jobs for the unemployed, and security for the nation. Each of Roosevelt's successors—even Dwight Eisenhower, who preferred that government play a less active role—was forced to take on greater federal responsibilities.

In addition to altering public expectations, Roosevelt, with the acquiescence of Congress, also changed the institutional form of the executive branch. Not only was the bureaucracy greatly expanded during his twelve-plus years in office, but, on the recommendation of the Brownlow Committee's Report (which expressed Roosevelt's personal viewpoint), the institutional framework of the modern presidency was established.[8] The Executive Office of the President (EOP) was created as an institutional arm of the president, providing the Chief Executive with the much needed "help" that the Brownlow Report had identified. This proved to be but a first step. Over the next half-century, such major positions as the Chief of Staff and the President's Adviser for National Security Affairs would be created within the White House. The Council of Economic Advisers, the National Security Council, the Congressional Liaison Office, the Council on Environmental Quality, and others units would also be established in the White House. Some of these, like the National Security Council and the Council of Economic Advisors, were initially designed by Congress to limit presidential power.[9] Whatever the original intent, however, these new institutions quickly provided presidents from Roosevelt on with a greater ability to influence policy formulation. The development of the administrative presidency strategy during the Nixon administration was but another link added to this constantly growing chain.

Besides altering public expectations regarding the proper role of the president and guiding the expansion of the institutional presidency, the administration of Franklin Roosevelt also had a major impact on the perceptions of presidential scholars. Roosevelt essentially redefined consideration of the role of the president in the scholarly literature from that of a passive player to that of a strong, active participant. Clinton Rossiter wrote of the "veneration, if not exactly reverence, for the authority and dignity of the Presidency."[10] Herman Finer added that "the presidential office is no trifle, light as air, no bauble; it belongs rightfully to the offspring of a titan and Minerva husbanded by Mars."[11] James MacGregor Burns wrote that the "stronger we make the Presidency, the more we strengthen democratic procedures."[12]

Other scholars also promoted the notion of a more powerful presidency. Probably the most influential of these was Richard Neustadt, who wrote that expectations about the role of the president had changed: "Everybody now expects the man inside the White House to do something about everything."[13] In addition to focusing the attention of scholars on the need for a stronger and more effective presidency, Neustadt offered a series of recommendations regarding how presidents could best increase their influence and power to deal with altered expectations. Yet, as the power of the presidency expanded, it was virtually inevitable that critics would surface who would argue that the presidency had grown too powerful. The presidencies of Lyndon Johnson and Richard Nixon provided the justification for this view.

Limiting Presidential Power

In his text on the presidency, Thomas Cronin raised a legitimate concern about the role of increasing expectations.

> We ask our presidents to raise hopes, to educate, to inspire. But too much inspiration will invariably lead to dashed hopes, disillusionment, and cynicism.[14]

As the demands on the presidency proliferated from the 1930s on, presidents were required to do more in order to insure reelection. Presidents who could not accomplish the many tasks that the public demanded were at a severe disadvantage. Thus, there was increasing pressure to further expand presidential influence over the various political institutions in and out of government. At the same time that public demands on the presidency were expanding, fundamental changes were occurring in the other institutions of government. By the 1970s a weakened leadership in Congress was no longer able to deliver congressional votes, as it had been able to do during the time of Franklin Roosevelt. The political parties were weaker, the bureaucracy had expanded, and the press was much more willing to openly defy the will of the president and his top advisers. As Charles Walcott and Karen M. Hult have argued, this political environment forced presidents to establish new "governance mechanisms" in an attempt to limit political certainty.[15]

The concomitant phenomena of ever-expanding public demands

and an increasingly uncertain political environment led presidents to adopt new and often risky strategies for advancing presidential leadership. Elsewhere I have argued that leadership strategies, such as the centralization of greater authority in the White House, have offered presidents expanded influence over the policy process by increasing the level of responsiveness to their programs.[16] At the same time, however, these strategies have also increased the risk that presidents will fail in their policy pursuits if they remove the political insulation that can protect them from policy fiascoes. Yet, due to the increasing level of public demands, presidents have opted to employ these new strategies despite the political risks. Given this relationship between an increasingly uncertain political environment and the development of risky new strategies for the promotion of presidential influence, it was inevitable that some president would eventually be accused of going too far in the pursuit of presidential power. Although there had been no scarcity of criticism of Franklin Roosevelt and Harry Truman, the presidencies of Lyndon Johnson and Richard Nixon became virtual lighting rods for opponents of expanding presidential power.

Both Johnson and Nixon were strong presidents. Both acted in a manner which, at least temporarily, strengthened the role of the presidency. Each had major accomplishments. Johnson had the many legislative achievements of the Great Society. Nixon had a number of foreign policy successes, including the dramatic diplomatic opening with China and improved relations with the Soviet Union. Yet both men were also perceived as having exceeded their constitutional authority. Johnson's Vietnam War policies in particular created the impression that the presidency had grown too powerful and even too arrogant. Nixon's impoundment of appropriated funds, his reliance on an increasingly powerful White House staff, and the various related Watergate crimes furthered this impression. In response to these abuses, the public and the press argued that the power of the presidency had to be restrained: Congress would have to reassert its constitutional role.

Likewise, in the scholarly literature, a number of studies were highly critical of the growing power of the presidency. In his analysis of the "imperial presidency," Arthur Schlesinger, Jr., argued that "the pivotal institution of the American government, the Presidency, has got out of control and badly needs new definition and restraint."[17] Other scholars criticized the rapid proliferation of the White House

Staff as symptomatic of the ills of the presidency.[18] George Reedy, formerly Lyndon Johnson's press secretary, argued that presidents had grown more and more out of touch with reality; Reedy's book was appropriately and somewhat apocalyptically entitled *The Twilight of the Presidency*.[19] Charles M. Hardin also expressed the crisis environment that the presidency faced:

> In 1973 America was gripped by its gravest political crisis since the Civil War. The president all too often was out of control. . . . The heritage of Washington, Jefferson, and Lincoln—so long miraculously intact—was crumbling to dust.[20]

After the drum roll of support for a strong presidency, the literature suddenly reflected a new theme: there were too many demands on the presidency. How could any person handle the difficult job of being president? These studies reflected that public expectations regarding the job of the president had simply become too demanding. Stephen Hess, a former aide to Presidents Eisenhower and Nixon, recommened that the burden on the presidency should be reduced.[21] I. M. Destler advanced a similar argument with regard to issues of national security, stating that public concerns should reflect the reality of presidential leadership rather than the illusion of presidential government.[22] Fred Greenstein, using the Eisenhower presidency as a model, argued that presidents should attempt to lower public expectations about the legitimate role of the presidency by concentrating on only a few selected issues.[23] Milton Eisenhower recommended that two additional vice-presidents were needed to help manage the affairs of government.[24] Bruce Buchanan described an institution of government which, by its very nature, promotes deceptive behavior that can ultimately threaten the foundations of democracy.[25] The questions were no longer whether there should be a strong presidency, but rather whether the presidency in its current form could ever succeed.

In this atmosphere of doubt and despair, Richard Neustadt in 1980 defended the strong presidency model in the second edition of *Presidential Power*.[26] Neustadt argued that his intent in the first edition was not to imply that presidents should have unlimited power; rather, presidents should use their power and influence wisely so as to achieve their basic goals and objectives. Johnson and Nixon had abused their power in such a fashion that they eventually reduced their influence over the policy process. Therefore, the Johnson and Nixon presidencies were not evidence condemning the strong presidency model but were instead a demonstration of how presidents can abuse and eventually expend their limited resources.

Further support for the concept of a strong presidency resulted from the election of Ronald Reagan. After two generally weak presidencies, the public and scholars once again focused their attention on the need for a stronger Chief Executive. Reagan affirmed that a strong presidency was possible, although it too had its failures, in particular the Iran-Contra debacle.

As a result of the Reagan presidency, concern for constraining the role of the president once again took a back seat to a concern for how presidents can best increase their influence over the policy process. Although somewhat more restrained than the post–Franklin Roosevelt presidential literature, the focus was once again upon what presidents can do to manage the federal government more effectively.

The Administrative Presidency and Presidential Leadership

How does the administrative presidency strategy fit into this brief history of the evolution of the modern presidency? First, like the establishment of the Executive Office of the President and other developments in the expansion of the institutional presidency, the administrative presidency strategy was designed to increase presidential influence so as to satisfy increasing public demands. As demands on the presidency escalated, it became necessary for presidents to have a responsive bureaucracy. Accordingly, the administrative presidency strategy emphasized "responsive competence" rather than "neutral competence." The failure of many of Lyndon Johnson's Great Society programs demonstrated the important role that bureaucratic responsiveness plays in the implementation of presidential policies.[27] Presidents who could not count on the bureaucracy as a political ally could not guarantee that their policies and programs would be properly implemented.

Second, the administrative presidency strategy was a response to the massive proliferation of the bureaucratic state. During the presidency of Franklin Roosevelt and again during the presidencies of Johnson and Nixon, the bureaucracy had expanded dramatically.

Nixon's strategy was a reaction to this growth and to continuing presidential skepticism about the neutrality of the bureaucratic state. Such skepticism had been growing during the presidencies of John Kennedy and Lyndon Johnson.[28] Under Richard Nixon it would come to complete fruition. The administrative presidency strategy was established to deal with the fact that the expanding bureaucracy often did not support the president's programs and in some cases actively opposed presidential initiatives.

Third, the evolution of the administrative presidency came at a time in which the abuse of presidential power was of greater public and scholarly concern than the promotion of presidential influence. The title of Richard Nathan's 1975 book which introduced the strategy, *The Plot That Failed*, reflected the general mood of the period: the presidency had grown too powerful.[29] In content, however, the book generally endorsed Nixon's major innovations in presidential-administrative relations. The exception was Nathan's criticism of the Nixon administration's highly centralized White House staff system; centralization, Nathan argued, did not serve the needs of the president and should be avoided.

In 1983, in the new political environment of the Reagan presidency, Nathan published *The Administrative Presidency*. In the preface, Nathan distinguished the new book from the old.

> This new volume is different from the earlier book. . . . It takes a much stronger position, arguing that elected chief executives . . . and their appointees should play a larger role in administrative processes.[30]

Nathan's second analysis, in both title and substance, was much more reflective of the strong presidency model. Nathan argued that presidents need to increase their influence over the bureaucracy in order to have greater control over the policy process. This argument was not without foundation. As Richard F. Fenno, Jr., argued, the president's cabinet has not always, or even often, been responsive to presidential demands.[31] Because cabinet secretaries have their own constituencies, both in Congress and among the clientele they serve, it is often difficult for them to serve the needs of the president. In a political environment in which the demands on the presidency were limited, this was not a major problem. When the public began to demand that presidents solve all of the country's problems—from the economy and poverty to the environment and worker safety—a lack of bureaucratic responsiveness became a serious threat to presidential leadership. Presidents simply had to be able to count on their subordinates. Presidents who could not would not be able to achieve their major objectives.

It was in this environment that the Nixon administration developed the administrative presidency strategy. The strategy evolved over Nixon's first term in office. His dissatisfaction with the traditional cabinet style of government, and his inability to work with a Democratic Congress, forced Nixon to search for alternatives that would maximize the probability that his policies would be adopted. The administrative presidency strategy filled this description. It placed a heavy emphasis on loyalty to the president, rather than loyalty to Congress or interest groups. Subordinates served the president and were therefore expected to be responsive to the president's needs, not the needs of those outside the administration.

The administrative presidency strategy was designed as a means of expanding presidential leadership. Although developed by Nixon, the strategy was never fully implemented during his presidency; after only a few months in operation, it was abandoned as Nixon became more concerned with survival in office than with influencing policy. Variations on the strategy, however, have been adopted since Nixon's departure from office. Jimmy Carter successfully employed a limited variation in such agencies as the Interstate Commerce Commission and the Civil Aeronautics Board. Ronald Reagan then adopted the strategy on a much broader scale. Examining the experiences of the Nixon, Carter, and Reagan presidencies for evidence of the success of the administrative presidency strategy in promoting presidential influence, will be the task of this book.

The Focus of this Book

In reappraising the administrative presidency strategy, my intent is not to refute Nathan's approach to the expansion of presidential influence, but rather to refine it. Nathan recommends, for example, that the Chief Executive should appoint individuals who will be loyal to the president and the president's programs. Under which circumstances has this approach resulted in increased presidential influence? On the other hand, when has it failed to serve the interests of the president? Then, under which circumstances should future presidents consider adopting the appointment strategy? These are the types of questions that will concern me here.

To evaluate the effectiveness of the administrative presidency strategy I will examine four federal agencies under three presidents: the Nixon administration and the Department of Housing and Urban Development (HUD), the Carter administration and the Interstate Commerce Commission (ICC), the Reagan administration and the Environmental Protection Agency (EPA), and the Reagan administration and the Nuclear Regulatory Commission (NRC). These case studies will examine the risks that the administrative presidency strategy entails, as well as the political benefits of the approach.

I have chosen the four case studies for different reasons. Those on Nixon and HUD and Reagan and EPA were selected because Nathan refers to them specifically in his analysis of the administrative presidency strategy; in fact, he characterizes the case of the EPA as an example "where Reagan appointees successfully took on the bureaucracy to pursue the administration's policy goals."[32] I find, instead, that the Reagan strategy actually reduced long-term presidential influence in the area of environmental policy.

I selected the case of the Carter administration and the Interstate Commerce Commission for two reasons. First, the case study reveals the inaccuracy of Nathan's claim that Carter did not use an administrative approach in advancing the policy of deregulation.[33] Indeed, the administrative approach was the centerpiece of the Carter administration's strategy to promote the deregulation of both the airline and the trucking industries. Second, the case of the Carter administration and the ICC demonstrates that a selective use of the techniques of the administrative presidency strategy—particularly the employment of the president's appointment power—can be an effective means of promoting presidential objectives.

The final case study on Reagan and the NRC was selected because it represents the limitations of the administrative presidency strategy in promoting presidential objectives. In this case, the policy change desired was neither politically nor economically feasible. The administrative strategy alone could not change this political reality.

Before beginning the analysis, I offer two important caveats. One is that Richard Nathan's most vehement defense of the strategy and the Reagan administration's management style came in 1983, when Ronald Reagan had been in the White House for only two years. Subsequent events, such as the experiences of Anne Burford and her subordinates at the EPA and the Iran-Contra scandal, might have induced Nathan to come to somewhat different conclusions. His most recent work on the subject, however, suggests that even after the Burford scandal at the EPA, he is still a strong supporter of the concept:

> It is my view that Reagan's administrative strategy could not have avoided some of these kinds of incidents. However, in the larger context, the benefits of pushing Reagan's ideas into the bureaucracy through this administrative appointment process outweigh the costs in terms of the tempests they cause.[34]

My response is the counter-argument that the risks of the administrative presidency strategy have often outweighed the benefits.

The other caveat is that the case studies in this book are not meant to suggest that Democratic presidents succeed while Republicans fail or that Jimmy Carter was brilliant in his management of the bureaucracy while Richard Nixon and Ronald Reagan were inept. Many studies of Carter's bureaucratic experiences have concluded that his administration was ineffective in dealing with the bureaucracy.[35] That this apparently was the case can be seen from my examination of some of the limitations of Carter's management style in the chapters on the Environmental Protection Agency and the Nuclear Regulatory Commission. In the concluding chapter I provide an explanation as to why the Carter administration encountered so many problems in its attempts to manage the bureaucracy.

Reagan's management style was successful in a number of cases. The Reagan administration succeeded in altering the goals of such agencies as the Office of Surface Mining[36] and the Occupational Safety and Health Administration.[37] Elizabeth Sanders has even stated that "when the dust has settled, it is likely that Reagan will have had more influence on the bureaucratic state than any other president except Roosevelt."[38] This book does not argue that the administrative presidency strategy promotes failure. Rather, my intent is to adumbrate the benefits of the administrative presidency strategy, while also demonstrating that the strategy entails significant political risks which can result in reduced presidential influence.

In advancing the thesis that the administrative presidency strategy is not a panacea, am I also arguing in favor of a more constrained presidency, in the spirit of the post-Watergate literature? The answer is an unequivocal *no*! Like Nathan, I endorse the strong presidency model. My argument here is that presidents faced with increasing demands must have the power and authority to successfully influence the bureaucracy. My disagreement with Nathan is not one of ends, but rather one of means. Where Nathan proposes a more confrontational approach, the analysis in this book supports a more cooperative approach.

Chapter 1

Justifications for Presidential Influence

As the bureaucratic state has evolved and expanded, presidents have attempted to extend their influence over it,[1] justifying this expanded influence on several constitutional grounds. The Constitution, however, is sufficiently vague on the matter of the president's control over the executive branch that each justification for presidential influence is open to debate and interpretation. Rather than presenting a clear case for presidential influence over the administrative state, the best that has been offered to date has been a series of justifications. What emerges is the disposition that presidents share responsibility for managing the executive branch with the Congress. As with executive-legislative relations, the politics of presidential-administrative relations is the politics of shared power.

This chapter will examine the various justifications for presidential influence over the administrative state. It will also present a critique of the two major models to be analyzed throughout this book: Nathan's administrative presidency strategy and a variation of Neustadt's approach to bargaining and compromise.

Justifying Presidential Influence

One manner in which presidents have attempted to justify their influence over the executive branch has been to advance the argument that under the Constitution the president is the only official, other than the vice-president, who is elected by a national constituency. Thus, as Nelson Polsby has stated, "political choice by the executive branch is legitimized only insofar as it can be plausibly seen to have radiated down from a presidential choice or preference."[2] According to this view the president's national constituency sets the president apart from all other governmental officials and imbues the president with a special authority other executive branch officials lack. For example, unelected representatives, such as career civil servants, are legitimized only to the extent that they follow the will and intent of the president. To do otherwise would be to violate the precepts of democracy.

The present-day bureaucracy does not reflect such a strict hierarchical relationship. Presidents do not possess a special legitimacy that compels their subordinates to obey them, nor do we expect such a relationship to exist. The independent regulatory commissions are an example of executive branch officials whose legitimacy does not radiate down from a presidential choice or preference. Had Congress intended such a relationship to exist, it would not have sought to make the regulatory commissions largely independent from presidential influence.

An alternative view to presidential electoral legitimacy is the concept that legitimacy is conferred continuously through both elections and a constant interaction between a variety of decision-makers. According to this view, legitimacy is dispersed among elected, appointed, and career officials.[3] This dynamic process suggests that Congress, the courts, and the president's executive branch subordinates also play a legitimate role in the decision-making process. It is this view which better reflects the reality of Washington politics. The president is but one of many players in the administrative process, although assuredly the most important.

Another means by which presidents have justified their influence over the bureaucracy is by citing the vesting clause of the Constitution (Article II, Section 1), which declares that "the executive Power shall be vested in a President of the United States of America." Most presidents have interpreted this clause as a confirmation of their legitimate authority over the administrative state. Andrew Jackson, for example, cited the vesting clause in defending his right to fire his Secretary of the Treasury William J. Duane and to remove funds from the Second Bank of the United States.[4]

Some constitutional scholars have disagreed with this interpretation. Edward Corwin concluded that the vesting clause is nothing more than an introduction to Article II of the Constitution.[5] According to this view, the Founding Fathers did not envision anything approaching the present-day bureaucratic state and therefore did not intend for this clause to confer any legitimate presidential authority over the bureaucracy. Support for this contention can be found in the fact that initially Congress statutorily defined the structure of the executive branch. It also itemized every single office in the departments and agencies while simultaneously setting the salary of every employee.[6]

Despite Congress's initial control over the bureaucracy, the vesting clause has been widely translated as a constitutional justification for extending presidential influence over the bureaucracy. James Madison, in defending the president's right to remove officials from the executive branch without senatorial approval, stated:

> The constitution affirms, that the executive power shall be vested in the President. Are there exceptions to this proposition? Yes, there are. The constitution says that in appointing to office, the Senate shall be associated with the President unless in the case of inferior officers, when the law shall otherwise direct. Have we a right to extend this exception? I believe not. If the constitution has invested all executive power in the President, I venture to assert that the Legislature has no right to diminish or modify his executive authority.[7]

Madison's basic reasoning was that if the legislature infringed on the powers vested in the executive branch, then the doctrine of the separation of powers would be violated. The executive power would be unwisely commingled with that of the legislature, to the detriment of both branches of government.

The vesting clause does provide presidents with a strong justification for the exercise of their influence over the administrative state. It does not, however, give them free reign over the executive branch. Although the president is acknowledged to be the head of the executive branch, the vesting clause does not confer complete authority on the Chief Executive. The Congress too has significant influence over bureaucratic affairs — influence that I shall delineate shortly.

Other clauses of the Constitution have also been cited as justifications for presidential influence. Article II, Section 3 of the Constitution states that the president "shall take care that the laws be faithfully executed." This clause has been interpreted as meaning that presidents must have direct influence over the administrative state, since it is the bureaucracy which administers the laws. But, as Louis

Fisher points out, to "faithfully execute" does not mean the same thing as to carry out the law. He explains that, for example, "if a statute creates an independent officer and makes the officer's judgment final and conclusive, and the officer faithfully executes the assigned statutory duty, the President's responsibility is at an end."[8] In this case, executive authority is delegated to a presidential subordinate and the president himself has no direct influence. According to this interpretation, the "take care" clause should not be considered as an unlimited grant of presidential authority regarding the supervision of the bureaucratic state.

Beyond these broad constitutional justifications for presidential influence, the Constitution does not specifically grant the president the direct means for controlling the bureaucracy. In fact, the word *bureaucracy* is never mentioned in the Constitution.[9] The president's constitutionally enumerated authority is limited. The Constitution does not grant the president the authority to submit a budget to the Congress nor to reorganize executive branch agencies. The Constitution says nothing about the president's right to remove officials from office. Even regarding appointments the president is given only the authority to nominate federal officers and to seek out the opinions of his appointed agents "in writing . . . upon any subject relating to the duties of their respective offices."

Since the Constitution does not specifically deal with the subject of the administrative state, everything regarding presidential influence over it must be implied from the few passages that relate to the subject. Accordingly, there has been great uncertainty regarding the president's true rights, responsibilities, and power. With regard to what can be inferred from the Constitution, Peri E. Arnold has written:

> The formal mandate of agencies, their organization, their funding and subsequent discretion in spending, the specification of the number of positions they might fill, the qualifications attached to those positions, and the precise definition of the actual jurisdiction of that agency all rest upon congressional will. If anything, it is Congress and not the presidency that is the institution intended by the Constitution to exert predominant responsibility over administration.[10]

Congress has extensive influence over the bureaucracy through its ability to appropriate funds. Congress can influence the behavior of executive branch agencies by reducing their level of funding or merely by threatening to do so. R. Douglas Arnold's analysis of congressional-bureaucratic relations demonstrated that agencies often adapt their programs to the needs of key congressmen and committees so as to ensure continuous funding.[11] Such activity makes executive branch agencies more responsive to Congress and less alert to presidential cues.

Congress draws legitimate authority over the bureaucracy from several sections of the Constitution. Article I, Section 8 grants Congress the power "to regulate commerce with foreign Nations, and among the several States." This allows Congress to play a vital role in the management of the economy and the control of business practices. Although Congress has invested much of this authority in executive branch agencies, such as the independent regulatory commissions, and the Federal Reserve Board, Congress has not detached itself from the regulatory process. It still can play an active role in regulatory oversight. It also has the power to enact legislation which can force executive branch agencies to comply with the will of Congress.

Congress's greatest grant of authority over the bureaucracy comes from the implied powers of the "necessary and proper" clause of the Constitution. This is particularly true with regard to the structure of the executive branch, for Congress has the authority to "create, alter, or abolish departments, agencies, commissions, and bureaus within the executive branch and to determine the powers of each."[12] Congress can delegate specific or broad grants of authority. It can also specify the functions of the officers of the agency. In other words, Congress has tremendous potential to influence the activity of the executive branch agencies that it creates.

For much of the nineteenth century, Congress did indeed exert considerable influence over the then diminutive administrative state. As the bureaucracy evolved and expanded, however, it became obvious to most congressional observers that the legislative branch lacked the discipline to adequately oversee the administrative state.[13] As a result, Congress itself began to delegate authority over the administrative state to the president.

The enactment of the Budget and Accounting Act of 1921 was the first substantial delegation of legislative authority to the executive. This act gave the president the responsibility for submitting a budget to Congress. Although this may not have seemed like a tremendous grant of authority at the time, it has profoundly increased the president's ability to set the agenda and thus expand the president's influence over the administrative state. Throughout the decades following the passage of the Budget and Accounting Act, much of the justification for presidential influence over the bureaucracy was derived directly from legislation. Since Congress could not exert the internal discipline necessary to administer the bureaucracy, a strong executive was seen as a necessity. The logic for this delegation of authority from the legislative to the executive branch was first spelled out by Alexander Hamilton in Federalist #70:

> A feeble executive implies a feeble execution of the government. A feeble execution of the government is but another phrase for a bad execution: And a government ill executed, whatever it may be in theory, must be in practice a bad government.

Through a series of legislative actions, Congress delegated greater authority to the president over administrative affairs. Along with the delegation of budgetary authority, Congress created the Executive Office of the President and allowed presidents to submit reorganization plans to Congress. Together, these and other reforms greatly increased the president's ability to influence bureaucratic behavior.

In the 1970s this trend was reversed somewhat. After the terms of Lyndon Johnson and Richard Nixon, critics began to argue that the presidency had grown too powerful. Rather than calling for greater presidential control over the bureaucracy, these critics turned their attention to the need for Congress to reassert its influence over the executive branch.[14] Congress reacted by enacting the War Powers Act of 1973 and the Budget and Impoundment Act of 1974. These acts were designed to constrain presidential influence and to reassert Congress's constitutional role in the areas of budgeting and national defense, although in the long run they may have exactly the opposite effect. For example, the War Powers Act legitimized for the first time the president's right to commit troops. Likewise, the Budget and Impoundment Act legitimized the president's right to withhold appropriated funds, within certain strictly delineated boundaries. These were powers the presidency had not officially possessed before.

Despite the passage of these acts, the presidency today has substantial influence over the administrative state. Much of this influence, however, was delegated by Congress to the president and thus can be removed. Thus Congress can and has retained a legitimate role in the oversight of the bureaucracy, although whether Congress actually does perform an active role in oversight is a matter of some considerable debate.[15] Still, Congress does retain the ability to oversee presidential-administrative relations, and the very fact that it can perform this function means that presidential influence over the bureaucracy is not unlimited.

The Chief Executive?

Since the Constitution does not unambiguously delegate authority to the president to manage the administrative state, how can presidents control the bureaucracy? Are presidents Chief Executives in name only or do they have palpable means at their disposal to extend their influence over the bureaucracy? For many years experts on both the presidency and the bureaucracy argued that presidents had limited influence over the administrative state. Rather than being its master, a president had to struggle constantly with an unruly beast.

In his classic book *The American Presidency*, Clinton Rossiter asserted that the most difficult task most presidents face is trying to sell their programs—not to Congress, but to the bureaucracy. This is the case even when an agency is headed by an official selected by the president.[16] Richard Fenno delineated a variety of reasons why presidents have been unable to use their cabinet members as an effective means of controlling the very executive branch departments these members head.[17] Louis W. Koenig stated that "even more resistant [than Congress] to the President's quest for dominion over the executive branch is the giant bureaucracy itself, with its layers of specialists, its massive paper work . . . , lumbering pace, [and] addiction to routine."[18] Similarly, Thomas Cronin wrote, "The federal bureaucracy . . . is one of the most visible checks on a president."[19] Roger Noll went even farther, arguing that "although the President could exercise authority . . . there is little evidence that he or his administration makes much of an attempt to do so."[20] Bruce Yandle, Jeffrey Cohen, and Nathaniel Beck provided evidence that suggested that presidents have not been able to influence the policies of the Federal Trade Commission, the Interstate Commerce Commission, and the Federal Reserve Board.[21]

One reason why the president was seen as lacking influence over the administrative state was that the Chief Executive had in effect been removed from the policy loop. A number of scholars argued that administrative policy was determined by an iron triangle relationship that bound an administrative agency with a particular interest group and a limited number of congressional committees.[22] In this policy process, the president was on the outside looking in. Thus, when giving an order, the president had neither an institutional base of support at the bureaucratic level nor the support of the relevant interest groups and congressional committees. As a consequence, the president lacked real influence over the bureaucratic state.

The capture or iron triangle theory of bureaucratic relations has come under attack in recent years as such events as the passage of a series of deregulation bills and the creation of a number of social regulatory agencies, such as the Environmental Protection Agency, have exceeded the ability of the theory to explain political behavior.[23] The theory has failed to explain, for example, such developments as the administrative adoption by the Interstate Commerce Commission of motor carrier deregulation (see ch. 4). As a result, a more dynamic view of the bureaucracy has surfaced, one that includes the president as a more active participant in bureaucratic politics. Although iron triangle relationships can indeed limit presidential influence, these triangles are not necessarily made of iron nor are they able to endure permanently.

In recent years, a number of scholars have argued that despite the various factors constraining them, presidents have indeed been able to extend their influence and to affect the policies of such diverse agencies as the National Labor Relations Board, the Federal Trade Commission, the Securities and Exchange Commission, the Federal Communications Commission, the Environmental Protection Agency, and the Office of Surface Mining.[24]

Although presidents are indeed at a disadvantage in attempting to control the bureaucracy, they are not impotent. They do have various tools at their disposal which they can employ to increase their influence over administrative behavior (see ch. 2). Although they cannot use these techniques unilaterally, presidents since Franklin Delano Roosevelt have attempted to increase their influence over the bureaucracy.[25] As Thomas Cronin has stated, "The problem of how to control the bureaucracy has become a major preoccupation of presidents."[26] The reason is clear: presidents need the bureaucracy if they are to see their most coveted programs adopted and properly implemented. Only by having the bureaucracy as an ally can presidents hope to accomplish their policy goals. As public expectations of what presidents should be able to do have increased (e.g., presidents should be able to balance the budget and eradicate poverty), they have relied even more on the bureaucracy.[27] Presidents are at a clear policy disadvantage without some form of control over the bureaucracy.

Given this need, the question once again becomes how presidents can extend their influence over the bureaucracy. The most influential author with regard to this particular question has been Richard Nathan. It is to an analysis of his recommendations that I now turn.

The Administrative Presidency Strategy

Richard Nathan introduced the concept of the administrative presidency strategy, the main focus of which is the belief that presidents should actively use the various sources of authority at their disposal to gain greater control over the bureaucracy.[28]

The administrative presidency strategy was formulated during the presidency of Richard Nixon. Although the Watergate-related scandals forced the Nixon administration to abandon the strategy, Ronald Reagan adopted a variation of the approach when he assumed office in 1981. This variation consisted of five main "ingredients":[29]

1. The president should select cabinet secretaries who agree with the president's policy positions.

2. The president should select subcabinet officials who also share the president's views on policy.

3. The president should motivate cabinet and subcabinet officials to pay attention to agency operations and administrative processes.

4. The budget should be used as the central organizing framework for policymaking.

5. Presidents should avoid an over-reliance on a centralized White House staff clearance and control system.

The essential recommendation that Nathan offers is that presidents should appoint individuals who are loyal to them and their policy choices. According to Nathan, the presidential appointment process should be political:

> Under an administrative presidency strategy a political executive should be just what the name indicates—political and executive. The basic premise is that management tasks can and should be performed by partisans. This concept is not only appropriate, but necessary, to a functioning democracy in a large and technologically advanced nation such as the United States.[30]

Not only is the president advised to appoint partisans to cabinet level positions, Nathan also recommends that the president appoint them to the various subcabinet posts, including the regulatory agencies. By appointing partisans who support the president's policy choices, the president increases the probability that the appointees will diligently work for the president's program, while simultaneously reducing the likelihood that the appointees will be won over by opposing forces within the bureaucracy. In this manner presidential influence will be advanced.

Nathan also recommends that loyal appointees should try to cooperate with career bureaucrats in the formulation and development of administration policy.[31] This recommendation creates a conundrum in that loyal appointees are supposed to stay in step with the president as well as to cooperate with career civil servants. It is not explained how loyal appointees can perform both of these tasks at the same time. It would appear that the only time loyal appointees could manage to do both tasks simultaneously would be when career civil servants already agreed with the president's program. In all other cases, appointees would be drawn in different directions at the same time. Thus, if appointees are to remain loyal to the president, they would have to side with the president in policy disputes and not with the career bureaucracy.

Another major recommendation offered by Nathan is that presidents should make the budget the central framework for policymaking. In this regard Nathan states that "the role of the budget as a vehicle for policymaking and management in government is bound to be important as long as resources are scarce, and this is bound to be a long-term—even perpetual—condition."[32]

Nathan's strategy places a heavy emphasis on loyalty to the president and the employment of the budget as a device for advancing the president's policy objectives. Although the strategy may not by design recommend confrontation politics, this is often the result. Presidential appointees loyally promoting the president's objectives can come into sharp disagreement with subordinates who oppose these goals. In these cases, the potential for conflict is greatly increased. The removal by appointees of disloyal subordinates or the reorganization of agencies so as to diminish the influence of certain bureaucrats can also promote confrontation politics. Under such circumstances, one institution that disgruntled bureaucrats can turn to for redress is Congress.

Since Congress is an active partner in the budgetary process, using the budget as a political technique can run the risk of increasing congressional opposition to presidential programs, which can in turn lead to greater congressional supervision of presidential budgets and reduced presidential influence. Threats of budgetary reductions can also promote greater resistance to presidential initiatives at the bureaucratic level. Such resistance can take the form of leaks to congressional committees, interest groups, and/or the press. Thus, one of the principal risks of the administrative presidency strategy is that it can increase external opposition to presidential programs by promoting an environment of confrontation politics. The case of the Environmental Protection Agency (see ch. 5) is a clear example.

The Power of Persuasion

If Nathan's recommendations threaten to increase the risk that presidential influence will be diminished by involving the president in disputes with Congress, the courts, and the bureaucracy, what then is the alternative? According to Richard Neustadt:

> The power to persuade is the power to bargain. Status and authority yield bargaining advantages. But in a government of "separated institutions sharing powers," they yield to all sides. Command has limited utility; persuasion becomes give-and-take.[33]

The above quotation would be readily confirmed if the topic of discussion were presidential-congressional relations, but in the realm of presidential-administrative relations, it is often assumed that presidents can and should have the power to command. The reality, however, is that many of the institutions that compose the executive branch are protected from too much presidential influence. For example, presidential removal power over certain members of the executive branch (e.g., civil servants and regulatory commissioners) has been strictly limited by Congress. Congress purposefully enacted legislation designed to ensure that many executive branch agencies are more concerned with the "public interest" than the transitory interests of any particular president. Although these provisions have not always safeguarded the public interest,[34] Congress has been convinced that too much presidential influence can be detrimental. As a result, presidents do not have the power to unilaterally force executive branch agencies to comply with presidential directives.

In order to accomplish their goals, presidents must be willing to bargain, to compromise, and to sell their program initiatives to subordinates within the executive branch. One means by which they can promote their policies is to follow Nathan's advice with regard to the president's appointment power, the one constitutionally enumerated tool of the administrative presidency strategy. Appointees who support the president's program can help sell the president's agenda to civil servants and thereby can be useful in building bureaucratic support for the president's policies.[35] Since such appointees testify to the fact that the president is committed to the program, bureaucratic support can be further promoted.

Although the appointment of loyal individuals is an important first step, it is not alone sufficient to ensure presidential influence. Presidents must also be willing to work with key elements within the bureaucracy to advance their programs. This means that presidents have to be willing to bargain and compromise with their own subordinates to determine what is politically feasible. Although compromise means that presidents will not ordinarily get all of what they want, it improves the probability that they will get much of what they want. This was the case with Jimmy Carter and the ICC (see ch. 4). On the other hand, confrontation can promote bureaucratic resistance, which can severely impede, or even halt, progress on presidential initiatives. Such was the case with the Reagan administration and the EPA (see ch. 5).

Compromise has other benefits as well. It can reduce the likelihood of conflict with the legislative branch. By avoiding such potentially confrontational techniques as the president's removal and reorganization authority, or at least limiting their use, presidents can avoid politically costly confrontations with Congress—confronta-

tions that can promote congressional opposition to presidential programs. By working with the bureaucracy, presidents can also take
advantage of the institutional memory of the administrative state.[36]
Career civil servants who have been in Washington for many years
have seen a number of presidents come and go. Since they retain
knowledge about what those presidents have done, they can help
the current president avoid making the same mistakes. Presidents
who ignore the bureaucracy run the risk of losing valuable time
learning lessons that could more easily have been taught by experts
within the bureaucracy.

Like the administrative presidency strategy, compromise and the
use of persuasion is not a panacea. In some cases, presidents may
have no other alternative than a more confrontational approach.
The decision to use such an approach, however, can wait until less
drastic measures have been exhausted. When diplomacy fails, presidents can then resort to a more confrontational management style.

Although a reliance on compromise and persuasion does not
guarantee presidential influence, it reduces many of the political risks
of the administrative presidency strategy. It also does not foreclose
the use of the more confrontational command and control techniques of that strategy. Command can be used when all else fails.
Yet, according to Richard Neustadt:

> Truman was quite right when he declared that presidential power is the
> power to persuade. Command is but a method of persuasion, not a
> substitute for everyday employment.[37]

Conclusion

Presidents do not have an unlimited grant of constitutional authority over the executive branch. Congress also has considerable influence. Thus presidents must share power with Congress and even
with their own subordinates within the executive branch. Presidents are not in a position to influence the administrative state
merely by invoking command and control techniques. Rather, presidents must be willing to bargain and compromise to get what they
want. In the next chapter I will examine in greater detail the various
sources of presidential influence over the administrative state and
the constraints which limit presidential power.

Chapter 2

The Tools of the
Administrative Presidency Strategy

Richard Nathan has identified several techniques used by presidents to extend their influence over the administrative state.[1] These tools of the administrative presidency strategy include the president's powers of appointment, removal, and reorganization, together with the presidential budgetary authority. Presidents can also transfer program authority to the states. Two more sources of presidential influence — central clearance and the use of cost-benefit analysis — should be added to those enumerated by Nathan. Both strategies were employed by Presidents Richard Nixon, Jimmy Carter, and Ronald Reagan in their attempts to alter bureaucratic behavior.

This chapter will examine the state of the literature with regard to each of these tools of the administrative presidency strategy, focusing on what each presidential power entails and on the potential benefits and limitations of each technique in advancing presidential influence.

Appointment Power

Of the various tools of the administrative presidency strategy, the power of appointment is the most prominent. It is the first among equals — a necessary but not a sufficient means of influencing agency goals and behavior — for, unlike the other tools of the administrative presidency strategy, the president's appointment power is derived directly from the Constitution. Article II, Section 2 provides that the President of the United States

Shall nominate, and by and with the Advice and Consent of the Senate, shall appoint Ambassadors, other public Ministers and Consuls, Judges of the Supreme Court, and all other Officers of the United States, whose appointments are not herein otherwise provided for, and which shall be established by Law, but the Congress may by Law vest the Appointment of such inferior Officers, as they think proper, in the President alone, in the Courts of Law, or in the Heads of Departments.

Congress by law has augmented presidential appointment power as the government has expanded. For example, presidents have been delegated new authority to nominate judges to the Federal District and Appellate Courts as well as the members of the independent regulatory commissions. These increases in the number of presidentially appointed positions have, over the years, proven to be extensive. By the time Jimmy Carter assumed the office of president in 1977, the president was responsible for nominating individuals to over 1,500 governmental positions.[2] With less than three months from election to inauguration, presidents have found it difficult to render considered judgments in the selection of each and every one of these appointees. As a result, most presidents have limited their active participation to no more than 500 or 600 positions, and other positions have generally been filled by cabinet secretaries, the White House staff, or agency chairmen.

The rapid escalation in the number of presidentially appointed positions has made it exceedingly difficult for presidents to select individuals who are properly qualified and who reflect the president's political philosophy. This situation has led one scholar to recommend that there should be a reduction in the number of presidentially appointed positions.[3] Paul Light's argument that there are so many layers of political appointees that it is making it more difficult for top appointees in an agency to get to know, and therefore benefit from the experience of, career civil servants[4] has a similar implication.

To deal with the proliferation of appointed positions, presidents have devised new organizational mechanisms which have provided more information on prospective appointees. Harry S Truman became the first president to name an aide whose primary function was to review candidates for appointive office. Truman's innovation was later expanded by John F. Kennedy, who set up the first permanent staff specifically designed to assist the president on personnel matters. Kennedy's innovation has been adopted by each of his successors.[5]

The development of a unit in the White House dedicated to the task of locating qualified individuals to serve in the government has served the purpose of providing presidents with more information about the qualifications of prospective appointees. This information is not confined to their technical qualifications for office. Over time presidents have also received greater information regarding the political philosophy of the various individuals under consideration for appointed positions. This factor was a particularly important development in the evolution of the administrative presidency strategy.

Without the development of a more sophisticated personnel management system within the White House, presidents were forced to nominate individuals without access to a great deal of information concerning the prospective appointee. With a large number of positions to fill, many in specific areas of expertise, most presidents simply did not personally know enough people to fill all of these positions. They had to rely on subordinates within the executive branch, members of Congress, and other influential politicians to help them select individuals for many important positions. As a result, appointees often reflected the divergent views of the president's subordinates or of members of Congress. Since many of the president's subordinates, especially cabinet officials, had been selected for a variety of political reasons (including geography or placating the disgruntled wing of the president's party), such appointees often did not reflect the president's political philosophy. Thus, appointments often failed to promote presidential influence.

With the development of new organizational mechanisms to locate and evaluate prospective appointees, presidents were in a better position to appoint individuals who shared their political philosophy. Lyndon Johnson, for example, created a dual organizational structure, one formal and one informal, to provide information regarding prospective appointees. One clear concern was an individual's loyalty to the president. As Johnson's Vietnam War policies exacerbated public criticism, loyalty became the primary consideration in nominating individuals to office.[6] Likewise, both Nixon and Reagan used their personnel management systems extensively as a means of locating and screening individuals for appointive office.

As a result, both presidents were able to appoint a greater number of individuals on the basis of loyalty to the president.

The appointment of loyal individuals to the bureaucracy has had one clear benefit. According to Jeffrey E. Cohen, loyal appointees tend to stay in office longer and consequently provide presidents with a more stable bureaucratic structure.[7] Presidential influence is advanced because presidential appointees are no longer constantly coming and going (the average tenure for appointees is approximately two years) and can thus learn the intricacies of their jobs. They can then use this knowledge to promote the president's programs.

Although the appointment of loyal individuals can be helpful to presidents seeking to increase their influence over the bureaucracy, it does not guarantee expanded influence. According to Linda Fisher, "appointing people who support the president's philosophy is not enough to ensure presidential control of the bureaucracy."[8] Loyal individuals who lack political experience can do the president more harm than good. Motivated by the best of intentions (e.g., serving the president) such officials can produce disastrous political consequences which can ultimately reduce presidential influence.[9] Thus, Fisher recommends that presidents should be concerned with the competence of their nominees as well as their loyalty to the president. Richard Neustadt commented, "A president is likely to want loyal support but not to relish trouble on his doorstep."[10]

But what is competence? Individuals who are substantively competent—that is, technically well trained—are not necessarily politically competent. As Richard Fenno wrote with regard to cabinet members, "An expert in terms of substantive knowledge may turn out to be a very poor departmental administrator."[11] More than substantive knowledge is necessary to manage a bureaucracy in Washington. Fenno recommends that presidents also look for individuals who have management experience. In addition, they should seek individuals with prior experience in the federal government. It takes appointees without prior governmental experience a great deal of time to learn the important details of governmental management, such as how to deal with an omnipresent Congress, how the budgetary process works, what to say and not to say to the press, and how to deal with interest groups and the public.[12] Because of these many factors, presidents who can appoint experienced and loyal individuals are at a distinct advantage.

Unfortunately, it is often difficult to find qualified individuals who not only share the president's personal political philosophy but are at the same time willing to serve. The trials and tribulations associated with government service scare many qualified individuals away. Many turn down government service because of financial considerations; the remuneration is quite low compared to that in the private sector. Moreover, the hours of work are long: in a recent survey of presidential appointees, 73 percent of all respondents reported working 61 hours or more per week.[13]

In addition to inadequate pay and long hours, reporting requirements under the 1978 Ethics in Government Act have also kept many qualified individuals from accepting appointments. The act demands that appointees provide detailed information regarding their finances and severely limits their post-government employment options. More critically, since appointees are often forced to sell stock and other holdings that might be considered a conflict of interest, they may suffer severe financial losses on stock sales and extremely high capital gains taxes. In some cases, appointees have been forced to lose millions of dollars as the cost of accepting a government job.[14]

Because of all of these factors, a president is often forced to select a candidate who is neither first nor even second choice. The lack of a constant pool of qualified potential candidates is thus a factor that can constrain presidential influence, because presidents often are unable to get the people that they really want.

Other factors also constrain the president's appointment power. For example, appointments are subject to confirmation by the Senate. Although most presidential appointees are routinely confirmed, the confirmation process is by no means a rubber stamp.[15] Jimmy Carter's selection of Theodore Sorenson as director of the Central Intelligence Agency was opposed, Richard Nixon had two nominees to the Supreme Court rejected by the Senate, and Ronald Reagan's appointment of Edwin Meese for Attorney General, though eventually confirmed, met with intense opposition. Reagan's nominee for the Supreme Court, Robert Bork, and George Bush's choice of Secretary of Defense, John Tower, were also rejected by the Senate. Presidents must thus consider potential Senate opposition when nominating individuals for office.[16]

In recent years the Senate's role in the appointment process has actually expanded. Committees have increased the amount of time they spend on nominations and are holding hearings for a greater number of positions. However, there are still no uniform rules for the nomination process, and wide variations exist across committees regarding the times dedicated to presidential appointments.[17]

The Constitution also constrains presidential power by giving Congress the right to place the power of appointment for certain inferior officers in the hands of individuals other than the president: According to Article II, Section 2, "Congress may by Law vest the Appointment of such inferior Officers, as they think proper, in the President alone, in the Courts of Law, or in the Heads of Departments." As a result, Congress has created executive branch positions in which the president's power of appointment has been severely curtailed. Nowhere is this more evident than with the independent regulatory commissions. Appointments, for fixed terms of lengthy duration (up to seven years), are staggered so that a president can name a large number of members to any one agency only if the president serves for a long period of time or if there is a quick turnover rate. Moreover, most agencies require a partisan balance, meaning that presidents cannot exclusively nominate members of their own party to a particular agency.[18] Rather, presidents must select a certain number of appointees who are either members of the opposition party or have no party affiliation. In practice, these constraints can often be circumvented. For example, presidents usually can find members of the opposition party who support their programs. Also, since the turnover rate on the regulatory commissions is usually quite high, presidents will have a realistic opportunity of appointing a majority of the seats on a commission.

Other constraints historically have also limited presidential appointment power. Interest groups have played an important role in selecting individuals to serve in the federal regulatory commissions. In years past, the regulated industry's opposition was sufficient to block a particular appointment.[19] Although interest group vetoes will not always prevent presidents from naming their preferred candidates, interest groups still have the option of presenting their cases before the Senate and the American public. This pressure can lead a president to select someone more amenable to the relevant interest groups, particularly if the groups involved are important to the president's reelection.

Even when presidents are able to name individuals that they most prefer for particular positions, presidential influence can be constrained. Appointed officials do not owe their loyalty solely to the president. Once they assume office, appointed officials must perform certain legally mandated functions which are enumerated in detail in congressional legislation. Appointed officials cannot simply do as the president wishes. Rather they have an obligation to enforce the law consistent with congressional intent. This often draws presidents and their subordinates into open conflict over policy. In 1833, for example, President Andrew Jackson attempted to force his Secretary of the Treasury, William J. Duane, to remove government funds from the Second Bank of the United States. Duane's resistance led to the following exchange:

> *President Jackson*: A secretary, sir, is merely an executive agent, a subordinate, and you may say so in self defense.
> *Secretary Duane*: In this particular case, congress confers a discretionary power, and requires reasons if I exercise it. Surely this contemplates responsibility on my part.[20]

In direct response to this disagreement, President Jackson replaced Secretary Duane with Attorney General Roger B. Taney, the man who had been the strongest advocate of removing the bank funds. The Senate reacted by refusing to confirm Taney and by voting to censure President Jackson, an act the Senate later repealed. Although Jackson eventually got what he wanted, the removal of government deposits from the bank, he encountered intense resistance from both his own executive branch subordinates and Congress.

In other cases the resistance that presidents have encountered from subordinates within their own executive branch has been less overt. Rather than openly challenging the president on policy matters, appointed officials have dragged their feet to stall the implementation of the president's program. In such cases the need for the president to follow up can be crucial. If a president does not follow up on an order, then no action may ever be taken to implement the policy. If a president does check back to see that the policies are being implemented, then the president can increase the probability that recalcitrant officials will be forced into action. Unfortunately, a president's time is bounded and the ability to follow up on each and every order is therefore limited. Even with the assistance of their White House staff, presidents are constrained in their supervisory capability. Accordingly, subordinates have a great deal of leeway in following the president's actual intent.

Although the president's power of appointment is the most important source of influence, it is not an absolute power. Presidential appointment power is constrained in a variety of different ways. Presidents can increase their influence over the bureaucracy by appointing loyal and competent individuals, but they cannot force subordinates to comply with their policy demands.

Removal Power

Even though the Constitution delegates the power of appointment to the President of the United States, it does not entrust presidents with the power to remove officials from office. In Federalist #77, Alexander Hamilton wrote that the consent of the Senate "would be necessary to displace as well as to appoint." In debate before the House of Representatives in 1789, James Madison disagreed with this constitutional interpretation. He argued that if the power of removal were vested jointly in the Senate and the presidency, it would destroy the "great principle of unity and responsibility in the Executive department, which was intended for the security of liberty and the public good."[21] Hamilton himself came to agree with this position, writing in an advisory memorandum to President George Washington that

> the executive power of the United States is completely lodged in the President. This mode of construing the Constitution has indeed been recognized by Congress in formal acts upon full consideration and debate; of which the power of removal from office is an important instance.[22]

Despite the explicit decision of the Congress in 1789 that the president should have the authority to remove officials from the executive branch, this question came to dominate the political debate throughout much of the 1800s. Attempts to limit the president's removal power included the passage of legislation which set staggered four-year terms for executive officials dealing with appropriations. Though the act was signed by President James Monroe, every living ex-president at the time — Madison, Jefferson, and Adams — viewed the act as unconstitutional (eventually even Monroe himself came to the same conclusion).

In March 1867, Congress went further in attempting to constrain the president's authority to remove officials from office. Congress enacted the Tenure of Office Act, over President Andrew Johnson's veto. The act prohibited a president from removing any official whose appointment had required Senate confirmation from office without Senate authorization. Andrew Johnson directly challenged the validity of the act when he demanded the resignation of Secretary of War Edwin Stanton. When the Senate refused to concur, Johnson fired Stanton, thus precipitating a major constitutional clash between the president and the Congress. Three days later the House voted to impeach Johnson. The trial in the Senate resulted in a vote that threatened to alter the balance of power between the presidency and Congress. By a vote of 35 to 19, one vote shy of impeachment, a constitutional crisis was averted. Still, the issue of whether the president had the legitimate right to remove officials confirmed by the Senate was not resolved until 1926, when the United States Supreme Court finally decided the question. In *Myers v. United States*,[23] Chief Justice and former President William Howard Taft ruled that presidents do indeed have the constitutional right to remove officials from the executive branch of government. Although the Court would later qualify the president's right to remove officials from office, this decision represented a major victory for advocates of expanded presidential power.

The debate over the extent of the president's removal power has continued from the days of the Founding Fathers to the present. Although it is now understood that presidents have the right to remove the members of their cabinet, many other appointive positions are protected from the capriciousness of the Chief Executive. For example, Supreme Court and other federal judges can be removed only through the impeachment process. This guarantee of life tenure insulates judges from the vicissitudes of everyday politics.

Members of the independent regulatory commissions also are protected from removal by the president. Presidents have the power to remove most of the chairmen of the independent regulatory commissions. When officials are removed from the chairmanship, however, they still remain as active members of the commission until their terms have expired. Likewise, commissioners cannot be removed from office by the president. When Franklin Delano Roosevelt fired Commissioner William Humphrey of the Federal Trade Commission (FTC), he challenged the constitutionality of regulatory statutes that limit a president's removal power. Roosevelt justified his action on the basis that Humphrey's philosophy was not in accord with administration policy. In the case of *Humphrey's Executor v. United States*,[24] the Supreme Court ruled unanimously that an FTC Commissioner could be removed from office by the president only for malfeasance in office, neglect of duty, or inefficiency. Since Roosevelt had not justified the termination on the basis of any of these criteria, the removal of William Humphrey was overturned. This decision provided a strong precedent limiting presidential removal power. Nonetheless, the *Humphrey* decision placed restrictions only on presidential removal of executive branch officials who exerted "quasi-legislative" or "quasi-judicial" functions. The president could remove, for any reason, other appointed officials serving in the executive branch.

The largest category of federal employees protected from presidential removal is the civil servants. After the assassination of President James Garfield by a disgruntled job seeker, Congress passed the Civil Service Act of 1883. The act created the Civil Service Commission, established the merit system as a means of selecting and promoting administrative employees, and also limited removal from office to certain specific violations such as malfeasance in office. The civil service system was an attempt to separate administration from politics by limiting the direct influence of the president over the bureaucracy.[25] Although it did not succeed in separating politics from administration, it has greatly limited presidential removal power. Still, as the experiences of the Nixon and Reagan administrations attest, it has not prevented presidents from removing individuals from office. Nixon skirted—and may have violated—the provisions of the original civil service act. Reagan, on the other hand, was able to use the new provisions of the Civil Service Reform Act of 1978, particularly those relating to the new Senior Executive Service (SES), to transfer civil servants from offices in Washington, D.C., to remote locations around the country.

The 1978 act was designed to increase presidential influence over the bureaucracy by creating a new level of civil servants, the Senior Executive Service. Approximately 7,000 positions were created throughout the government. Presidents were also granted the authority to appoint an additional 800 or so individuals from outside the government to serve within the bureaucracy.[26] In addition, the act replaced the Civil Service Commission with the Office of Personnel Management (OPM), which is headed by a single executive appointed by the president. This latter reform was similar to the one requested by Franklin Roosevelt and the Brownlow Committee Report in the late 1930s.

The new provisions of the 1978 act should provide presidents with greater influence over the civil service in the future. The act increased the president's ability to transfer and even terminate civil servants. It did not, however, extend total control to the president. The Merit Systems Protection Board was also created to investigate alleged abuses of the civil service system and to air employee grievances.[27] Presidential influence over career civil servants who do not hold SES rank is also still strictly limited. Therefore, though they do have more influence over civil service employees, presidents are still greatly constrained in terms of their direct influence over the career bureaucracy.

Budgetary Power

Gerald Ford wrote in his memoirs that "a president controls his administration through the budget. The document reflects his basic priorities."[28] Budget expert Lance LeLoup also stated that "the budget offers the President promising opportunities to achieve his policy goals."[29]

The budgetary process gives the president tangible powers and real influence over the administrative state. The fact that the president submits the budget to Congress is in itself a major agenda-setting power. Presidents can set the tone for the budget, such as increased defense spending, reductions in social welfare programs, and so forth. They can also influence the fate of a particular agency by proposing increases or reductions in funding, initiating new programs, and vetoing appropriations. Of course, in flexing these powers, presidents must be aware that Congress plays a very active role in determining the final budgetary figures.

Even after Congress has appropriated funds, there are still a number of techniques availabe to presidents and their subordinates for determining how that money will be spent. Presidents can impound funds through the rescission or deferral processes, but only subject to congresssional action.[30] Funds can be transferred across or within agencies. Since Congress is often limited in its ability to force agencies to spend funds exactly as specified in the budget, presidents and their subordinates have a great deal of freedom to determine how funds will be allocated after the budget has officially been set.[31]

Perhaps the greatest source of presidential budgetary power is the personal commitment the presidents themselves make to the process. According to Lance LeLoup:

> The greater the personal involvement of the President, the greater the constraints on subsequent decisions in the bureaucracy. On the other hand, the less active the President's role, the greater the discretion of other actors.[32]

Presidential interest in the budgetary process has varied according to who has been in the White House. Gerald Ford was intensely interested in the budgetary process. Jimmy Carter's interest was quite substantial in the beginning but waned over his term of office. Richard Nixon initially had little interest in budgets. As inflation came to dominate the domestic political agenda, however, he adopted a much more vigorous role in the budgetary process.

Institutionally, the president's greatest asset in the budgetary process is the Office of Management and Budget (OMB), formerly the Bureau of the Budget (BOB). OMB, which is located in the Executive Office of the President (EOP), provides the organizational means by which presidents can gain greater control over the budget. By requiring all departments and agencies to submit their proposed budgets to OMB, the Nixon and Reagan administrations gained greater influence over the budgetary process. In the case of the Reagan administration, OMB went so far as to inform various agencies of the exact amount of funding they would receive and how much they had to cut out of their proposed budgets.[33] OMB also included detailed plans regarding the number of layoffs for each department and proposals for the reorganization of functional units.

By providing a point of central clearance for all executive branch budgetary requests, OMB has reduced the ability of individual agencies to make an end run around the president and request more money from Congress. It has thus increased the president's influence over the budgetary process. At the same time, however, hostility toward OMB from within the executive branch has increased. Many agencies feel that they are being unfairly singled out for budget cuts. This increased hostility may in the long run promote even closer agency relations with congressional committees and interest groups as a means of circumventing OMB's control over the budget.

Even though presidents have a great deal of influence over the budgetary process, it is not easy for them to use the budget as a means of influencing administrative behavior. Presidents are limited with regard to which programs they can actually cut. A large percentage of the federal budget is made up of entitlements (such as Social Security and Medicare), which can be reduced or increased only if legislation is adopted that changes the basic requirements and benefit levels. Many programs, particularly defense systems, are framed with multi-year appropriations; accordingly, it is more difficult to substantially alter the budgets for these programs. Finally, there are programs which for political reasons are virtually untouchable. These programs have the strong support of powerful interest groups. Tobacco subsidies, for example, are considered by most governmental officials to be a virtual untouchable item in the budget. Jimmy Carter's ill-fated decision to scrub several ongoing dam and water projects demonstrated what can happen to presidents who attempt to cut such programs from the budget: this decision greatly weakened Carter's future bargaining power with Congress.

Other factors can also constrain a president's influence over the budget. A sudden downturn in the economy, a poor wheat crop, or an oil embargo can force a president to radically alter budgetary priorities. Economic trends such as rising deficits can also limit a president's discretion. It is more difficult to advocate new social welfare programs in the face of a widening budget deficit.

Allen Schick has argued that due to these various constraints, presidents have actually lost much of their power and influence over the budgetary process.[34] In a period of retrenchment politics, however, the opposite argument can also be advanced. Record high budget deficits increased the Reagan administration's ability to demand cuts in the programs that it opposed. This was particularly important when it came to justifying cuts in popular programs, as the administration was able to argue that deep budget cuts were necessary for the good of the economy as a whole.

As with presidential removal power, using the budgetary process as a means of promoting presidential objectives at the administrative level can entail political risks. By politicizing the budgetary process, presidents can lose a valuable source of bureaucratic advice or what Hugh Heclo calls "neutral competence."[35] Proposed reductions in popular programs can also increase congressional oversight as well as bureaucratic resistance to presidential initiatives. Although budgetary reductions can be a powerful tool in altering agency goals, they can also increase congressional and bureaucratic opposition to presidential objectives.

Reorganization

Organizational structure is not neutral. The manner in which an agency or department is organized can have a major impact on policy outcomes. In a highly decentralized agency, it can be very difficult for a president to extend personal influence over the agency's policy choices. Centralized agencies tend to be more amenable to presidential influence because greater authority rests with the agency's head and potential sources of opposition within the organization are easier to circumvent or remove entirely. In a centralized agency a president's appointees are thus in a stronger position to advance the president's program at the administrative level.

Whether an agency shares jurisdiction for a certain program with other agencies can also have a tremendous impact on presidential influence. If an agency has sole jurisdiction over a program, rather than sharing responsibility with several other agencies or departments, it has a greater freedom to initiate a policy without being constrained by its external environment. If, on the other hand, an agency must share program responsibility with one or more other agencies or departments, it must negotiate and compromise before decisions can be reached. This can slow progress toward policy change.

As each of these organizational factors suggests, the structure of an agency can "help or hinder the president in performing his pivotal role within our constitutional system," as Harold Seidman has stated.[36] Presidents thus have attempted to alter organizational structures as a means of promoting their objectives. Their primary methods are two: presidential reorganizations, initiated by the president, and administrative reorganizations, initiated by the president's subordinates within the bureaucracy.

Since organizational structure matters, reorganization—whether a change in the organizational structure of government agencies or departments or a change in the location of programs—also matters. The president was first afforded the authority to reorganize the executive branch in 1932. Following the recommendation of Franklin Roosevelt's Committee on Administrative Management, better known as the Brownlow Committee, the president's reorganization authority was greatly expanded. The Reorganization Act of 1939 gave the president the power to transfer, consolidate, or abolish governmental agencies unless both Houses of Congress vetoed the president's plans within a period of sixty days after they were submitted to Congress. Since 1939, presidential reorganization authority has been extended and redefined on a number of occasions, including the Legislative Reorganization Act of 1949, which encompassed a number of recommendations from the first Hoover Commission.

Presidential reorganization authority is established by Congress for a specified period of time, after which the reorganization authority must be renewed. The provisions of the various reorganization authorizations have changed over time. Presidents have been granted the authority to establish new units within the Executive Office of the President and to create new departments subject to congressional disapproval, usually within a period of sixty days. Congressional disapproval has varied from a one-house to a two-house legislative veto. In 1964, Congress amended the president's reorganization authority to prevent the president from creating or abolishing cabinet-level departments.[37] In 1977 presidents were excluded from reorganizing the independent regulatory commissions.[38] These latter constraints on presidential authority demonstrate how fluid the president's reorganization authority has been. Rather than giving presidents a fixed and permanent power, Congress has consistently changed the rules under which presidents can seek reorganizations. These changes have reflected not only the president's need to control the organization of the executive branch, but also Congress's unwillingness to grant presidents too much reorganization authority.

In 1984, following the Supreme Court's 1983 *Chadha* decision,[39] in which the legislative veto was ruled unconstitutional, the president was given the right to reorganize subject to congressional approval, rather than disapproval. Because Congress must now approve presidential reorganizations within a ninety-day period, presidential attempts to reorganize the executive branch should be even more constrained.[40]

Presidents do have other options beyond congressional reorganization authority. They can also seek to reorganize the executive branch by submitting legislation directly to Congress and can make some organizational changes via Executive Order. The latter was the means by which the Nixon administration created the Environmental Protection Agency. The use of Executive Orders is constrained by the fact that future presidents can countermand the reorganization by issuing a new Executive Order. Given the limitations of Executive Orders, and given the change in presidential reorganization authority following the *Chadha* decision, presidents in the future may rely to a greater extent on the legislative alternative in reorganizing the executive branch, especially since Congress is not constrained to accept legislation within a ninety-day period. Presidents may also rely more on administrative level reorganization.[41]

With such constraints, why have presidents sought to reorganize the executive branch? They have initiated reorganizations for a variety of reasons. Lester M. Salamon has identified three types of reorganization goals: economy and efficiency, policy effectiveness, and tactical political advantage.[42] Existing law requires that presidents defend reorganizations on the basis of economy and efficiency; that is, a reorganization should result in net savings over the existing organizational structure by removing duplication and unnecessary programs. The first Hoover Commission espoused the idea that programs should be structured so as to promote maximum efficiency.[43] Although economy and efficiency are the legally sanctioned reasons for presidential reorganizations, the goal of many reorganizations has been policy effectiveness or tactical political advantage.[44] Often these last two goals are interrelated.

The Brownlow Committee took the view that reorganization should improve the president's ability to manage the government. Economy and efficiency should not be the only legitimate goals for a presidential reorganization. The Committee's report stated:

> Managerial direction and control of all departments and agencies of the Executive Branch . . . should be centered in the President; that while he now has popular responsibility for this direction . . . he is not equipped with adequate legal authority or administrative machinery to enable him to exercise it.[45]

The unabashedly pro–executive power views of the Brownlow Committee's report were not greeted enthusiastically by Congress. Although Congress eventually did create the Executive Office of the President, congressional dissatisfaction with the Brownlow report underscores a major limitation of the presidential reorganization strategy: reorganizations can and often do provoke deep hostility from congressional committees and from various other groups. As Robert E. DeClerico states:

> Any time a President seeks to transfer, abolish, or consolidate government agencies, he is likely to face formidable opposition from three sources; those within the agency, those congressional committees exer-

cising oversight over the agency, and finally, those clientele groups served by the agency.[46]

Bureaucratic employees may see their interests threatened. A reorganization could weaken their program authority or even force layoffs. Interest groups may see their interests threatened by the elimination of a favorably disposed agency and its replacement by a less sympathetic entity. Congressional interests can also be threatened. According to Harold Seidman, "Reorganization of the Executive Branch can't achieve very much unless there is a parallel reorganization of Congress."[47] Executive branch reorganization often is accompanied by reorganizations in congressional committee jurisdiction because changes in the structure of the executive branch force Congress to adopt a new committee structure that is consistent with the new goals and programs of the new executive units. When reorganizations of this type occur, they can threaten long-entrenched relationships between congressional committees, interest groups, and agency officials. Presidential reorganizations that entail congressional committee reorganizations have thus long met with intense resistance. Reorganizations that do not require congressional committee reorganization usually have a much higher probability of being approved by Congress.

In an analysis of the president's reorganization authority, Louis Fisher and Ronald C. Moe have argued that the reorganization process tends to "degrade the institutional relationship between the president and Congress."[48] According to this view, not only can the president's reorganization authority increase conflict between the president and Congress but there are few benefits derived from the use of the strategy. Most reorganization proposals, badly prepared, and hastily written are unlikely to be accepted. Fisher and Moe conclude that the president's reorganization authority may not be worth the costs of increased conflict between the president and Congress. Indeed, when such conflict occurs, the reorganization strategy may actually constrain presidential influence rather than promote it.

Reorganizations initiated by the president often receive the most attention in textbooks on organizational structure. Often overlooked is administrative level reorganization or reorganizations initiated by a president's subordinates within the bureaucracy. Administrative reorganization is an important tool for promoting presidential influence over the administrative state, particularly within the independent regulatory commissions, where presidents lack reorganization authority. Yet, even this source of reorganization authority has been constrained, as Congress has at various times limited the ability of the independent regulatory commissions to reorganize their internal units without congressional approval. Still, administrative reorganization authority can be effective. In his study of the federal regulatory commissions, David Welborn found only one case in which a reorganization plan initiated by an agency's chairman was rejected by his fellow commissioners. In this case, involving the Federal Communications Commission, the chairman himself expressed ambivalence about the reorganization plan at a crucial juncture, thus dooming the proposal.[49]

Since the chairmen of the regulatory agencies are appointed by the president, administrative reorganization can promote presidential objectives. A president can count on an agency's chairman to remove sources of administrative opposition to the president's program. This can pave the way for administrative action which promotes the president's program. If the appointee's action is controversial, as was the case of the Environmental Protection Agency under Anne Burford, administrative reorganization can threaten to reduce presidential influence by increasing interest group and congressional opposition (see ch. 5). Thus, administrative reorganization, like its presidential counterpart, is not risk-free.

Delegation of Program Authority

The delegation of program authority to the states is another means by which presidents have sought to increase their influence over the administrative state. Program delegation advances presidential influence by limiting an agency's ability to initiate policies that are detrimental to a president's program. Both Presidents Nixon and Reagan advanced "New Federalism" proposals which called for the transfer of various federal functions to the states.[50]

David Walker provided a strong justification for program delegation.[51] His idea of "sorting out" federal activities is a means of determining which programs should be implemented at the national level and which can best be administered at the state or local level. The criteria for sorting out are based on cost considerations and whether a function can better be handled at the federal or local level.

The Reagan administration endorsed the idea of sorting out federal activities as a justification for its delegation of various programs to the states. Yet the administration did not always delegate authority on the basis of cost or an evaluation of which function can and should be handled by local governments. Rather, decisions were often made on the basis of whether the administration supported a particular program. Such considerations invite congressional intervention as well as criticism from state governments and sometimes the industries affected. Consequently, the strategy of delegating program authority to the states for political reasons can run the risk of increasing opposition to presidential initiatives.

Further, the delegation of program authority can have unanticipated consequences. Although a particular delegation of authority may be intended to reduce the level of governmental oversight, it may actually result in increased governmental activity. Since program delegation means that at least fifty functional units of government will be involved in the development of policy, rather than one, there are new opportunities for various state agencies to enact stronger restrictions than the federal government previously required. Under such circumstances the relevant industries may actually find themselves in a less advantageous position. As the case of the Environmental Protection Agency demonstrates, the delegation of environmental program authority to the states has in some cases had exactly this unanticipated consequence (see ch. 5).

Along with the traditional notion of delegating program authority to states or local governments, the Reagan administration recommended the delegation of authority to private enterprises. This idea of privatizing federal functions derived from success on the local level in privatizing such functions as garbage collection. Reagan's contribution was his recommendation that the concept be extended to a variety of federal programs, such as the post office and prisons. Under these proposals, private entrepreneurs would not be denied access to certain markets now monopolized by federal and state governments. Thus, for example, if a private company wanted to set up a more cost-effective prison, it would have the right to compete with federal, state, and local governments.

The idea of privatizing the post office, prisons, and other federal functions will likely raise a spirited debate. Certainly, moral questions could be raised about the idea of making money off prisoners. Although the idea of privatization was raised by Reagan and a number of his top subordinates, it is doubtful that there will be an immediate rush to privatize a great deal of federal functions.

Central Clearance

Besides their administrative activities, departments and agencies also prepare legislative proposals. Most of these are rather mundane, requiring only minor modifications of existing law. On occasion, however, bureaucratic units prepare major legislative proposals. To increase their knowledge and control over such administrative initiatives, presidents have long used a process known as central clearance.

Central clearance is a means of reviewing all department, agency, and commission legislative proposals before they are transmitted to Congress. Clearance of administrative proposals was performed for many years by the old Bureau of the Budget (BOB). When the Nixon administration reorganized the Bureau in 1970, its successor, the Office of Management and Budget, assumed this responsibility.

The central clearance technique was first instituted, following congressional passage of the Budget and Accounting Act of 1921, as a means of keeping track of agency legislative proposals. It also ensured that these proposals were in accord with the Harding administration's budgetary goals. The first presidents to employ the technique extensively were Calvin Coolidge and Herbert Hoover, who used central clearance solely as a means of keeping track of appropriations bills.

Franklin Roosevelt became the first president to employ the technique as a means of providing greater presidential control over all legislative initiatives.[52] Not only did he ask the Bureau of the Budget to examine all proposals dealing with appropriations, but he also asked that purely policy related bills be reviewed. This practice was followed by Roosevelt's immediate successors, Harry Truman and Dwight Eisenhower.

John Kennedy and Lyndon Johnson also employed central clearance, but in a slightly different manner from their predecessors. Rather than using the BOB to review agency legislation, Kennedy and Johnson relied on their own White House staffs to perform the clearance function. Nixon later placed central clearance under the watchful eye of the Domestic Council.[53] The experiences of Kennedy, Johnson, and Nixon with central clearance indicate that like many other sources of presidential influence, each president is likely to employ the central clearance technique differently. Presidential preference about how the technique is employed reflects the system with which each president is most comfortable.

In January 1985 the Reagan administration adopted another new variation of the central clearance technique to screen all ongoing administrative rule-making procedures. Executive Order #12498 required that all department and agency rule-making proceedings, with the exception of the independent regulatory commissions, must be reviewed by the Office of Management and Budget to ensure that the new rules and regulations were consistent with the goals of the Reagan administration. All rules—even those in the very earliest stages of development—were subject to review. This innovation was greeted with a great deal of skepticism by some members of Congress who were concerned that the president was intruding on the independence of the regulatory agencies and other bureaucratic entities.

The development of administrative central clearance procedures will likely come to have a major impact on bureaucratic activity. Administrative proposals for new rules and regulations will have to be submitted to administration officials for review before a rule has even been written, rather than when the rule is ready to be promulgated. This change has the potential for increasing presidential influence over the administrative state, since presidents and their subordinates will be in a stronger position to veto or alter administrative proposals. It will also provide presidents and their appointees with more information regarding agency activities. Thus, it will be more difficult for agencies to adopt regulations without the knowledge or acquiescence of the administration.

Interestingly, the Reagan administration's new, innovative employment of the central clearance function was simply an extension of a variety of accretions in the use of the technique over time. Originally used only for appropriations bills, the technique later was extended to include policy-related bills. It is not surprising, then, that the technique has been extended to include agency rule-making proceedings. Perhaps the most surprising aspect of the Reagan administration's innovation was that it did not come earlier.

Given the concern of recent presidents with control over the bureaucracy, an extension of the central clearance function to agency rule-making would seem to be a natural and astute maneuver.

Cost-Benefit Analysis

Although cost-benefit analysis has been utilized for many years by various government agencies, particularly the Army Corps of Engineers, it did not achieve prominence until the 1960s when the Johnson administration institutionalized a variation of the technique, cost-effectiveness analysis, within the Defense Department. Cost-effectiveness analysis is designed to help administrators to choose the best, most monetarily efficient alternative from the options available. Later, Johnson attempted to expand the employment of cost-effectiveness analysis to the government as a whole through the Planned Program Budget System (PPBS). PPBS was not successful, largely due to bureaucratic confusion over how the technique was supposed to work, but also because of strong resistance from career civil servants.

With the failure of PPBS, cost-benefit analysis did not again achieve prominence until Richard Nixon instituted the "Quality of Life" review process in 1971. Under the review, agencies were instructed to submit a comparison of the anticipated costs and benefits of proposed regulations, particularly those dealing with the environment, safety, and health.

When Gerald Ford became president, he continued the "Quality of Life" review process. In 1974, President Ford institutionalized the use of cost-benefit analysis within the Office of Management and Budget (OMB) and the Council on Wage and Price Stability (CWPS) via Executive Order #11821.[54] The order required agencies of the executive branch to file Inflation Impact Statements (IIS) for all new regulations. Although the administration's experience with cost-benefit analysis was checkered,[55] Ford reauthorized the employment of the technique before he left office.[56] Ford's successors, Carter and Reagan, then continued to use cost-benefit analysis as a means of controlling regulatory spending. According to Edward Paul Fuchs,

> The use of cost-benefit analysis as a management tool was an attempt to alter the institutional framework of regulatory decision making to

broaden presidential discretion. It evoked an intense political struggle both because of the important interests involved and its economic
consequences.[57]

If cost-benefit analysis were value-free (that is, if no bias was involved in determining the results and the method was purely scientific), then it could be argued that the technique does not really promote presidential influence or constrain bureaucratic activity at all.
Rather, it would simply promote cost-consciousness at the administrative level. Unfortunately, there are questions about whether cost-
benefit analysis is really value-free. The measurement of costs and
benefits is not an exact science; indeed, it is difficult to find adequate measures for many benefits. How, for example, does one adequately measure such intangible benefits as saving a life or a limb?
Although formulas exist that provide monetary figures for such
benefits,[58] the determination of a dollar value is far from value-free.

The serious problem of adequately quantifying costs and benefits has led critics to charge that cost-benefit analysis has become
a weapon designed to prevent bureaucratic entities from adopting
pro-safety and pro-environmental regulations.[59] As these criticisms
suggest, cost-benefit analysis has the strong potential for increasing
conflict among the White House, the bureaucracy, and Congress.
It has also led to a number of court challenges. The courts have
been forced to determine whether presidents can avoid implementing certain safety requirements on the basis of cost. The courts have
also been asked how much influence the president legally has over
certain regulatory agencies, in particular the independent regulatory commissions. The employment of cost-benefit analysis, in once
again raising the question of who controls the bureaucracy, therefore threatens to put presidential regulatory programs on a collision
course with both Congress and the courts.

Conclusions

Of the various tools of the administrative presidency strategy, the
power of appointment stands out as the president's most potent
weapon. Presidents can use their constitutional authority to influence administrative behavior by appointing loyal but competent in-

dividuals to the bureaucracy. Although this does not guarantee presidential influence, it is an important first step.

Other tools of the administrative presidency strategy can also increase presidential influence, though at the same time they have the potential for increasing congressional, bureaucratic, and interest group opposition, as well as promoting court challenges that can permanently limit presidential discretion. The budget can be a powerful contributor to presidential influence. The president's reorganization authority, by limiting or removing authority from the various competing factions within the bureaucracy, can increase presidential influence, but by challenging entrenched interests the reorganization authority can also reduce presidential influence. The same can be said of the president's ability to delegate program authority to the states. Other tools of the administrative presidency strategy— particularly the president's removal power—threaten to reduce presidential influence, often without palpable benefits.

The next four chapters, which examine the various tools of the administrative presidency strategy in actual practice, analyze in detail the experiences of the Nixon, Carter, and Reagan presidencies with this strategy. These case studies suggest that some of the tools of the administrative presidency strategy—in particular, the power of appointment—can advance presidential objectives but also that some tools of the strategy can reduce presidential influence. Command is one means of persuasion but not the only one.

Chapter 3

Nixon and the Department of Housing and Urban Development: The Evolution of the Administrative Presidency Strategy

During his first term in office, Richard Nixon experimented with a number of different management styles and techniques in an attempt to centralize greater authority over domestic policymaking. Through this process of experimentation, the Nixon administration developed what Richard Nathan has labeled the administrative presidency strategy.[1] To illustrate the development of the strategy, and the criticism it engendered, I will focus on the Nixon administration's attempts to alter the policies of the Department of Housing and Urban Development (HUD). Unlike the other case studies in this book, which concentrate on one agency or department, this chapter will also examine the broader management style of the Nixon administration by tracing the evolution of the administrative presidency strategy.

Appointments

When Richard Nixon first assumed office in January 1969, he decided to employ a traditional cabinet style of government. This management style involves a highly decentralized decision-making structure in which administration goals and policy objectives are set by the president but the details of the everyday management of the government are left to the individual cabinet secretaries. The result is that presidential influence over the executive departments is often severely constrained, since the president's personal involvement in the policy process is limited. Consequently, the success or failure of this approach depends to a great extent on the president's choice of cabinet members and personal relationship with them.

Rather than appointing individuals who were loyal to him, Nixon first appointed individuals who had their own policy agendas and programs. Nixon chose to adopt this appointment strategy because he wanted to surround himself with men of independent mind rather than a chain of yes-men. Independent-minded cabinet secretaries, Nixon argued, would be able to handle the various problems within their departments without constantly involving the president in minor details.[2] Accordingly, more of Nixon's time could be devoted to his real interest, foreign affairs.

Nixon's search for men of independent mind led him to select a combination—former friends as well as other individuals who had no personal loyalty to him. Robert Finch, named to head the Department of Health, Education, and Welfare (HEW), and John Mitchell, Nixon's choice for Attorney General, were long-time friends who were exceedingly loyal to the president. On the other hand, Walter Hickel, the ex-governor of Alaska, chosen for Secretary of the Interior, John Volpe, the ex-governor of Massachusetts, selected to head the Department of Transportation, and George Romney, the ex-governor of Michigan, appointed Secretary of Housing and Urban Development, came to Washington with their own political constituencies and their own political agendas. It was therefore not surprising that they advanced their own views on domestic policy rather than following the president's lead. At the Department of Housing and Urban Development, this appointment strategy promoted a progression of serious disagreements between Nixon and Secretary George Romney.

Cabinet Government and HUD

George Romney, the president's first Secretary of Housing and Urban Development, had been an early competitor with Nixon for the 1968 Republican presidential nomination. Romney had even been considered the front-runner at one point. However, a comment attempting to justify his early support for the Vietnam War—that he had been "brainwashed" on the issue—effectively undermined his campaign. Despite his failure to win the nomination, Romney retained a great deal of support within the Republican party, especially within Nelson Rockefeller's more liberal wing. By naming Romney to a cabinet position, Nixon hoped to reach out to Romney's and Rockefeller's supporters.

While this move made infinite political sense, there were serious policy repercussions associated with the selection of George Romney as Secretary of HUD. Romney was much more liberal and, as a former governor, more favorably predisposed toward many of HUD's programs than was the new president. Given these policy differences, Romney perceived Nixon's comment that he wanted men of independent mind as a promise that he could pursue his own more liberal agenda. Romney therefore felt justified in raising his voice in protest against the president at cabinet meetings, a practice Nixon came to detest.[3]

The decision to allow Romney to select his own subordinates further exacerbated tensions between the White House and HUD. Romney was allowed to surround himself with loyal associates. For example, his Under Secretary, Richard Van Dusen, was a former colleague from his home state of Michigan. As such, Dusen was more likely to be loyal to Romney than to Nixon. Other HUD appointees did not fit in with the many conservatives within the Nixon administration. Even though many of those close to the president considered Floyd Hyde, the former mayor of Fresno, too liberal, he was nonetheless selected to be the Assistant Secretary in charge of the Model Cities Program. Hyde's appointment was warmly greeted by Ralph Taylor, Hyde's predecessor under Lyndon Johnson, who called the Hyde appointment a "good signal" that the Nixon administration would be sympathetic to the Model Cities program.[4] By allowing Romney to appoint his own subordinates, the Nixon administration gave up any chance of constraining Romney's more liberal policy views.

Nixon and Romney's views diverged on a variety of specific issues. George Romney supported the continuation of the Model Cities Program, while Nixon desired its termination. The Model Cities Program, one of Lyndon Johnson's Great Society programs, was originally designed to assist the rebuilding of older cities. To ensure the program's long-term success, however, projects were chosen with an eye toward important congressmen on influential committees. In other words, the program quickly devolved into a quintessential example of pork barrel politics. As such, it was bitterly opposed by conservatives within the Republican party. Although Model Cities was almost the prototype Great Society program that the Nixon administration was committed to canceling, Romney, who as Secretary of HUD represented the country's big city mayors, was determined to preserve it.

Floyd Hyde, the Assistant Secretary in charge of Model Cities, convinced Romney that the program could be saved if the rationale for the program was altered to conform with the Nixon administration's political philosophy. Hyde argued that the old rationale for the program—urban renewal—was unattractive to the new administration, but the program could be repackaged and sold as a means of strengthening local governmental control, since the program would decentralize responsibility for construction to local officials. This new rationale would be consistent with the administration's New Federalism proposals.[5] In a meeting of the Urban Affairs Council on April 7, 1969, Romney presented a report prepared by HUD, which suggested that the program could be continued with greater local control and with a 4 percent reduction in funding.[6]

In the summer of 1969, Romney put further pressure on the president to support the program. In a press conference Romney stated that "the Model Cities Program cannot possibly succeed unless it has the backing of the President . . . and unless the departments involved are agreed on the policies that are going to be applied."[7] Faced with Romney's adamance, Nixon backed down from his opposition and instead offered his tentative support for the program's continuation.[8]

The White House formed two separate task forces to investigate whether the program should be continued. The first group, the President's Task Force on Model Cities, was chaired by Edward C. Banfield, a conservative Harvard University professor. The Banfield Task Force, though highly critical of the program, recommended continuing it.[9] A second task force, the Blair House group, which was composed mostly of administration officials, also recommended that the program be continued. At the same time, it suggested that a limited number of model cities should be chosen to test a new program called "planned variations," which would further reduce federal involvement while simultaneously increasing local autonomy.[10]

As a result of Romney's support, and Nixon's unwillingness to oppose his own Secretary of HUD, the Model Cities program was allowed to continue until 1973. Thus, a program that Nixon had personally wanted to terminate resulted in the expenditure of $2.3 billion between 1969 and 1973.[11]

The Model Cities Program was not the only instance in which Romney and Nixon disagreed over policy. In 1969, Romney joined Arthur Burns and Vice-President Spiro Agnew in opposing the Family Assistance Program, the cornerstone of Nixon's early welfare reform plan. Romney also joined Transportation Secretary John Volpe in outspoken criticism of the Ash Council's Report on the reorganization of the executive branch.[12] In March 1971, Romney infuriated Nixon by setting up a rump special session of the cabinet to hear the report of the chairman of the Council of Economic Advisers on the wage-price problem. The meeting was organized because Nixon had refused to hold general cabinet meetings where economic issues were debated. Nixon characterized the meeting as a "cabal" and accused Romney of being its leader.[13]

The Section 235 Housing Scandals drove in the wedge between Romney and Nixon still further. In 1971 and 1972 a number of congressional committees examined various improprieties involving the Section 235 program of the Housing Act of 1968, which was designed to assist lower-income individuals who wanted to purchase a home.[14] These investigations produced evidence of poor administration by the Federal Housing Administration and the Department of Housing and Urban Development. Romney's response was to downplay criticisms of HUD, while concomitantly urging that reforms be made to correct administrative problems.[15] The Nixon administration, which generally opposed the program, had desired a much stronger stand, and Romney's reaction was not considered strong enough by conservative critics. Later, following Romney's departure from the administration in 1973, and under the stewardship of Nixon loyalist James Lynn, HUD released a report which was much more critical of the Section 235 and 236 programs. The report argued that rather than meeting the needs of the poorest of the poor, the programs had assisted those with higher incomes. The report endorsed a Nixon proposal to provide cash subsidies directly.[16]

The immediate effect of the numerous conflictual exchanges between Romney and Nixon was that the president threatened on several occasions to fire his HUD Secretary. On May 25, 1970, Nixon informed Ehrlichman that he planned on replacing Romney in November after the midterm elections. This came in response to a statement by Romney that he would voluntarily take a cut in pay to assist in reducing the budget deficit. Nixon was furious, arguing that the move was nothing more than political "grandstanding."[17]

Following the 1970 elections, Nixon sent Attorney General John Mitchell to talk with Romney. Mitchell did not ask Romney to resign but left him with the definite impression that the president wanted him to. Romney, in turn, let the administration know that he would vehemently resist any attempts at removal. Nixon, who planned on naming Donald Rumsfeld as Romney's replacement, decided not to create another political controversy, like the one that had followed Interior Secretary Walter Hickel's forced departure. Thus, Romney was retained and did not leave office until 1973, following Nixon's reelection.[18]

The case of Romney and HUD points out a major problem with Nixon's initial decision to utilize a highly decentralized cabinet style of government. Since Romney was allowed to have an independent base at HUD, only a strong-willed president could have constrained Romney's more liberal policy objectives. But this was not Nixon's personal style of problem-solving. Nixon did not like having to make a decision on a particular matter in front of his cabinet. Rather, he preferred to listen to debate, even when he had already made up his mind, and then render a decision in writing or through a subordinate at a later time. Romney liked to challenge the president at cabinet meetings, thus forcing the president to commit himself on issues that he otherwise would never have agreed to, such as Model Cities. Although Romney's perseverance preserved such liberal programs as the Model Cities, his actions and those of other independent cabinet secretaries, especially Volpe and Hickel, convinced Nixon and his top lieutenants that the decentralized cabinet-style government was not achieving the administration's objectives.

Why Did Nixon Select A Decentralized Cabinet Government?

Given the problems that resulted from Romney's appointment at HUD, and other similar problems at the Departments of Interior and Transportation, why did Nixon originally decide to rely on a highly decentralized cabinet style of government? Why didn't he initially employ an appointment strategy that emphasized loyalty to the president's programs?

The reason is that Nixon came to office without clearly articulated domestic policy choices; that is, he had no specific program for domestic affairs. Moreover, he had little personal interest in domestic policy, preferring instead to concentrate on foreign affairs. He therefore felt that he could leave the business of domestic policy to his cabinet, while taking an active role in foreign affairs. This naive view of domestic affairs was exemplified in a comment Nixon made early during his first term in office: "All you need is a competent Cabinet to run the country at home. You need a President for foreign policy."[19] This quotation suggests that Nixon had little interest in managing a large and expanding administrative state or in proposing specific domestic programs. His conception of domestic policy management contrasted sharply with his more sophisticated political understanding of foreign affairs, an area in which he seemed fully aware of the importance of controlling bureaucratic operations.

In the area of foreign affairs Nixon initiated a sophisticated means of centralizing decision-making authority in the White House at the very beginning of his term in office. This management style not only insulated foreign policymaking from the vicissitudes of the State Department but also allowed the president to devise policy in the White House without constant interference from State Department officials and other career civil servants.[20]

Nixon also made deft use of his appointment power in the area of foreign affairs. For example, he named a friend, William Rogers, to head the State Department. Rogers' lack of expertise in foreign affairs had the expected effect of weakening the State Department's influence in foreign policymaking. At the same time, Nixon took full advantage of the institutional capacity of the National Security Council (NSC) by naming Henry Kissinger to assist in the formulation of a consistent foreign policy. This policy was directed from the White House, often without the input or knowledge of the State Department.

Since Nixon clearly understood the need for a centralized decision-making structure for foreign affairs, why then didn't he initially adopt a similar appointment strategy for the control of domestic policy? In order for Nixon to construct a management style for domestic policymaking that was similar to the one he employed for foreign affairs, it was first necessary for him to offer a clearly articulated domestic policy. Without such a program, it is exceedingly difficult for a president to name like-minded individuals to the cabinet, that is, individuals who will vow to support the president's policy agenda. In order to be able to follow the president's lead on domestic affairs, cabinet members must know what the president's views are. If a president has no clearly articulated programs or policies, cabinet members are free to act on their own, filling the void created by the lack of presidential leadership. Because Nixon had neither clearly enunciated programs nor much personal interest in domestic policy, the void was considerable. This situation encouraged Romney and other cabinet members to initiate their own policies based on their own political views.

A New Appointment Strategy Emerges

Nixon's experiences with Romney, Hickel, Volpe and other first-term cabinet secretaries led the administration to search for a new appointment strategy. Rather than relying on a strategy which encouraged the selection of a cabinet on the basis of independence of mind, future nominations would be made on the basis of loyalty to the president. But before such a strategy could be adopted, an institutional mechanism had to be found to locate candidates for appointive office, and Nixon had to develop clearly articulated domestic policy choices. Without both of these developments, it would be difficult for Nixon to surround himself with loyalists who would be committed to his administration's policies and programs.

The first factor, the development of an institutional mechanism to promote a new appointment strategy based on loyalty, was initiated in late 1970. Nixon's Chief of Staff, Harry Robbins (H. R.) Haldeman, like Nixon, had been dissatisfied with the existing management style. He thus sought advice on various alternative appointment mechanisms. During December 1970, Haldeman received a 45-page report prepared by Frederick Malek, the Deputy Under Secretary of Health, Education, and Welfare. The report, entitled "Management of Non-Career Personnel: Recommendations For Improvement," included a series of recommendations for bringing greater accountability to appointed officials. The report stated:

> In the two years of the Nixon Administration, the difficulty in effectively managing the Federal Government has become increasingly apparent. The Executive Branch has not galvanized sufficiently as a team implementing Presidential policy. In some cases, Presidential directives have not been carried out, and counter-productive efforts have taken place within a number of Departments. While the causes of this problem

are varied and complex, the President can do much to solve it by increasing his direct management control over appointees to non-career positions in the Executive Branch. *Such management control can be achieved by attracting the best qualified individuals who are philosophically compatible with and loyal to the President and placing them in leadership positions, motivating them by recognizing and promoting outstanding performers, and removing any whose performance is poor.*[21]

Haldeman was impressed with the report's recommendations and with Frederick Malek, whom he named to assume control of the White House Personnel Office (WHPO). With Malek in charge, WHPO developed a number of new techniques for locating and selecting potential candidates to serve in the Nixon administration. First, it increased the number of potential candidates by searching across the country for qualified candidates — that is, loyal and philosophically compatible. Second, it kept in touch with the departments and agencies concerning lower-level positions. This was a major change. In the past, department and agency heads had automatically been given the right to appoint their immediate subordinates. By 1970, the White House's concern with political loyalty was extending further down the hierarchical ladder.[22]

A third major innovation was WHPO's constant surveillance of appointees after they assumed office. Malek felt it imperative for the administration to ensure that its appointees were living up to expectations concerning loyalty and competence.[23] Appointed officials who ended up "marrying the natives," to use Ehrlichman's term, would be subject to the penalty of removal from office. Loyalty was not meant to be a transient quality.

Malek's ideas on the development of a personnel system designed to appoint Nixon loyalists to cabinet and sub-cabinet positions, made the administration's second-term appointment strategy possible. Now the administration had the organizational means to locate and appoint individuals who would loyally serve the president. But one additional element was necessary for the Nixon administration to take full advantage of the strategy: Nixon had to develop clear and consistent domestic policy choices.

As persistently high inflation, high unemployment, and escalating budget deficits came to dominate the political agenda during the early 1970s, Nixon's concern with domestic affairs intensified. The emerging fiscal crisis, which Nixon could no longer ignore, demanded strong action. These economic factors encouraged the development of more consistent policy choices based on the notion that government spending should be constrained and that new programs were no longer needed. Government wasn't the solution, it was the problem. As Nixon developed more conservative views, he found himself in a stronger position to recruit and appoint individuals who shared his views on domestic matters. In his memoirs he wrote,

> I regretted that during the first term we had done a very poor job in the most basic business of every new administration of either party: we had failed to fill all the key posts in the departments and agencies with people who were loyal to the President and his programs. Without this kind of leadership in appointive positions, there is no way for a president to make any major impact on the bureaucracy.[24]

Nixon made it clear that he would not make the same mistake in his second term. Following the 1972 election, he appointed a number of loyalists to important governmental positions. Unlike the independent-minded individuals of the first term, second-term cabinet secretaries included such loyalists as Caspar Weinberger at Health, Education, and Welfare and James T. Lynn at Housing and Urban Development.[25] Lynn's performance in a variety of different positions within the administration had impressed the president during the first term. When it came time to name a replacement for the petulant George Romney, Lynn's loyalty to the president made him a perfect candidate.

In addition to naming loyal individuals to the cabinet, the White House also took over responsibility for the appointment of lower-level officials. Accordingly, during the second term a greater number of Nixon loyalists controlled positions throughout the bureaucracy. No longer could an independent-minded secretary like George Romney completely dominate the policies of his department. From now on, the president's policy views would be adopted.

Reorganization

Nelson Polsby has argued that the change in Nixon's appointment strategy reflected a fundamental alteration in Nixon's overall political goals. His early concern was with "constituency-building." His second term appointments, in contrast, reflected his concern with "centralizing power in the White House,"[26] a concern that is also reflected in the administration's reorganization proposals.

After his unsatisfactory experience with the highly decentralized cabinet style of government, as exemplified in his various confrontations with HUD Secretary Romney, Nixon decided to adopt a new organizational mechanism for the day-to-day operation of domestic affairs. In foreign affairs the National Security Council had the dual benefit of centralizing presidential control while also reducing the number of individuals with whom the president personally had to deal. Nixon wanted a similar arrangement for domestic affairs.[27] The Nixon administration's first experiment with this type of organizational unit came in 1970 with the establishment of the Domestic Council.

The Domestic Council was created via Reorganization Plan No. 2 of 1970. The president served as Council chairman, which was similar to his position as head of the NSC.[28] John Ehrlichman was selected as the first head of the Domestic Council.[29] Other members included the Vice-President, the Attorney General, and the Secretaries of Interior, Agriculture, Transportation, Treasury, HEW, and HUD. As originally envisioned by the Ash Council, the Domestic Council was supposed to include both professional and nonprofessional staff who would interact with departmental secretaries.[30] In practice, the Council centralized domestic policymaking, thus isolating cabinet secretaries from the policy formulation process. Interagency task forces reported directly to the Domestic Council rather than to department heads. Since the Council was staffed by only about thirty employees, it did not have the manpower to handle all domestic policy questions. Consequently, other power centers quickly emerged. Specific domestic policies became the personal kingdoms of members of the White House staff. Mini-bureaucracies developed around such individuals as Charles Colson, Donald Rumsfeld, Daniel Moynihan, and Bryce Harlow. As Nixon's first term came to an end, it became clear that the Domestic Council had failed in its attempts to centralize presidential authority. Instead, domestic policy had been placed in the hands of individual members of the White House staff, without any mechanism for policy coordination.[31]

George Romney and other cabinet secretaries were highly critical of the Domestic Council because it removed authority for policy development and management from their departments, while providing White House staff with greater authority. The creation of the Domestic Council and the attempt to centralize greater authority in the White House exponentially increased the level of hostility between Nixon and his more outspoken cabinet secretaries.

As a result of the failure of the Domestic Council, the Nixon administration searched for an alternative organizational structure that would centralize domestic policymaking within the White House. On another recommendation of the Ash Council, the administration turned to a comprehensive proposal to reorganize the executive branch of government.

By the middle of his first term, Nixon had begun to learn what could and could not be done within the executive branch. According to former Nixon aide William Safire, the extreme effort required to make the "monster government move confirmed his worst suspicions."[32] Because he was disillusioned with the existing organizational structure, Nixon asked Roy Ash, the president of Litton Industries, to work closely with H. R. Haldeman in "developing a plan for a more efficient way to manage the Executive Branch, [thus] coming to grips with the duplication, overlaps, and essentially making possible policy direction from the man elected to make policy."[33] In other words, Nixon wanted an organizational arrangement that would eliminate redundancy and centralize greater authority in the White House. In response to this request, the Ash Council returned with a comprehensive proposal to reorganize the executive departments that were related to domestic policy.

These proposals were opposed by members of the cabinet. George Romney and John Volpe were particularly adamant in their opposition; both feared that the strategy would further remove authority from their departments. Their opposition to the Ash Council recommendations further alienated them from Nixon and his top lieutenants.

On March 25, 1971, Richard Nixon presented a series of reorganization proposals to Congress. Had they been adopted, these proposals would have represented the most comprehensive restructuring of the federal government in U.S. history. In his message accompanying the proposals, Nixon explained the reason for the reorganization:

> The major cause of the ineffectiveness of government is not a matter of men or money. It is principally a matter of machinery. It will do us little good to change personnel or to provide more resources unless we are willing to undertake a critical review of government's overall design.[34]

According to Nixon, there was a serious problem with the basic "machinery" of government. Government was unresponsive due to organizational limitations, not through any fault of elected or appointed officials. The basic problem was that it no longer made any sense to organize on the basis of methods, such as letting one department deal with all policies related to labor while another dealt with housing policies. Instead, organization needed to be on the basis of means, which represented broad-based policy areas, such as economic policy or community development. Nixon described the difference between methods and means in his message to Congress:

> As we look at the present organization of the Federal Government we find that many of the existing units deal with methods and subjects rather than with purposes and goals. If we have a question about labor we go to the Labor Department and if we have a business problem we go to the Commerce Department. . . . The problem is that as our society has become more complex, we often find ourselves using a variety of means to achieve a single set of goals. We are interested, for example, in economic development. . . . But which department do we go to for that?[35]

Nixon's solution to this problem was to reorganize the executive departments so that they reflected broad policy areas rather than narrow methods. Thus, he offered a proposal to reorganize seven executive departments and several independent agencies, all dealing with domestic policy, into four new super-departments: the Departments of Community Development, Natural Resources, Human Resources, and Economic Affairs. Each of these would represent a broad policy area; for example, policies related to the national economy would be under the jurisdiction of the Department of Economic Affairs, and policies dealing with poverty, such as food stamps, would be under the jurisdiction of the Department of Human Resources.

Reorganization and the Department of Community Development

To fully comprehend the extent of Nixon's reorganization proposal, it is useful to look at the specific proposals for the creation of one department: the Department of Community Development (DCD).

This super-department would have absorbed the Department of Housing and Urban Development, the Rural Electrification Administration, the Appalachian Regional Commission, the Economic Development Administration, the Regional Commission programs from the Commerce Department, Agriculture Department programs dealing with water and waste disposal grants and loans, urban mass transit programs from the Department of Transportation, OEO's Community Action Programs, and the Farmers' Home Administration.[36] The reorganization proposal was justified on the basis that it would have included many similar types of programs within one department, thus reducing interdepartmental competition.

The reorganization proposal, however, also threatened many entrenched interest groups. Big-city mayors and the poor, who had fought for the creation of the Department of Housing and Urban Development during the Kennedy and Johnson administrations, did not like the idea of having their department superseded by a federal entity that might not be as responsive to their demands. The constituency of HUD was fairly narrow. The constituency of DCD would have been much broader. Thus, a specific interest group, such as the mayors of the major cities, would have potentially had less access to officials within the federal government if DCD had been established.

Given the broad scope of the structural change that Nixon's comprehensive reform proposals would have involved, it is not surprising that they met with intense congressional opposition as well.[37] What the Nixon administration did not seem to understand, or take seriously, was that a reorganization plan of this magnitude threatened numerous existing interests, such as those of interest groups and governmental organizations. The reorganization proposals also threatened congressional interests. A massive reorganization of congressional committee jurisdiction would certainly have been required to match the cabinet-level changes. This not only would have disrupted existing relationships between congressional committees and interest groups but also very likely would have reduced the influence of individual members of Congress over specific domestic policies.

Although the administration seemed to understand these facts on a conceptual level, it never examined the political consequences which emanated from this reorganization of authority. The administration was thus unprepared to adequately defend its proposals in

Congress. As Peri E. Arnold has written, "Even in late 1971, as the first of the super-department bills met intense opposition during committee consideration, the administration acted as if its strongest weapon was the good sense of the proposal."[38] Unable to assuage the fears of various powerful interests, the administration watched as its reorganization proposals died in committee.

Following the failures of the Domestic Council and the super-department reorganization proposals, the Nixon administration sought to find another means of centralizing authority in the White House. Shortly after Nixon's reelection victory, the administration adopted a third approach. In his memoirs Richard Nixon wrote,

> Congress had smothered my attempt in 1971 to streamline the government, so I had asked Ehrlichman and Roy Ash, the incoming Budget Director, to set up task forces and consult with constitutional lawyers to determine how much reorganization I could legally do on my own. They advised that I could in fact create by executive authority a system closely resembling the one I had requested in the 1971 reform proposal.[39]

As the second Nixon administration prepared to assume office in January 1973, a new reorganization strategy was prepared. This reorganization created four general management groups, similar in scope to the four super-departments. Again there would be organizational arrangements for Human Resources, Natural Resources, Community Development, and Economic Affairs. But this time, instead of cabinet-level departments, they would be informal management groups overseeing and approving all domestic policy initiatives.

Heading these four management groups would be what the administration came to call the four Super Secretaries or Counselors to the President. James Lynn, the president's new Secretary of Housing and Urban Development, was selected as the Counselor to the President for Community Development. George Schultz held the same post for Economic Affairs. Earl Butz and Caspar Weinberger were chosen as the Counselors for Natural and Human Resources, respectively. The main idea behind the creation of the Super Secretaries was the perceived need to centralize domestic policymaking authority within the White House. Under this organizational arrangement, the administration would not have to depend on the executive departments for advice. Rather, the administration could effectively run the government directly from the White House without fear of bureaucratic resistance or a recalcitrant cabinet secretary like George Romney.

Soon after the Super Secretaries experiment commenced, external factors forced the Nixon administration to abandon the approach. By the end of April 1973, the plan's two most enthusiastic advocates, Haldeman and Ehrlichman, had been forced to resign from office. Ehrlichman's successor, Melvin R. Laird, the Nixon administration's former Secretary of Defense, was not nearly so committed to the new organizational arrangement as his predecessor had been. When Laird departed, Ehrlichman's former deputy, Kenneth Cole, took command. By this time, the administration was fighting for its own survival and Cole found little opportunity to make use of the new organizational arrangement.[40]

Although short-lived, the idea of the Super Secretaries was highly controversial, as had been Nixon's earlier reorganization proposal. Again, critics argued that the reform was an attempt to centralize domestic policymaking authority directly within the White House.

Haldeman has suggested that the establishment of the Super Secretaries was one reason why Nixon's enemies were so willing to use Watergate as a means of attacking the president:

> What would happen if Nixon's reorganization went through, and Nixon remained in office? Washington insiders shuddered. Not only would he tightly control all reins of the government through eight top officers in the White House, he would plant his own "agents" in key positions in every agency of the government. It was too much for those who feared Nixon. Then suddenly, like a ripe plum dropping from a tree Watergate split wide open in late January 1973.[41]

Haldeman's view is conspiratorial and ignores the very real concerns that were the basis for the Watergate investigations. It nevertheless raises an important point. Many of the means by which the Nixon administration attempted to increase its influence over the administrative state eventually led to increased congressional oversight and a decline in the president's actual influence. Clearly, the reorganization strategy had the effect of increasing external opposition to the president's programs without providing palpable benefits. Had Nixon remained in office, would the benefits have eventually exceeded the costs? Since the Super Secretaries strategy provoked intense criticism from officials within the Nixon administration, even during its limited period of implementation, this possibility seems unlikely. For Nixon, the strategy did not achieve its objectives. However, Ronald Reagan would later employ a variation of the strategy—with much greater success—during his two terms in office (see ch. 5). One reason that Reagan was more successful was that he adopted a variation of the Super Secretaries at the very beginning of his term of office, rather than waiting until cabinet secretaries had developed their own entrenched interests.

Removal Power

The president's various reorganization proposals not only failed to centralize greater control over domestic policymaking but also increased congressional concern regarding the ultimate objectives of the Nixon administration. Other administration activities in the area of domestic policy also increased the level of congressional criticism. One such area in which the Nixon administration overstepped its Constitutional authority was in its use of the president's removal power.

The Nixon administration believed that the electoral process had conferred legitimacy on the president and as Nelson Polsby has stated, "a kind of illegitimacy upon many of the very people with whom a President ordinarily does business."[42] This was especially true of the career civil service. Bureaucrats lacked an electoral mandate. Thus, according to administration belief, their opposition to Nixon's policies represented a rejection of democratic values.

Coupled with this rationalization about presidential influence was the administration's belief that, as Polsby puts it, the "elite political stratum in this country . . . was out of touch with the dominant mood of conservatism in the country at large."[43] In other words, the bureaucracy was populated predominantly by liberal Democrats, whose views had been rejected by the public in the previous election. Furthermore, these liberal Democrats, lacking an electoral or popular mandate, reverted to obstructionist techniques to block the will of the people (i.e., the Nixon administration's programs). In a manual prepared for its new political appointees, the administration warned:

> Because of the rape of the career civil service by the Kennedy and Johnson Administrations . . . this Administration has been left a legacy of finding disloyalty and obstruction at high levels while those incumbents rest comfortably on career civil service status.[44]

Viewing career civil servants as nothing more than an obstructionist force blocking the will of the people, the Nixon administration felt entirely justified in removing them from office, even if this violated the spirit, and possibly the letter, of the law. The fact that career civil servants were protected by the Civil Service Act of 1883 seemed irrelevant to administration officials.

Examples of this disregard can be found in the White House personnel manual, which was distributed to political appointees shortly after the 1972 election. This manual was replete with suggestions for skirting the civil serviced statutes — for example, that appointees transfer civil servants to new offices, thus forcing them to relocate or to resign. When firing career civil servants, appointees were also told to inform them that they should remove themselves from the premises immediately; the manual warned, however, against firing a civil service employee in the presence of a witness.[45] Such recommendations blatantly ignored the various legal protections guaranteed civil servants by the 1883 statute.

Although the Nixon administration went beyond the letter of the law in formulating and carrying out these recommendations, according to Frederick Mosher, the Civil Service Commission failed to "attack, or growl, or even bark until the affair had run most of its course."[46] Consequently, the Nixon administration was able to implement its plan to remove recalcitrant civil servants without much immediate protest. Later, though, congressional investigations focused attention on the Nixon administration's violations of the Civil Service Act. The Carter administration then proposed major changes in the management of the civil service system, and these reforms were eventually adopted by Congress with the passage of the Civil Service Act of 1978. Thus, the Nixon administration's removal strategy may have temporarily advanced presidential influence, but it also increased congressional oversight, a potentially significant long-term cost.

The fact that this oversight did not come until later suggests that increased attention to this issue may have been related to increased congressional supervision of the executive branch following the Watergate-related crimes. Because Watergate was so close in time to President Nixon's use of his removal authority, definitive statements regarding the effect of the strategy cannot be provided. Rather, it will be necessary to examine the experiences of another administration with the removal strategy. I will return to this subject in chapter 5 when I examine Reagan and the Environmental Protection Agency.

Presidential Removal at HUD and other Social Service Agencies

The Department of Housing and Urban Development and the other social service agencies were particular targets of the Nixon administration's removal strategy. HUD, for example, was regarded as a new agency populated by zealots who believed in the original goals and objectives of the Johnson administration and the Great Society. In other words, the civil servants within HUD tended to be liberal in their policy views and thus not in agreement with the evolving conservatism of the Nixon administration. Nixon and his top aides viewed such agencies as HUD with disdain: the unelected civil servants within HUD were determined to promote and protect their liberal programs no matter what the electorate had decided in the 1968 or 1972 elections. Consequently, the Nixon administration felt entirely justified in removing many of these liberal civil servants from HUD and the other social service agencies.

What benefits did the removal strategy achieve? The evidence suggests that the benefits were not substantial. According to Joel D. Aberback and Bert A. Rockman, prior to the implementation of the strategy, civil servants within HUD, HEW and the Office of Economic Opportunity (OEO) were predominantly Democrats or Independents. Few Republicans were employed in these agencies, and those who were tended to be more liberal than Republicans in other types of agencies.[47]

Using Aberback and Rockman's analysis as a base point for comparison (most of their interviews had been conducted in 1970), Richard L. Cole and David A. Caputo reexamined the attitudes of HUD, HEW, and OEO employees after the Nixon strategy had been implemented. They found that Nixon had not been able to name a large number of new civil servants; approximately 85 percent of all the pre-Nixon civil servants were still on the job. The number of Democrats in such agencies, however, had decreased from 46 percent to 33 percent, while the number of Republicans had increased from 30 to 37 percent.[48] Thus, the extra-legal Nixon removal strategy did have some limited impact on personnel within such social service departments as HUD. The number of liberal Democrats in these departments did decline. But, in return for these modest benefits, congressional oversight increased. In addition, the strategy may have increased bureaucratic resistance to the Nixon administration's policies (e.g., through leaks to congressional committees and the media).

It is doubtful that the benefits emanating from the removal strategy were worth the long-term costs. Not only did it produce increased congressional scrutiny, but there was no clear evidence that civil servants in the social service departments were any more amenable to the Nixon administration's programs.

The Budget and Impoundments

Another means by which the Nixon administration attempted to increase presidential influence over domestic policymaking was through the use of the president's impoundment authority. Nixon's use of this technique provoked intense congressional criticism. In 1974, Congress overrode a presidential veto to pass the Budget and Impoundment Act, which was designed to reassert congressional influence in the budgetary process and to limit presidential use of the impoundment technique. Also in 1974, the House Judiciary Committee considered adopting an article of impeachment against Richard Nixon relating to his abuse of the impoundment technique. The president's impoundment authority was also challenged in a series of court cases, in most of which the courts ruled against the administration. In recompense for these extraordinary political costs, Nixon received few immediate benefits. With the Department of Housing and Urban Development, the impoundment strategy did produce some limited benefits. The administration was able to bring an abrupt halt to the escalating level of public housing construction. The administration even was able to get a housing bill from Congress which reflected the administration's views. But the high costs the strategy entailed were clearly greater than the benefits received. Again, however, it may be impossible to determine whether these costs were related solely to Nixon's use of the impoundment strategy or whether they were the result of the Watergate-related crimes. As unsatisfying as this conclusion may be, the high costs were likely a response to both.

HUD and the Impoundment Strategy

Within weeks of the 1972 election, the Nixon administration decided to impound funds for a variety of programs administered by the Department of Housing and Urban Development. On January 5, 1973, the administration announced an eighteen-month moratorium on low-rent public housing, rent supplements, home-ownership assistance, and rental housing assistance. Although the impoundments were publicly supported by outgoing HUD Secretary George Romney, he privately criticized the action. At one point, he even refused to make a public announcement of the proposed impoundments.[49]

The impoundment strategy was devised by James Lynn, who replaced Romney as HUD Secretary early in 1973. The impoundments were also supported by Kenneth Cole, Ehrlichman's assistant on the Domestic Council. Cole stated that there was "mounting evidence that the present (HUD) programs . . . have proved inequitable, wasteful, and ineffective in meeting housing needs."[50] To justify this conclusion, HUD officials spent a day and a half putting together a report demonstrating that the department's programs were indeed wasteful and inequitable. HUD's departing Deputy Secretary William Lilley characterized the report as "paper thin, highly subjective and totally unsupported by any back-up data."[51] U.S. District Court Judge Charles R. Richey later ruled the moratorium unlawful. The U.S. Court of Appeals for the District of Columbia, however, reversed the lower court's ruling, largely on the basis of HUD's hastily written report.[52] Later, in *Train v. New York*, a case involving the Environmental Protection Agency, the Supreme Court ruled that the Nixon administration's impoundment of funds had been improper.[53]

In addition to imposing a housing moratorium, the Nixon administration also impounded community development program funds. Many of these programs were administered by HUD. Specific grants affected included new commitments for water and sewer projects, public facility loans, and open space grants.[54] Nixon opposed these categorical grant programs, preferring that they be combined and replaced by a block grant. In 1973, the administration proposed a block grant program that became known as the Better Communities Act. The proposal included more money for water and sewer grants, public facilities loans, and open spaces grants in an attempt to assuage congressional opposition to the impoundment strategy, which intensified with each new Watergate revelation.[55]

All told, the Nixon administration was successful in withholding $970 million from the Department of Housing and Urban Development. Of this amount, the administration intended to spend only $6.6 million, for housing production and mortgage credit, after Fiscal Year 1973. The other 99.3 percent of the impounded funds was meant to lapse irrevocably.[56]

In response to the president's impoundment strategy, Congress attempted to force him to release the impounded funds. Legislation, however, could not get beyond conference.[57] Though Congress could not work out the details of a bill forcing the Nixon administration to release the impounded housing and community development funds, it did turn its attention to the passage of legislation that would force the president to spend at least some funds for housing and community development.

In 1974, Congress enacted the Housing and Community Development Act, which terminated a number of programs, including public facility loans, the water and sewer grant programs, open space grants, model cities, urban renewal, and the neighborhood development program. In return, Congress enacted general block grants, thus providing the Nixon administration with somewhat of a legislative victory just as the president was resigning from office. Even though the bill endorsed many of the president's objectives, Nixon preferred that no bill at all be adopted. Instead, he wanted to prevent Congress from expending the appropriated funds, thus protecting the president's right to impound funds and also continuing the housing moratorium. As pressure from Congress for impeachment began to build, Nixon decided to support the bill as a means of developing support within Congress in hopes of averting impeachment and conviction. Although that strategy failed, the bill was adopted and later signed by President Gerald Ford.[58]

It can be argued that the impoundment strategy was successful in forcing Congress to adopt changes in housing legislation that the Nixon administration advocated. Still, the long-term costs, which included court challenges and increased congressional oversight of the Nixon administration's public housing policies, were prohibitive. The Nixon administration's impoundment strategy no doubt also helped fuel the move to impeach the president, as well as promoting the passage of the Budget and Impoundment Act of 1974.

Like the reorganization proposals and the administration's removal strategy, Nixon's unprecedented use of his impoundment authority engendered greater political costs than the benefits ultimately derived. Presidential influence may have been temporarily increased, but in the long term the technique proved counterproductive.

What does Nixon's employment of the impoundment mechanism suggest regarding attempts to increase presidential influence over the administrative state? First, it suggests that attempts to centralize greater authority in the White House will meet with resistance. Because centralization of power in the president's hands necessarily means that some other policy actor's power will be diminished, there is likely to be an increase in congressional oversight or bureaucratic resistance or both. Second, the use of some techniques to increase presidential influence may entail more political costs than benefits. The rapid increase in congressional activity following the Nixon administration's attempts to centralize control via the reorganization, removal, and impoundment strategies suggests that presidents who are not careful in their use of the tools of the administrative presidency strategy may actually reduce their long-term influence.

Unfortunately, because of both the abbreviated nature of Nixon's second term and the various related Watergate crimes, it is impossible to fully evaluate the usefulness of the administrative presidency strategy. The fact that Nixon was involved in a scandal of historical proportions tends to obscure the actual effect of Nixon's innovations. Would his impoundment strategy have promoted the same retribution had he not been under investigation for various other impeachable actions? Would his reorganization strategy have been more successful following his unprecedented reelection victory had Watergate never come to the attention of the American public? Would his removal strategy have succeeded if he had served out his full term? Any answers to these questions can only be speculative. Although the Nixon administration's experience provides some clues regarding the usefulness of the strategy, a thorough evaluation of the approach cannot be extrapolated entirely from Nixon's term of office. The added effect of the Watergate investigations seriously complicates any attempt to evaluate the potentially negative impacts of the administrative presidency strategy. Were these negative effects related to the administrative presidency strategy, to Watergate, or to a combination of the two? We may never be able to fully untangle the interaction of one phenomenon with the other. Fortunately, for the sake of testing our theory, we do have the experi-

ences of the Carter and Reagan presidencies to analyze, and it is
to those that we will turn in the next three chapters.

Conclusions

Three basic points emerge from this examination of the evolution
of the administrative presidency strategy. First, Nixon's development
of clearly articulated policy choices was a prerequisite to the evolution of the administrative presidency strategy. This is particularly
true of the administration's strategy of appointing loyalists to cabinet
and sub-cabinet positions.

Second, the Nixon administration developed the administrative
presidency strategy as a means of centralizing domestic policymaking
authority in the White House. Nixon wanted to establish a structure
for domestic affairs that was similar to the organizational arrangement for foreign policy development. Consequently, the administration developed the Domestic Council. When this failed, the administration turned to other approaches, such as the Super-Secretaries.

Third, with the exception of the president's appointment power,
the use of the other tools of the administrative presidency strategy
entailed extensive political costs. The reorganization proposals threatened entrenched congressional and interest group influence over
specific domestic policies and generally increased suspicion about
the ultimate objectives of the Nixon administration. The removal
and impoundment strategies increased congressional oversight and
led to the passage of new legislation that constrained presidential
influence. Unfortunately, because Nixon and much of his administration was under investigation for a variety of Watergate-related
crimes, we will never be able to fully untangle whether it was the
crimes or the administrative presidency strategy that led to reduced
presidential influence during Nixon's tenure. To more fully evaluate
the strengths and limitations of the strategy, it will be necessary to
examine the experiences of Nixon's successors.

Chapter 4

Carter and the
Interstate Commerce Commission:
The Power of Appointment

The Nixon administration's experience suggests that the risks of the administrative presidency strategy may outweigh the benefits. Nixon's appointment of loyalists did bring about greater accountability, and the impoundment strategy did lead Congress to adopt legislation consistent with the president's views. By relying on command, rather than persuasion, however, the Nixon strategy also provoked congressional hearings, hostile legislation, and court challenges.

Jimmy Carter's employment of the administrative presidency strategy at the Interstate Commerce Commission (ICC) stressed persuasion over command. Although Carter took full advantage of his appointment power to build support for his policies at the bureaucratic level, he eschewed the more confrontational techniques, such as budget cuts, personnel removals, and reorganization plans. By building support at the bureaucratic level, Carter advanced his policy goals without engendering the hostile opposition that Nixon's approach elicited.

In this chapter I examine Jimmy Carter's experience with the ICC. This case is interesting for two reasons: it demonstrates that a variation of the administrative presidency strategy that emphasizes cooperation over command can be successful, and, in showing Carter's success in this case, it helps explain why Carter was so ineffectual in dealing with the bureaucracy in other policy areas. The latter theme is one I will develop further in the chapters that follow.

Before I examine the case of Carter and the ICC, I first define the issues involved.

Deregulation

Although the term *deregulation* has been widely employed by scholars, its precise meaning has been greatly misunderstood. Airline and trucking deregulation differ distinctly, in both scope and intent. Airline deregulation was designed to be total: rate control and entry restrictions were removed so that the free market prevailed. The Civil Aeronautics Board closed its doors on January 1, 1985. Even under this so-called total deregulation, however, certain safety standards remained in force. In addition, regulation of entry continued under the direction of the Federal Aviation Administration (FAA). Though predominantly due to the air traffic controllers' strike, this continued regulation demonstrates that total deregulation had not been achieved.

Trucking deregulation, in contrast, was not meant to be total. Although major regulatory reforms were envisioned, particularly in the areas of competition and rate setting, certain ICC restrictions were expected to remain in place. These differences in the scope and intent of the airline and trucking reforms suggest the need to define the term *deregulation* more precisely.

According to Alan Stone, there are a number of different types of deregulation. Deregulation can encompass "a complete restoration of market mechanisms and withdrawal of government intervention."[1] As the case of airline deregulation demonstrates, even when such terms as "total" and "complete" are used by policymakers, the result is not total deregulation. Consequently, most reforms can be viewed as a second type of deregulation: "a reduction in the extent of regulation," which Stone defines as an "increase in the number of activities over which firms and persons in a subject industry may exercise discretion without fear of government sanction."[2] We could include both airline and trucking deregulation under this definition.

Several issues became common themes in the debate over deregulation. The regulated industry (including air, truck, and bus) argued that entry requirements and rate-setting provisions were necessary prerequisites for continued economic vitality. Proponents of reform argued that deregulation would promote efficiency and lower prices.[3] Since the issues involved in the deregulation debate are highly technical, I will review them briefly before analyzing how the Carter administration promoted the policy of deregulation.

Competition

Competition or entry policy was one of the major issues raised during the debate over motor carrier deregulation. The original Motor Carrier Act of 1935 had given the ICC the power to grant operating certificates. Section 207(a) permitted the Commission to approve or deny certificates to carriers. Entry into the regulated market was limited to applicants whose service met the standard of "public convenience and necessity."[4] The ability to meet this standard depended on proof by the applicant that the new service to be provided was both needed by the community and could not be provided by existing carriers. This burden of proof on the part of the applicant proved extremely difficult for new carriers to meet and as a result limited the number of new entrants into the regulated market. From 1935 until 1977, the number of trucking firms did not change substantially, as few new carriers were granted certificates.

Despite the lack of new entrants, the American Trucking Associations (ATA), the representative of the regulated trucking industry, argued that the trucking industry was highly competitive. Of the 16,600 trucking firms, 12,453 had annual gross revenues of less than $500,000. The ATA cited these figures as evidence that many of the trucking firms were small companies.[5] In addition, the ATA claimed there was an "absence of concentration in the motor carrier industry."[6] The four largest companies accounted for only 10 percent of the industry's revenues, and the eight largest firms accounted for only 14 percent. These levels of concentration were much lower than in other major industries, such as steel.

On the other side of the debate, proponents of deregulation, such as Mimi Cutler of the Transportation Consumer Action Project, argued that although there were about 15,000 regulated trucking companies, there were "rarely more than two on any route combination. Thus, 15,000 shared monopolies were created in 15,000 little markets which were carefully isolated from one another by ICC regulation."[7] Companies were assigned a particular market by the ICC and could operate only within that limited market. In this way, companies did not have to compete with each other. They had virtual monopoly control over a particular route. If a company wanted to ship goods between St. Louis and Little Rock, for example, it could not choose from among thousands of trucking companies, but rather from only a handful. Supporters of deregulation believed that increased competition would break this monopoly control, thus lowering prices and providing for a more efficient market.

According to the supporters of regulation, increasing competition would have exactly the opposite effect. Although in the short run the number of competitors would increase, the long-term trend would be towards increased concentration.[8] Eased entry would lead to cutthroat competition, a rash of bankruptcies, and an eventual decrease in the number of trucking firms. The larger carriers, with more resources at their disposal, would move into new markets, forcing smaller firms out of business. The end result would be the concentration of trucking service in the hands of three or four large firms. Prices would skyrocket and service would diminish.[9]

Rate Setting

According to the regulated industry, increased competition was not the only factor which could lead to skyrocketing prices. Removal of the industry's ability to set its own rates would also lead to rapid price escalations. The Reed-Bulwinkle Amendment of 1948 had granted the motor carrier industry an antitrust exempt status, thus giving truckers the legal right to collectively set their own rates. According to Section 5(a) of the Interstate Commerce Act (the Reed-Bulwinkle Amendment):

> Parties to any agreement approved by the Commission under this section . . . [are] relieved from the operation of the antitrust laws with respect to the making of such agreement, and with respect to the carrying out of such agreement in conformity with its provisions and in conformity with the terms and conditions prescribed by the Commission.

The ATA claimed that the "exemption from the antitrust laws . . . is not an exemption in the truest sense of the word." Since rate agreements had to be sanctioned by the ICC "in furtherance of the National Transportation Policy," the exemption did not "represent a free ticket for carriers to ignore the antitrust laws."[10] Section 216(a) of the 1935 act required that rates had to be "reasonable." In cases where shippers felt that unreasonable rates were being charged, the Commission could force the motor carrier industry to charge a lower rate. Under this rate-setting system, the antitrust laws had been replaced by a regulatory system.

The organizational structure used by the trucking industry to set collective rates was a system of ten regional rate bureaus, upon which industry representatives were permitted to sit together and to set rates on both single and joint lines.[11] With ICC approval, trucking firms could then legally charge customers these collectively derived rates. The motor carrier industry argued that the ICC's approval power constituted a serious constraint on rate bureau activity; in other words, rate bureaus could not simply set any rates they pleased. However, according to President Carter's first Secretary of Transportation, Brock Adams, the Commission received "hundreds of thousands of motor freight tariffs per year" (containing millions of proposed freight rate changes) and rejected "less than one percent of these" proposals.[12] These figures suggest that ICC rate approval did not provide a serious constraint on rate bureau activity.

Small Community Service

Although competition and rate setting were the primary issues of concern to the motor carrier industry, the issue which received the most attention from Congress was the availability of service to small, predominantly rural communities. Transportation Secretary Brock Adams told the Senate Commerce, Science, and Transportation Committee that "probably the most frequent argument this Congress will hear by opponents of trucking reform is the one dealing with service to small communities."[13] According to this argument, a majority of rural routes were unprofitable. Service was provided to these areas only because the Interstate Commerce Commission forced certified carriers to provide service. In return for bearing this economic hardship, the ICC gave these firms permission to serve other highly profitable routes. Through this process of cross-subsidization, small communities were guaranteed service at an affordable or reasonable price. According to the regulated industry, if ICC controls were removed, the economic incentive for trucking firms to provide service to these rural areas would vanish. Thus, service to many small communities would diminish and the prices for those retaining service would increase dramatically.[14]

Both critics and supporters of deregulation raised the experience of airline deregulation (enacted in 1978) as an example of what would happen if the trucking industry were deregulated. Critics argued that some rural areas had already lost airline service due to deregulation. Supporters countered that smaller airlines had quickly moved into these rural markets, replacing the larger airlines that had left. The result was that few communities had actually lost their airline service. With less than two years of experience to examine, the airline industry did not yet provide a clear indication of the possible effects of deregulation on rural areas. Other evidence, however, was available.

Supporters of deregulation claimed that service to rural areas would not be adversely affected by regulatory reform. In support of this claim, they cited studies conducted by the Department of Agriculture involving exempt agricultural commodities.[15] The exemption of food products by the ICC was temporarily abandoned in the early 1950s, and, for a period of time, agricultural commodities were shipped by common carriers. These commodities were deregulated again shortly thereafter. As a result of this temporary period of regulation, it was possible to perform a controlled study on the effect of regulation on service to small communities. These studies, conducted by the Agriculture Department, found that after deregulation, service had not been abandoned and prices had actually decreased. These studies, however, dealt only with food products which have to be shipped within a very short period of time and for which a large unregulated trucking market already existed. They did not demonstrate that regulatory reform would have a beneficial effect on non-agricultural commodities.

In an attempt to provide more concrete evidence on the subject, the Department of Transportation (DOT) conducted several studies on the potential effects of deregulation.[16] A study conducted in 1979 found that 70 percent of rural communities were not served by the trucking firms authorized to provide service for that area. Many of these communities had switched to private carriers (unregulated motor carriers owned and operated by a specific company) and to United Parcel Service.[17] Another DOT study found that operating certificates issued by the ICC for rural areas were being sold at a positive rate of return.[18] This finding indicated that these rural routes were profitable.[19]

Studies conducted by academics and other government offices also showed strong support for deregulation. Ann F. Friedlander and Richard Spady, in an article that was widely cited in congressional testimony, examined 306 ICC common carriers and found no evidence to support the industry's cross-subsidization argument.[20] A study by the Congressional Budget Office argued that "it does not appear . . . deregulation of [the] trucking [industry] would lead to large-scale discontinuation of service or greatly increased rates in such communities."[21] The evidence provided by these studies did not support the trucking industry's contention. Rather, it appeared that service would likely continue and at lower prices.

Although these studies indicated that service to small communities would not be impaired, many legislators remained deeply concerned. Congressional hearings were held in a number of rural areas by the House Subcommittee on Surface Transportation to collect information on the subject.[22] Senator Howard Cannon, chairman of the Senate Commerce, Science and Transportation Committee, commissioned a study of the potential effects of deregulation on rural service in a number of states, including his own state of Nevada.[23] The regulated industry hoped that congressmen representing predominantly rural states and communities would oppose deregulation out of a concern that service would be impaired. In a study of Senate voting on the Motor Carrier Act of 1980 and related amendments, John P. Frendreis and I found that the urban-rural composition of the senator's state did have a significant impact on the senator's vote, though the relationship was not nearly so strong as for such other factors as whether or not a senator received a PAC contribution from the American Trucking Associations.[24]

The issues of competition, rate setting, and small community service dominated the debate over trucking deregulation. Interestingly the Interstate Commerce Commission was both an early advocate of the trucking industry's stand on these issues and ultimately the strongest proponent of deregulation.

The ICC's Organizational Structure

The Interstate Commerce Commission was established in 1887 as an arm of the Interior Department to regulate the nation's swiftly developing railroad system. With the election in 1888 of President Benjamin Harrison, an ally of the railroad industry, Congress reestablished the ICC as an independent regulatory commission, thus removing it from the jurisdiction of the Interior Department.[25] More importantly, this move greatly weakened the president's direct influence over the Commission. Although the president was still given the right to appoint members of the Commission, he was not delegated the authority to remove the commissioners from office or to select the Commission's chairman. This latter duty was left to the commissioners themselves. They were granted the authority to select the chairman from among themselves to serve for a period of one year. Commissioners served fixed seven-year terms, which were staggered so as to diminish the likelihood that any one president could appoint all eleven commissioners.

Although the ICC was originally created to regulate the railroad industry, its mandate was extended with the passage of the Motor Carrier Act of 1935 to include the trucking industry. The trucking industry initially opposed regulation by the ICC, fearing that it would be the second among equals to the railroad industry, with which it competed. With the rate of bankruptcy rapidly escalating due to the Great Depression, and with the promise that existing trucking firms would receive a favored status over potential new competitors, the trucking industry ultimately endorsed the 1935 act.[26] Within the next five years, the bus and barge industries were also included under the ICC's jurisdiction.

At the recommendation of the first Hoover Commission, an attempt was made in 1950 to grant the president greater authority over the Interstate Commerce Commission.[27] The reorganization was designed to allow presidents to appoint the chairmen of the ICC and the other regulatory commissions. Although Congress adopted the reorganization plan, thus giving presidents greater authority to select agency chairmen, Congress specifically exempted the ICC. This exemption was the result of strong interest group pressure from the railroad industry, which had opposed the change.[28]

In 1969, President Nixon submitted a new reorganization plan to Congress, once again calling for the direct appointment of the ICC's chairman by the president. This time Congress adopted the proposal. The railroad industry was not quite the political force it had been in 1950, and resistance to the proposal was minimal. Reorganization Plan No. 1 of 1969 was to greatly alter the relationship between the president and the Commission. From now on the chairman would unambiguously be the president's man.

Of equal or perhaps even greater importance was that the reorganization plan radically increased the authority of the chairman by officially designating him the executive head of the agency. Before the adoption of the reorganization plan, the chairman had possessed limited formal authority and little influence over the direction of Commission policy, as industry behavior before the Commission demonstrated. Prior to 1969, when industry representatives pleaded their case before the Commission, they usually approached a number of different commissioners. Following the adoption of the 1969 reorganization plan, industry representatives came to present their case directly and exclusively to the ICC's chairman.[29]

According to David Welborn, as a result of the reorganization, the chairman of the Interstate Commerce Commission now had authority over:

(1) the over-all management and functioning of the Commission, (2) the formulation of plans and policies designed to increase the effectiveness of the Commission . . . , (3) prompt identification and early resolution, at the appropriate level, of major substantive regulatory problems, and (4) the development and improvement of staff support to carry out the duties and function of the Commission.[30]

This delegation of authority over management allowed the chairman to reorganize units within the ICC. The right to formulate plans and policies and the ability to identify regulatory problems gave the chairman control over the Commission's agenda, which in turn enabled him to set the agency's priorities and programs. The final delegation allowed the chairman to select staff who supported his policies. The extension of these formal powers played a critical role in promoting the Carter administration's regulatory reform agenda.

Besides granting the chairman of the ICC greater authority, the reorganization plan also provided the means for reducing the influence of the powerful ICC division chairmen.[31] These officials, comparable to bureau chiefs, not only had a history of strong opposition to deregulation but before 1969 had the power to unilaterally kill a deregulation proposal by bottling it up within their division. Reorganization Plan No. 1 of 1969 gave the chairman the means to remove this obstacle to deregulation. The principal means was the power of administrative reorganization, a power that Carter's first chairman, A. Daniel O'Neal, would use to great effect to limit internal ICC opposition to the administration's deregulation proposals.

Through the adoption of Reorganization Plan No. 1 of 1969, Richard Nixon contributed as much to the final adoption of the

Motor Carrier Act of 1980 as did Jimmy Carter. Nixon's reorganization plan provided the organizational basis for regulatory change. Without the increased influence of the chairman over Commission policy, and without the extension of presidential appointment power over the chairmanship, it is unlikely that the Carter administration's deregulation proposals would have been formulated and adopted. Why neither Nixon nor Ford used the ICC chairman's new authority as a means of promoting deregulation at the administrative level is unclear.

Early Deregulation Proposals

The issue of deregulation was first placed on the governmental agenda in 1955 when the second Hoover Commission recommended the elimination of the Interstate Commerce Commission.[32] There was little congressional response to the Hoover Commission's report. This can be attributed partially to the fact that the Commission's 1955 recommendations were much more ideologically based and broader in scope (of proposed change) than were its more modest 1949 recommendations. A second reason why the recommendations were not pursued is that the Eisenhower administration seemed less committed to the goals of reorganization in 1955 than it had been two years earlier when the Commission had commenced its work. Third, the Democrats had rebounded in Congress, scoring impressive victories in both the House and the Senate. By the late 1950s there were a greater number of liberal Democrats in Congress. Thus, the Eisenhower administration was not politically in a strong enough position to offer a bold new reorganization proposal.[33]

The Kennedy administration was the first to offer a comprehensive legislative proposal for reform. Following the recommendations of the Landis Report,[34] and the Senate Commerce Committee's Special Study Group on Transportation,[35] the administration proposed legislation which attempted to provide greater coordination in the area of transportation policy. According to Robert Bernard, the main purpose of the Kennedy reform package was to "plug the loopholes" in transportation regulation or, failing this, to "remove all regulation" entirely.[36] The proposal was not high on the administration's agenda and thus received limited congressional attention. Congress examined the issue briefly during 1962, but no action was taken. The Johnson administration followed up on Kennedy's proposals, later creating the Department of Transportation (DOT).[37] DOT did not assume the tasks of railroad, motor carrier, bus, or barge regulation, although it did take the responsibility for several tasks previously performed by the ICC, such as supervision over cargo insurance, the requirements for vehicle safety, and limiting the number of hours truck drivers could work.[38]

The next proposal for reform came in 1971 with the Nixon administration's Transportation Regulatory Modernization Act. Based on the Ash Council's recommendations, the bill was "premised on the belief that increased reliance on competitive forces and the ability of regulated surface transportation carriers to respond to these forces free of unheeded constraint is an essential prerequisite to the revitalization of a privately-owned transportation system," a top Nixon aide said.[39] Like Kennedy's reform proposal, the Nixon bill received little attention in Congress, partly because of ICC opposition to reform initiatives and partly because of the Nixon administration's limited commitment to reform (that is, it was not high on the administration's legislative agenda).

Once the Nixon administration's Reorganization Plan No. 1 of 1969 gave the president the right to appoint the ICC's chairman, Nixon exercised his new presidential prerogative and appointed George Stafford, an ardent critic of deregulation. This decision can be partially explained by the fact that Nixon initially decided to surround himself with independent-minded men, rather than yesmen. Moreover, Richard Nixon was not only more concerned with foreign policy than domestic policy but also appeared to be even less interested in regulatory policy than in most other domestic policies. As ICC resistance to the administration's reform agenda continued, however, a dissatisfied President Nixon proposed that the ICC be eliminated and its functions transferred to the Department of Commerce.[40] This proposal, like many of Nixon's other reorganization proposals, went nowhere in Congress.

After the Nixon administration's reform attempts, deregulation was again assigned to the legislative agenda by the Ford administration. Following the recommendation of an overwhelming majority of the twenty-three economists who participated in the administration's September 1974 Summit Conference on Inflation, President Ford announced his intention to propose legislation deregulating the trucking, railroad, and airline industries.[41] In 1975 legislation was introduced in Congress, but once again the proposal failed to make it out of committee.[42]

The Ford administration did not put forward a concerted effort to procure congressional approval of its trucking bill. Concerned with the upcoming 1976 election, Ford backed away from his reform proposal, even apologizing to an ATA conference for initiating the trucking bill. The proposal also was vehemently opposed by the regulated trucking industry, the Teamsters Union, and, more importantly, by the Interstate Commerce Commission. In a report entitled "A Cost Benefit Evaluation of Surface Transport Regulation," the Commission maintained that deregulation would "reduce efficiency" in the trucking industry by "introducing destructive competition."[43] In testimony before the House Subcommittee on Surface Transportation, ICC Chairman George Stafford argued that "it has not been demonstrated that the sweeping revisions" proposed by the Ford administration's bill "are responsive to a public demand for such changes in motor carrier regulation, and there is also a clear lack of objective evidence to support many of the proposals for change contained in it."[44] Stafford defended his statement by citing a Department of Transportation Industrial Shipper Study which indicated that 84.7 percent of all shippers "found the present number of motor carriers to be entirely adequate to maintain good service."[45]

ICC opposition to deregulation contributed to the defeat of the Ford administration's reform proposal much in the same manner as it had undermined all previous reform initiatives. Without the support of the Commission, the presumed experts on motor carrier regulation, it was difficult for members of Congress to endorse an abstract theoretical concept. Consequently, Congress had repeatedly ignored administration proposals to substantially alter the manner in which the trucking industry was regulated. In addition, ICC opposition to deregulation provided the regulated industry with a potent ally before Congress and imbued its defense of regulation with a strong sense of credibility. Therefore, a prerequisite in the strategy to gain congressional approval for trucking reform was to somehow neutralize ICC resistance toward deregulation.

Ford had attempted to neutralize this resistance by naming as commissioners Robert J. Corber and Betty Jo Christian, both of whom were pro-reform, and by attempting to replace George Stafford with his own chairman. In February 1976, Ford nominated

Warren Rudman to serve as the new ICC chairman. Partially because 1976 was an election year, the Senate failed to act on Rudman's nomination. After four months of waiting, Rudman withdrew his name from consideration, leaving Ford with no replacement for Stafford.[46] The attempt to remove Stafford did, moderate his behavior, however;[47] for example, Stafford applied the mild rate-setting provisions of the Railroad Revitalization and Regulatory Reform Act to the trucking industry. Real reform, however, would not come under George Stafford's leadership. It would have to await the appointment of a new chairman who supported the goals of deregulation.

When Jimmy Carter assumed the office of president, the major problem with which he was confronted was how to neutralize the Commission's opposition to his deregulation proposals. Carter's proposals would likely have failed, as had the initiatives of his predecessors, if he had not removed this source of opposition. Carter could have employed the tools of the administrative presidency strategy to neutralize ICC opposition. He could have reduced the Commission's budget or attempted to reorganize the ICC by transferring its functions to the Department of Transportation. In other words, he could have challenged the ICC directly. Instead, Carter selected a strategy which emphasized his power of appointment. He also worked with the career bureaucracy to fashion a deregulation proposal. Instead of taking the confrontational approach, Carter adopted a cooperative approach.

Carter and His Appointments

The selection of A. Daniel O'Neal to serve as the ICC's new chairman seemed at first to signal that Jimmy Carter was not committed to the goal of deregulation. After all, O'Neal as an ICC commissioner had distinguished himself over the years for his opposition to deregulation. He had also served as a staff assistant to Senator Warren G. Magnuson (D-Washington), who was himself opposed to deregulation. At his confirmation hearings in 1973, O'Neal stated,

> I think that . . . there are some dangers in complete deregulation that . . . we have to be aware of. I am not sure what it means if you trust in the virtues of pure competition and rely solely on the antitrust laws for protection for the public. It seems to me that the Commission was established to carry out vigorous enforcement of regulatory laws and that probably is the best course to follow.[48]

O'Neal's opposition to deregulation did not appear to be a transient belief. He later expressed his opposition in scholarly articles and in testimony before the U.S. Congress concerning the Ford administration's regulatory reform bill.[49] At the same time that O'Neal expressed opposition to deregulation, however, he also voiced support for consumer protection. These views, consistent with those of O'Neal's mentor Warren Magnuson, apparently had an effect on Jimmy Carter's decision to designate O'Neal as the Commission's new chairman.

Although Carter was committed to replacing the ardently anti-deregulatory George Stafford, he wanted to select a chairman who would not offend the established interest groups: the American Trucking Associations and the Teamsters. The designation of O'Neal as chairman avoided the interest group opposition which would have developed had Carter initially appointed an outwardly pro-deregulatory chairman. The O'Neal appointment also provided the Carter administration with a strategic advantage over the regulated industry. The ATA expected the Carter administration to offer a deregulation proposal. What they did not anticipate was that deregulation would be initiated by the Interstate Commerce Commission. O'Neal's radical policy reversals caught the industry entirely off guard. As a result, the ATA was not able to effectively respond to the ICC's initial reform initiatives.

That O'Neal's elevation from commissioner to chairman well served the Carter administration is apparent. What is not so obvious is the reason why O'Neal, a consistent opponent of deregulation, was willing to initiate a regulatory reform program. Unfortunately, evidence on this point is at best circumstantial. In my interveiws with officials from the Interstate Commerce Commission, the regulated industry, and the Carter administration, it was suggested that O'Neal altered his personal viewpoint in order to be consistent with the president's regulatory philosophy. For an office-holder with ambitions of advancing to more important governmental positions, this change of heart makes complete sense. Alternatively, it has been suggested that O'Neal's views on deregulation had matured slowly over time. As a result of his combined experiences as a congressional staffer on the Senate Commerce Committee and over three years as an ICC commissioner, he had come to view deregulation more favorably. Yet his writings and congressional testimony do not seem to support this interpretation. Whatever the source of his conversion, there is no doubt that he vigorously implemented the president's program.

After making the decision to elevate A. Daniel O'Neal to the chairmanship of the Commission, the Carter administration embarked on an unusual strategy for influencing Commission goals and behavior. Rather than taking an active role in appointing new commissioners, the Carter administration refused to fill Commission vacancies. Over the next two years, four commissioners departed and were not replaced. These four vacancies were meant to serve as a symbol of Carter's commitment to deregulation. By allowing the Commission to contract from eleven to seven, Carter was demonstrating his commitment to smaller government and less government regulation. The strategy also prevented the regulated industry from using the congressional hearings process as a means of attacking the Interstate Commerce Commission's reform initiatives.

Carter was assisted in his pursuit of this strategy by President Ford's decision to name commissioners who supported the goal of deregulation. As the terms of opponents of reform expired, Ford's pro-reform commissioners had more influence over Commission policy. When the Carter administration turned its attention from administrative to legislative change, however, Carter adopted a new appointment strategy.

In December 1978 at a meeting before a business conference, President Carter signaled that a new appointment strategy would soon be adopted:

> I am very proud that the ICC Chairman, Dan O'Neal, has been very staunch in deregulating the trucking industry. I back him in this. I realize the independence of the regulatory agencies but with my own voice and influence, my future appointments to the ICC, my intention [is] to continue this trend.[50]

As 1979 approached, two factors induced Carter to make a positive use of his appointment power. First, A. Daniel O'Neal's term was coming to an end. Although O'Neal had supported the president's program, he was not enthusiastic about the Carter administration's planned legislative proposal.[51] He preferred instead to promote reform only at the administrative level.

A second reason why Carter decided to adopt a more active appointment strategy in 1979 was that the administration had just successfully promoted the deregulation of the airline industry. During

1977 and 1978, the Carter administration had focused most of its political resources on the deregulation of the airline industry.[52] This was a calculated move. The administration felt that airline reform would meet with less resistance from the regulated industry and Congress. It would thus have a better chance for congressional adoption than motor carrier or railroad reform. With the passage of the Airline Deregulation Act of 1978, the Carter administration judged that there was now sufficient momentum behind the deregulation issue to move forward with its trucking and railroad bills. It thus made sense to nominate a number of pro-reform individuals. Such nominations demonstrated to Congress both that the administration was fully committed to reform and that the newly constituted Commission would be capable of carrying administrative deregulation forward even if Congress did not act. Because of these factors, Carter proceeded to nominate a number of pro-deregulatory individuals to the Interstate Commerce Commission and to other agencies that had a stake in the administration's reform proposal.

In 1979 Carter nominated Darius B. Gaskins to serve as the new chairman of the ICC and Marcus Alexis and Thomas Trantum as commissioners. Together the three would become known as the "free marketeers." These new appointees had impeccable credentials. Darius B. Gaskins was an economist who had prior governmental experience with the Department of Energy, the Civil Aeronautics Board, and the Federal Trade Commission.[53] Particularly relevant was his experience as director of the Office of Economic Analysis at the Civil Aeronautics Board between 1977 and 1978, where he served as the right-hand man of Alfred Kahn, the CAB chairman. Gaskins' office was responsible for initiating many of the reform proposals that later formed the basis for the CAB's administrative deregulation program. Thomas Trantum and Marcus Alexis were also well qualified to serve on the Commission: Trantum had spent nine years as a securities analyst specializing in the airline and motor carrier industries, and Alexis was chairman of the economics department at Northwestern University.[54]

Besides having excellent qualifications, each had expressed support for the policy of deregulation. At his confirmation hearings, Darius Gaskins expressed his support for O'Neal's administrative deregulation agenda:

> My experience with airline deregulation indicates that there may be substantial advantages to relying on competition. I am also encouraged

by the recent steps taken by the Commission under Chairman O'Neal to ease regulatory restrictions in the motor carrier industry. I certainly support this deliberate and thoughtful attempt to strike a better balance between competition and regulation by increasing opportunities for entry, easing route and carriage restrictions, and circumscribing the role of rate bureaus.[55]

Trantum and Alexis also voiced their support for reform. Trantum stated that "every effort should be made to minimize artificial barriers that tend to inhibit the responsiveness of truck service to shippers."[56] Alexis said that he favored open entry to increase competition but did not support the sudden abandonment of ICC rate and route restrictions. Rather than blanket action he preferred a case-by-case examination of the issues so as to avoid any serious dislocations, such as abandoning service to small communities.

The nomination of Gaskins, Trantum, and Alexis to the Commission greatly concerned the regulated industry. The American Trucking Associations asked the Senate Commerce, Science, and Transportation Committee to delay action on the three nominations until Congress had acted on the Carter administration's motor carrier deregulation bill.[58] Despite this opposition from the regulated industry, Carter's appointees were easily confirmed.

Carter's support for deregulation did not end with the appointment of the "free marketeers." Carter also nominated Neil E. Goldschmidt to serve as the new Secretary of Transportation. Carter's first Transportation Secretary, Brock Adams, had opposed deregulation of the motor carrier industry while serving in the House of Representatives.[59] Although Adams supported the Carter administration's deregulation proposals in congressional testimony, his commitment to reform was still suspect, particularly among ardent supporters of deregulation. In fact, the Carter administration itself had circumvented Adams in formulating the initial deregulation proposals for the airline and trucking industries.[60] Carter's nomination of Neil Goldschmidt demonstrated to supporters of deregulation that the administration would vigorously promote the policy of regulatory reform.

Unlike Adams, Goldschmidt was quick to endorse the Carter administration's regulatory reform agenda. At his confirmation hearing, Goldschmidt characterized the administration's railroad and motor carrier reform proposals as "essential in improving productivity, fighting inflation, and improving energy conservation."[61] After his confirmation by the Senate, Goldschmidt played an active role in promoting the administration's reform agenda.

Carter also appointed economist and ardent deregulator Alfred Kahn as the new chairman of the Council on Wage and Price Stability (COWPS). As the chairman of the Civil Aeronautics Board, Kahn had helped to lead the administration's efforts to deregulate the airline industry. With his new job, which afforded him greater access to the Oval Office, Kahn was in a strong position to leave his personal imprint on the administration's motor carrier deregulation proposals as well.

Carter's active use of his appointment power was the fulcrum of his efforts to secure the deregulation of the motor carrier industry. By naming *qualified* individuals whose commitment to deregulation was beyond reproach, Carter was able to successfully advance the policy of deregulation both at the administrative level and in Congress. Not only were Carter's appointees committed to the goal of deregulation, but *they were also qualified both in terms of prior experience and training to promote the Carter administration's reform agenda.*

The conversion of the Interstate Commerce Commission from an active opponent of motor carrier deregulation to its strongest proponent played a critical role in promoting the policy of deregulation in Congress. Unlike Nixon (and later Reagan), Carter did not unduly rely on his budgetary or reorganization authority to alter ICC policy. His activity in these areas was minimal.

The ICC and Its Budget

Carter's appointment strategy was not supplemented with direct cuts in the ICC's budget or its number of employees. The budget for the Interstate Commerce Commission increased steadily during the Carter years (see Table 4-1). In addition, the number of employees remained approximately the same throughout most of Carter's tenure and did not begin to decline until 1980, two years after the ICC had initiated many of its administrative reform proposals.

Carter's approach suggests that budget and personnel reductions are not a necessary or sufficient condition for altering the behavior of regulatory agencies. When staff resistance is high, such reductions may be necessary to weed out opposition within an agency

APPROPRIATIONS AND EMPLOYMENT FOR THE ICC

Year	Appropriation	Average Employment
1977	60,786,000	2,084
1978	65,575,000	2,040
1979	70,400,000	2,040
1980	79,400,000	1,946

Source: Interstate Commerce Commission, *1984 Annual Report:* 119.

or to intimidate prospective opponents. Since staff level support for motor carrier regulatory reform was already high, budget cuts and personnel layoffs might have been counterproductive, very likely disrupting the sense of unity. As a result of strong staff level support, budget and personnel reductions were neither needed nor necessarily prudent presidential strategy.

Reorganization and the ICC

Jimmy Carter did not use his reorganization authority with regard to the Interstate Commerce Commission to promote his policy of deregulation. A. Daniel O'Neal, however, employed his administrative reorganization authority to eliminate the last internal vestiges of ICC opposition to the policy of deregulation, the once powerful specialized divisional units. O'Neal also created the Office of Policy and Analysis to perform studies on the possible effects of deregulation, and most of these studies strongly advocated the deregulation policy. These organizational changes, though important, do not match the scope of structural change that occurred at the Environmental Protection Agency during Anne Burford's tenure as administrator, where strong staff level opposition to the Reagan reform agenda was present (see ch. 5).

As with budget and personnel reductions, the need to make extensive use of the reorganization strategy was largely mitigated by the presence of strong staff-level support. After the divisional units had been removed and an office created to analyze and promote deregulation, there was no further need to reorganize the ICC. The Nixon administration's Reorganization Plan No. 1 of 1969 had already enacted the major organizational changes that were needed to centralize greater authority in the office of the ICC chairman and to grant the president greater direct influence over the Commission. Consequently, by the time Carter was elected president, the organizational road had already been cleared for deregulation, and all he had to do was to take advantage of these generous provisions.

This is not to suggest that Jimmy Carter's contribution to the adoption to the policy of deregulation was minimal. Indeed, the opposite point needs to be made. By using the provisions of the 1969 reoganization plan to appoint committed and qualified individuals to the ICC, the Commission was able to adopt an administrative strategy for promoting reform, rather than relying on the legislative approach, which all of Carter's predecessors had utilized. The adoption of the administrative approach was the Carter administration's greatest contribution to the passage of the Motor Carrier Act of 1980. Administrative deregulation disrupted existing relations between the ICC and the regulated industry. It also provided clear evidence of the beneficial effects of deregulation, which Congress could then analyze. Finally, it greatly removed the burden of responsibility from Congress should the policy of deregulation have deleterious consequences; under such circumstances, Congress could simply put the blame on the ICC. These factors made it easier for Congress to adopt a motor carrier act in 1980. With these points in mind, we can now turn to the Carter administration's important innovation of administrative deregulation.

Administrative Deregulation

One of A. Daniel O'Neal's first acts as chairman of the ICC was the creation of a Staff Task Force on Regulatory Reform. On July 6, 1977, less than three months after its creation, the task force reported thirty-nine recommendations for reform. According to the ICC's Annual Report, these proposals served as the "primary agenda for efforts to improve entry regulation," one of the reformer's chief goals.[62]

The Task Force played a crucial step in altering the ICC's regulatory goals. It provided the agency with an agenda for deregulation that was consistent with President Carter's philosophy. It also gave the Commission direction — a clearly delineated strategy that could be followed in promoting reform. With these proposals in hand, the Commission could begin to ease entry requirements and increase competition within the regulated trucking industry.

Adhering to the recommendations of O'Neal's Task Force, the Interstate Commerce Commission enacted a radical policy of administrative deregulation between 1977 and 1980. These administrative reforms fall into two basic categories: the ICC acting to ease entry into the regulated industry, and the Commission attacking the trucking industry's antitrust exempt status, thus providing greater rate-setting freedom.

One of the main goals of the Carter administration and the Interstate Commerce Commission under Chairman A. Daniel O'Neal was the promotion of greater competition in the regulated trucking industry. This was to be accomplished by the easing of entry requirements, which would allow new carriers to provide trucking service.

The ICC had been under pressure from external forces to alter its entry policies. In 1977, the Second Court of Appeals ruled in the case of *P.C. White, Inc. v. United States*[63] that the Commission had to consider the potential benefit to the public of increased competition. This decision opened the door to increased competition, but it alone does not explain why the ICC altered its entry policy. The Commission could have appealed the decision to the Supreme Court or could have interpreted the decision narrowly, thus forcing another court action which likely would have taken years to resolve. Yet the Commission chose neither of these alternatives. Instead, over the next two years, it actively moved forward towards a policy of liberalized entry.

In the Commission's first decision of 1978, *P.C. White Truck Line Incorporated Extension–Atlanta,*[64] the ICC reversed an earlier decision denying the P. C. White Company a certificate of public convenience and necessity. In this reversal the Commission complied with the Second Court of Appeal's ruling. Although the Commission did not yet take the radical step of restating its entry policy, compliance with the court's decision provided an early signal that change was forthcoming.

By the end of 1978, the Commission had unambiguously enunciated a new entry policy. In its *Policy Statement on Motor Carrier Regulation,*[65] the ICC announced that applicants now had to demonstrate only that the service proposed was responsive to a useful public purpose and that they were fit to perform that service. In other words, the Commission had shifted the burden of proof in certificate application cases from the applicant to the protestant.

This new policy represented a clear and dramatic break with ICC entry policy over the past forty years.

In September 1978, the ICC decided the *Liberty Trucking* case, which officially altered ICC entry policy. In considering an application to grant the Liberty Trucking Company the right to provide night service to Atlanta, the Commission ruled that the Liberty Company should be granted a certificate extension because it was fit and because no other existing carrier could provide the service.[66] The American Trucking Associations asked the Commission to reconsider its decision. The ATA charged that the Commission had gone beyond the existing criteria established in 1936 in the *Pan American Bus Lines Operation* case,[67] which had provided the basis for ICC entry policy for over forty years.

In its decision on the reconsideration of the *Liberty* case, the ICC announced that it had not violated the spirit of the *Pan American* decision. But the Commission warned,

> The day is past when conflicting authority coupled with pertinent abstracts will alone suffice to deny an application for operating rights. It is reasonable to require a protestant more than a showing that the applicant might offer competition.[68]

By 1979 the Commission's new eased entry policy was reflected in the fact that the ICC was rejecting less than 2 percent of all certificate applications.[69] Only applicants with egregious past safety records were denied a certificate of public convenience and necessity. Consequently, by the beginning of 1979, ICC entry policy had been almost entirely returned to the free market. Congress had not yet been consulted. What every president from Kennedy to Ford had attempted legislatively, Carter and the ICC had achieved by administrative means.

Increased competition was not the ICC's only objective. Another issue of concern was the trucking industry's antitrust exempt status. During the Nixon and Ford administrations, the Departments of Justice and Transportation had investigated ICC rate-setting policy. Senator Edward Kennedy had also conducted hearings on the matter.[70] In 1976, with the passage of the Railroad Revitalization and Regulatory Reform Act (the 4R Act), Congress had attempted to alter the trucking industry's antitrust exempt status. The industry was successful in preventing any amendments to the act that would have altered existing motor carrier rate-setting standards. After the

Ford White House attempted to replace George Stafford with War-ren Rudman, and following the Kennedy hearings, which focused greater congressional attention on the issue, the ICC eventually acted to unilaterally apply the modest provisions of the 4R Act to the trucking industry.

In December 1977, as a means of promoting more extensive change, the Carter administration formed the fifteen-member National Com-mission for the Review of Antitrust Laws and Procedures. The Com-mission consisted of Assistant Attorney General John H. Shene-field, Federal Trade Commission Chairman Michael Pertschuck, CAB Chairman Alfred Kahn, three members of each house of Con-gress (including Senator Edward Kennedy), a U.S. District Court judge, and five people from the private sector.[71] In January 1979, the panel recommended that the trucking industry's antitrust ex-empt status should be removed.[72]

Following the recommendation of Carter's Antitrust Commis-sion, the ICC acted to alter its existing rate policy. O'Neal's first ac-tion, according to an Annual Report of the ICC, was to force all rate bureaus to "refile their agreements, subject to Commission re-view, to determine whether the agreements [warranted] continuous antitrust immunity."[73] On February 28, 1979, shortly after Carter's Antitrust Commission had released its recommendations, the ICC enunciated its new rate-setting policy. Just as in the decision on en-try, the new ICC policy represented a repudiation of its prior stand on the issue. In Ex-parte No. 297 the Commission decided to "pro-hibit collective voting on single-line trucking rates and to limit the voting on joint-line rates to those carriers that can 'practicably par-ticipate' in the movement under consideration."[74]

According to an official from the American Trucking Associa-tions, this decision had the effect of deregulating rate setting. With entry requirements practically abandoned and rate-setting standards radically altered, the ICC had administratively achieved the two ma-jor aims of deregulation by February 1979, sixteen months before Congress was to adopt the Motor Carrier Act of 1980. The Carter administration had accomplished this revolution by using its ap-pointment power to remove the last source of internal opposition, ex-Chairman George Stafford, from a vital position where he could block Commission support for deregulation. As the year 1979 con-tinued, and as the focus of debate moved to Capitol Hill, Carter used his appointment power again to name Darius Gaskins, Thomas

Trantum, and Marcus Alexis to the Commission. These appointments made it evident to legislators that if Congress did not act, the Commission would be capable of continuing the revolution in transportation regulation entirely on its own. This was a message that the regulated industry and members of Congress heard loud and clear.

Carter not only used his appointment power, but also personally promoted the issue of deregulation. John Kingdon has argued that Carter's interest in the issue was partially responsible for the increased political salience of the trucking issue among transportation experts. In 1978 only 16 percent of Kingdon's transportation interviewees stated that trucking deregulation was an important issue. By 1979 that number had jumped to 83 percent. A number of the respondents attributed their changed perspective to Carter's personal involvement.[75]

Carter's personal involvement was no doubt influential. Yet the administration's decision to promote reform at the administrative rather than at the legislative level was the essential step in the promotion of the policy of deregulation. It forced Congress to give the issue more than a perfunctory review. It also disrupted the close relationship between the ICC and the regulated industry.

The Interest Group Reaction

The regulated trucking industry reacted with outrage to the ICC reform agenda. Bennett C. Whitlock, Jr., the president of the American Trucking Associations, stated that the "ICC has embraced a policy of uneven ill-considered administrative deregulation."[76] Stressing that only Congress had the legal right to alter the system of motor carrier regulation, the ATA filed numerous lawsuits charging the ICC with violations of the Motor Carrier Act of 1935. Most of these lawsuits, however, were negated by the passage of the Motor Carrier Act of 1980.

The powerful Teamsters Union also opposed the ICC's reform agenda. Frank E. Fitzsimmons, the General President of the Teamsters, claimed that "under the chairmanship of A. Daniel O'Neal, the ability of the [motor carrier] industry to pay fair wages and benefits has been seriously threatened."[77]

The ATA and the Teamsters were the two largest and most influential groups opposing the deregulation of the motor carrier industry. The ATA raised over $2 million in an attempt to convince the Congress and the American people that deregulation was not in their best interests.[78] Of this sum, over $250,000 was contributed to members of Congress through the Truck Operator's Nonpartisan Committee, the ATA's political action committee.[79] The organization also hired a high-powered public relations firm at great expense to convince consumers that ICC regulation was beneficial to the public interest. This attempt proved unsuccessful, largely because it was difficult to demonstrate to the public the economic benefits of regulation. The ATA also tried to arouse public concern by arguing that if deregulation were adopted, service to small communities would be impaired. Although this argument was stressed repeatedly in congressional hearings, public interest in the issue was not perceptible.

It is interesting that despite this high level of opposition to ICC deregulation, the regulated industry's views on the subject were far from monolithic. The American Trucking Associations is composed of 13 separate conferences, each representing a different type of regulated carrier (e.g., private carriers and contract carriers). Each of these conferences had different interests and thus had somewhat different opinions on the deregulation debate. For example, although there was general agreement among the conferences that the ATA would have to compromise on either entry or rate policy in order to limit the movement towards deregulation, there was little agreement concerning whether the ATA should compromise on rates or entry. Some conferences argued that the ATA should compromise on rate policy and stand firm on competition, while others made the opposite agrument. This lack of unanimity considerably weakened the ATA's ability to counter the ICC's new agenda.

The deregulation debate also exacerbated some long-term disagreements, such as the conflict between the Private Carrier Conference and other ATA conferences. Private carriers, who provide trucking service for a firm owned and operated by a specific company, such as Sears, wanted to have the right to haul goods that were owned by a subsidiary company. Other conferences wanted to limit private carriers to hauling goods for subsidiaries that were 100 percent owned by the parent company. This disagreement had divided the ATA's conferences for years. The deregulation debate intensified this long-standing controversy, since one of the legislative proposals for reform was to allow private carriers to haul goods for a subsidiary company which was only 50 percent owned by its parent company. These sources of disagreement considerably weakened the ATA's ability to counter the growing momentum for regulatory reform.

Although the Teamsters were not internally divided over the issue of deregulation, the union was not so powerful by the late 1970s as it had once been. During the 1970s, the Teamsters Union suffered severe setbacks. The provisions of the Landrum-Griffin Act of 1959, for example, limited the union's ability to coerce non-union employees to follow the Teamsters' line. In addition, the Teamsters' strength had always been in the area of regular route carriers (those carriers who served specifically prescribed routes). In the 1970s there was a rapid increase in the number of irregular route carriers or those carriers who served geographic regions but not specific routes. These irregular carriers were predominantly non-union. There were also increases in the number of private and contract carriers. Again, both of these types of carriers were predominantly non-union. Accordingly, the increase in the number of irregular route, common, and private carriers provided greater competition for unionized regular route carriers. In many cases, the unionized carriers were unable to compete with the non-unionized competition.[80] Thus, the Teamsters Union found itself in a less politically influential position by the late 1970s than it had been in previous decades. Still, it would be incorrect to assume that the Teamsters had no influence. The Teamsters Union, along with the ATA, was still a powerful force opposing deregulation.

Although the greatest pressure on the ICC and Congress came from interest groups opposed to deregulation, a number of groups supported reform. The most prominent of these were the independent truckers, who, although only minimally subject to ICC regulation, stood to gain considerably if deregulation were adopted. Like the regulated industry, the independent truckers were unable to put forward a united front on the issue of deregulation. Their lack of unanimity emanated from another issue which was also consuming their time and resources: the gasoline shortage. At the same time that the trucking bill was before Congress, the independent truckers were involved in a number of often violent protests over the shortage of gasoline, the result of the Oil Embargo of 1979. This exogenous issue distracted the independent truckers from the deregulation debate, thus weakening their influence.

Of all the groups that supported deregulation, none was so well organized as either the ATA or the Teamsters. Most of the groups who were for reform were either badly divided over the various reform proposals — such as shipping groups over rate reform — or distracted by such exogenous factors as the Oil Embargo. They were not in a position to counter the tremendous effort mounted by the ATA and the Teamsters. Hence, it cannot be argued that these pro-consumer groups provided the necessary support for reform that would have independently forced the ICC and Congress to adopt deregulation. The greatest pressure on the ICC was to reverse its policy of administrative deregulation and to return to the traditional regulated market.

Interest group opposition to ICC deregulation raises several interesting points. First, this case study provides no evidence supporting the various iron triangle theories which postulate that the regulating commission is the pawn of the regulated industry. In this instance, the Interstate Commerce Commission initiated policies that were adamantly opposed by the regulated industry. Second, the regulated industry was not united in its choice of a strategy to halt the movement towards reform. Rather, the industry was seriously divided over which approach to adopt. Third, the regulated industry, despite a massive effort, was unable to interest the public in the issue of deregulation. Without public support, the regulated industry was unable to build an adequate coalition against reform. With the Carter administration and the ICC firmly behind deregulation, the regulated industry had only one place to turn for help: Congress. By 1980, Congress, like the ICC, had begun to move toward acceptance of a regulatory reform bill.

The Motor Carrier Act of 1980

Prior to 1979, neither the House nor the Senate had demonstrated much interest in the issue of trucking deregulation. Previous legislative efforts had died in committee. In January 1978, however, Warren Magnuson, a strident opponent of deregulation, resigned as chairman of the Senate Commerce Committee. Howard Cannon (D-Nevada), Magnuson's replacement, was not initially considered to be a proponent of reform, but concerns that Cannon would oppose deregulation quickly subsided as hearings commenced in the spring of 1979. Cannon, who wanted to be as closely identified with the issue of deregulation as his predecessor had been with consumer protection, indicated that he would support the passage of a bill and that he wanted to present one to the president no later than June of 1980.[81] Cannon's support, added to the already existing support from Senator Edward Kennedy, provided the Senate with two strong advocates for motor carrier deregulation.

In the House, support for reform was much more limited. The House Committee of Public Works and Transportation was sympathetic to the regulated industry's perspective on the issue and even allowed the American Trucking Associations to write its version of the deregulation bill. President Carter threatened to veto this bill if it were adopted. The White House also put pressure on Chairman James J. Howard (D–New Jersey) of the Subcommittee on Surface Transportation to repudiate the ATA-sponsored bill.[82] Despite its lack of commitment to deregulation, the House committee eventually recommended legislation to the full House and worked for the bill's passage. The Senate also passed a bill in March 1980. After a "fragile compromise" in conference committee, Congress officially adopted the Motor Carrier Act in June 1980.

Although both Senators Cannon and Kennedy were committed to the passage of the act, few other members of Congress were enthusiastic about trucking deregulation. It was also not an issue that the American public cared much about. Interest group opposition had been intense. Why then, without obvious sources of support, did Congress enact a deregulation bill in 1980? The answer can largely be found in the president's personal commitment to reform and in the ICC's administrative deregulation proposals.

While Carter was putting pressure on Howard to recommend a more favorable bill, the ICC was making it well known that if Congress did not act, the Commission would continue to deregulate unilaterally. In May 1979, the ICC's Motor Carrier Task Force published its initial report on regulatory reform. The report stated that further reform was necessary. The report also stated, however, that "it appears that the goals of this program can be reached through administrative actions alone. While legislation confirming the administrative actions could be drafted, we do not believe that it is necessary."[83] This statement reflected O'Neal's view that legislation was not needed. It also suggested that the ICC would do what Congress could not. This threat of unilateral action angered a number of congressmen who felt that promoting deregulation was the prerogative of the Congress and not of an administrative agency. Their anger was accompanied by a fear that if Congress did not act, then the ICC would be free to rewrite the existing standards, unbridled by congressional restraints.[84]

This threat was also taken seriously by the regulated industry. Whereas in past years the industry had preferred that Congress leave the business of regulating the trucking industry to the Commission, this time the regulated industry demanded that Congress enact legislation limiting the ICC's discretionary powers. The ATA and the Teamsters also wanted Congress to reverse the ICC's administrative reforms.

In responding to the ICC's threat of unilateral action, Senate Commerce Committee Chairman Howard Cannon asked the Commission to refrain from any further action until Congress had completed its examination of the deregulation issue. The ICC's incoming chairman, Darius B. Gaskins, agreed to give Congress until June 30, 1980, to adopt a reform bill. If Congress failed to act by that time, the ICC would recommence the process of administratively deregulating the motor carrier industry.[85] To demonstrate its commitment to further deregulation and to underscore its willingness to act unilaterally, the Commission in March 1980 rendered the *Arrow* decision, which further extended entry into the regulated trucking market.[86]

One other factor induced Congress to adopt a deregulation bill. Since many aspects of the proposed legislation had already been enacted administratively by the ICC, and since major disruptions had not occurred in the trucking industry, congressional uncertainty regarding the possible effects of reform had been greatly diminished. In addition, if deregulation proved to have negative consequences, members of Congress could always blame the ICC. In fact, in congressional oversight hearings on motor carrier deregulation, Congress has received generally high marks from the regulated industry for its role in enacting the Motor Carrier Act of 1980, while the ICC has been vehemently attacked for its administrative role in promoting deregulation.[87]

The Motor Carrier Act of 1980 endorsed most of the changes that the ICC had already enacted administratively. In both the administrative and the legislative efforts, the ICC played a major role. Had the ICC not altered its perspective on regulation, it is doubtful that Congress would have adopted a deregulation bill in 1980. The conversion of the ICC was a necessary component of the Carter administration's deregulation strategy.

Conclusions

The ICC's administrative deregulation of the motor carrier industry is a good example of a president successful in altering the goals of an agency, largely in this case through the use of his appointment power. A. Daniel O'Neal, who was elevated to the chairmanship by Carter, actively promoted the president's reform agenda. Carter's appointments of Darius B. Gaskins, Marcus Alexis, and Thomas Trantum ensured that Congress would not back down on the deregulation issue. The appointment of other pro-deregulatory officials, such as Neil Goldschmidt as Secretary of Transportation and Alfred Kahn as the head of the Council on Wage and Price Stability, further underscored Carter's commitment to deregulation.

Carter's appointment strategy would have been impossible had it not been for the Nixon administration's Reorganization Plan No. 1 of 1969. That plan provided the president with the authority to appoint the ICC's chairman. It also greatly expanded the chairman's formal authority and influence. As a result, Carter was able to encourage administrative change and then seek congressional approval.

Unlike Nixon, who tried to alter the policies of the Department of Housing and Urban Development and other social welfare agencies, Jimmy Carter did not attempt to employ the various confrontational techniques of the administrative presidency strategy, such as deep reductions in budget or personnel. The employment of these techniques, rather than increasing presidential influence, might actually have undercut staff support for reform.

The deregulation of the motor carrier industry was actively promoted by the regulating Interstate Commerce Commission over the vehement objections of the regulated industry. The president played a pivotal role in this process. According to the capture theory of regulation, which suggests that regulatory agencies are captured by the very industries they seek to regulate, the trucking industry should not have been deregulated. President Carter should not have been able to extend his influence over the ICC. That President Carter was able to influence the ICC's goals and that the ICC promoted the policy of administrative deregulation underscore serious limitations in the ability of the capture theory to predict regulatory outcomes.

This case study also disproves Richard Nathan's assertion that Jimmy Carter did not use an administrative approach to deregulate the motor carrier industry. Not only did Carter employ an administrative approach, but it was also the principal strategy for reform of the motor carrier industry. Carter's use of his appointment power, along with the Nixon Administration's Reorganization Plan No. 1 and A. Daniel O'Neal's administrative reorganization, represents a successful adoption of the administrative presidency approach. The approach succeeded because Carter made selective use of the various techniques of the strategy, rather than trying to force change by adopting the heavy-handed employment of the president's removal and budgetary powers.

Finally, this case study is an example of the successful use of the administrative approach in conjunction with the traditional legislative approach. In fact, the latter depended on the successful implementation of the former. By employing the administrative strategy, Carter was able to force Congress to pay attention to the trucking deregulation issue rather than to give it only a perfunctory review as it had in the past. Thus, the case of the Carter administration and the ICC demonstrates that presidents can use an administrative approach as a means of promoting their legislative agenda.

Chapter 5

Reagan and the
Environmental Protection Agency:
Revolution and Counterrevolution

When the Reagan administration assumed office in January 1981, it brought a new philosophy to the management of the federal government. This philosophy stressed, first and foremost, the notion of limited government or, as Reagan said on many occasions, "getting government off the backs of the people." A central component of the administration's program was the reform of the social regulatory agencies, including the Environmental Protection Agency and the Occupational Safety and Health Administration. The Reagan administration argued that the high costs of social regulation had produced few tangible benefits, while drastically contributing to the economic downturn in the 1970s.[1] To remedy this source of economic stagnation, the new administration declared its commitment to a serious reduction in new federal regulations, a withdrawal from enforcement of existing standards, and a reliance on voluntary compliance. These moves, the administration argued, would retain the government's commitment to social regulation, while simultaneously reducing the burden on U.S. industry. This in turn would stimulate economic growth, thus providing the nation with more jobs and lower inflation. A period of slowed economic growth, high interest rates, and escalating inflation could be reversed.

To accomplish this goal, the Reagan administration proposed radical changes in existing policies — changes which Congress could not be counted upon to adopt without a great deal of pressure. Since the traditional legislative approach was not a viable alternative, reducing the federal government's social regulatory role would have to be accomplished administratively. Although a legislative approach would later be pursued, the Reagan administration planned to initiate change through the bureaucracy and then seek legislative action. This chapter examines the techniques the Reagan administration employed in seeking the reform of environmental statutes. It also examines the various interest groups and other participants who opposed the administration's program. Because of the strong political backlash that the Reagan program provoked, this case study is an excellent example of the strengths and the limitations of the administrative presidency strategy.

A Brief History of the EPA

Although the Environmental Protection Agency (EPA) was established in 1970, it was not the federal government's first attempt at environmental management. The Water Pollution Control Act of 1956 attempted to define a role for the federal government in the area of environmental protection. This attempt was unsuccessful, largely because too much authority for the implementation of the environmental program was delegated to the states. Many states did not share the federal government's commitment to water pollution control or lacked the financial resources to adequately administer the program. As a result, implementation was sporadic at best.[2] Other congressional attempts at environmental management in the 1960s, including the Clean Air Act of 1963, the Water Quality Act of 1965, and the Air Quality Act of 1967, similarly delegated a great deal of authority to the states.[3] Because these programs had failed, environmental groups began to lobby Congress to adopt legislation that would give the federal government a more prominent role in environmental protection. By 1970, a growing number of influential politicians with environmental sensitivities had been elected to office. Consequently, the environmentalists' call for increased federal participation received a more favorable reception in Washington than it had in the past.

Another factor contributing to the expansion of the federal government's role in environmental politics was the emergence of greater public concern. In 1965 only 28 percent of the American public thought the problem of air pollution was very or somewhat serious, but by 1968 this fraction had increased to 55 percent. In the area of water pollution control there was a similar jump: from only 35 percent in 1965 to 58 percent by 1968.[4] The giant Earth Day demonstrations of 1970 were a clear indication that a growing number of Americans were committed to stricter federal regulation of the environment. As public support for environmental protection proliferated, there was an inevitable rush by politicians to curry favor with this new constituency. Unfortunately, popular support for environmental protection was a general concept. Politicians had no clearly delineated program for dealing with environmental problems; rather, as Charles O. Jones stated, the mood was reflective of "a majority in search of a policy."[5] The Clean Air Act of 1970 was written and the Environmental Protection Agency was established under these circumstances.

The Environmental Protection Agency (EPA) was established by President Richard Nixon via executive order on December 2, 1970, combining a number of federal pollution programs into a single agency. Among these were programs dealing with air pollution from the Department of Health, Education, and Welfare (HEW); water pollution from the Department of Interior; pesticide control from the Departments of Agriculture, Interior, and HEW; solid waste management from HEW; and radiation standards from the Atomic Energy Commission.[6] The new EPA also replaced the National Air Pollution Control Administration, which had been the federal government's primary environmental management agency.

In establishing the Environmental Protection Agency, a major concern of policymakers was that the new agency should not become the pawn of the regulated industry. For this reason, the idea of creating a federal regulatory commission was rejected.[7] In the academic literature, regulatory commissions were synonymous with the word *capture*. It was argued that the new environmental agency could avoid capture if it were set up as an independent agency, with its administrator selected by and serving at the pleasure of the president. To increase presidential influence, the administrator's term was designed to run concurrently with the president's. To ensure that the administrator would be accountable to the public and environmentalists, Senate confirmation was also required.[8]

The EPA's Organizational Structure

Largely because of the concern that a regulatory commission would be susceptible to capture by the regulated industry, the position of administrator of the Environmental Protection Agency was endowed with a great deal of authority and, perhaps more importantly, a great deal of discretion. The role of discretion is particularly significant in view of the degree to which scientific theories and evidence regarding the myriad problems EPA faces are often open to wide interpretation. The administrator can often choose between competing scientific theories in order to provide a rationalization for a particular decision. Anne Gorsuch Burford,[9] Reagan's first EPA administrator, supported the epigenetic theory of cell chemistry, which posited that a number of carcinogenic substances affect cell mechanisms in addition to DNA strands. This theory meant in practical terms that human beings could be subject to greater exposure to known carcinogens without fear of developing cancer. As a result, Burford decided to approve higher tolerance levels for several pesticides that were known carcinogens. According to the competing genotoxic theory endorsed by the Carter administration's EPA administrator, Douglas Costle, all carcinogens are thought to cause alterations in genetic cell materials, and therefore carcinogens should be strictly regulated.[10] Although the genotoxic theory was more widely supported, scientific backing for the epigenetic theory provided Burford with a strong justification for her decision.

The discretionary authority of the administrator extends beyond rule-making. The administrator also has wide discretionary authority to reorganize the offices of the Environmental Protection Agency and to develop the agency's budget. The administrator's discretionary authority has strong implications for the president's use of the administrative presidency strategy. Because the administrator possesses wide discretionary power over rule-making, reorganization, and the formulation of the agency's budget, the administrator can provide the president with strong administrative support. Despite this potential, administrators throughout the Nixon, Ford, and Carter presidencies distinguished themselves by their independence from the president. It was not until Reagan appointed Anne Burford that the administrator became an open and ardent advocate of the president's environmental program.[11]

Although the real authority of the agency rests with the administrator, the deputy administrator has often played an important role in EPA affairs. When the deputy administrator is not the personal selection of the administrator, such as was the case with John Hernandez during Burford's term at EPA, the authority of this office is considerably diminished.

Along with these top two officials, there are assistant administrators to oversee each of the functional offices of the agency: Air, Noise, and Radiation; Water and Waste Management; Planning and Management; Research and Development; Pesticides and Toxic Substances; and Enforcement.[12] The authority of each of these assistant administrators is greatly dependent on the discretion of the administrator. Still, it is not entirely dependent on the administrator, as the example of Rita Lavelle and the Superfund program during Anne Burford's tenure demonstrates. In this instance, Lavelle had internal White House support—reputedly from Edwin Meese— which gave her greater discretion than she likely otherwise would have possessed.

Among the EPA's over 10,000 other employees, a large number are scientists, engineers, attorneys, and other professionals, most of whom are career civil servants. The EPA has distinguished itself for acquiring an impressive cadre of experts on environmental affairs, and many of them have been strong advocates of environmental protection. It would be a mistake, however, to assume that the personnel of the EPA have constituted a giant monolith in support of a specific environmental approach. EPA employees have been deeply divided over a variety of issues, such as emission dispersion and the use of variances in State Implementation Plans.[13] In a particularly bitter dispute, the Office of Air, Noise, and Radiation and the Office of Planning and Management argued, for over two years, over whether industry should be compelled to use scrubbers.[14]

Although the focus of scholarly attention on EPA is usually its Washington office, most of its employees are dispersed around the country in one of EPA's ten regional offices. This geographical dispersion of employees, a decentralizing tendency, undercuts the direct authority of the administrator. Still, the regional offices are necessitated by EPA's strong intergovernmental component.

Another decentralizing tendency is that EPA is not the only agency responsible for the development of environmental policy. As many as a dozen other federal agencies can share jurisdiction with EPA on a particular regulatory issue. In some cases, EPA is even responsible for regulating other agencies, for example, the Tennessee Valley Authority (TVA). Although there are problems with such intergovernmental regulatory activity, the case of the TVA demonstrates that the problems of coordination are not insurmountable.[15]

In addition to interagency regulatory activity, EPA must also cooperate with the fifty states in the development of regulatory policy. Under the provisions of the Clean Air Act of 1970, states must submit State Implementation Plans (SIPs) to the Environmental Protection Agency. These plans suggest the method by which state governments will comply with the standards and deadlines enumerated in the act. EPA then must review the SIPs to determine if they adequately meet federal guidelines. Although this review process gives EPA oversight authority over state environmental agencies, it does not guarantee control. The EPA does not have enough personnel or resources to perform a comprehensive study of every state's environmental program. As a result, much authority is necessarily delegated to the states. Ann O'M. Bowman has argued that this intergovernmental component of environmental regulation has impeded progress in implementing environmental programs.[16] Coordination of decision-making is more difficult because different levels of government are involved. Despite this fact, or possible because of it, the pattern under the Reagan administration was towards greater delegation of federal authority to the states.

Consequently, the EPA is a curious blend of centralized control by the administrator and decentralized authority over its many functional responsibilities, the other federal agencies with which it shares responsibility, and the intergovernmental component of environmental regulation. Whereas the internal organization of EPA is amenable to presidential influence, the decentralized nature of environmental politics suggests that presidents will need to exert wide influence over a variety of federal and state agencies in order to successfully control the environmental agenda.

Nixon, Ford, Carter, and the EPA

It is commonly perceived that prior to the election of Ronald Wilson Reagan all presidents had unanimously supported the goals of the Environmental Protection Agency and that when Reagan was elected he broke faith with this tradition by espousing an anti-environmental platform. This generalization ignores the often tense relationship that existed between the EPA and the Nixon, Ford, and Carter administrations.

One reason for this tension was that the Environmental Protection Agency is primarily responsible for one broad task: protection of the environment. The president, in contrast, must consider a broad array of policies. Presidents must be concerned with unemployment, inflation, economic growth, and the nation's energy self-sufficiency. The EPA's activities may have a detrimental impact on each of these policy areas: spurring unemployment by forcing older facilities to close, raising the costs of production and thus exacerbating inflation while depressing economic growth, and limiting the use of energy sources such as high-sulfur coal that could help America become more energy-self-sufficient. In these circumstances, the potential for conflict with the Chief Executive is increased. As R. Shep Melnick has stated, "presidents, even those who start with strong positions on environmental protection, come more and more to seek what they call 'balance' and what their opponents decry as 'leniency.'"[17]

Each of the three presidents who occupied the Oval Office before Ronald Reagan came into conflict with the EPA. Richard Nixon, who established the agency via executive order in December 1970, later became concerned about the high cost of environmental regulation. As a result, Nixon vetoed the Federal Water Pollution Control Act Amendments of 1972, despite the recommendation of the EPA's first administrator, William Ruckelshaus, that the president sign the bill. Congress successfully overrode the president's veto. Again Nixon responded, this time by using his executive authority to impound congressionally appropriated funds. Ruckelshaus had stated that the new commitment to control water pollution would not prove inflationary, but President Nixon nonetheless ordered the EPA administrator to withhold $9 billion over a three-year period. Although the courts later ruled that the president's action had been improper, Nixon's impoundment of water pollution funds forced the EPA to delay various deadlines for compliance.[18]

Even though Ruckelshaus had been forced to go along with the president on the impoundment question, he felt that the EPA should be independent from the White House. He thus embarked on a mission to cultivate a favorable public image for the EPA, believing that if the general public supported the goals of the agency, then the EPA would be able to distance itself from White House pressure. Besides his public relations campaign, Ruckelshaus vigorously enforced existing statutes to demonstrate that the EPA would not bow down to industry pressure.[19]

Under both the Nixon and Ford administrations, the Office of Management and Budget coordinated the "quality of life review," which allowed agencies opposed to EPA to get a second hearing before a more sympathetic executive organization.[20] Despite this new institutional arrangement, EPA remained largely independent of White House pressure. Favorable media coverage and pro-environmental public opinion assisted the new agency in this quest for independence. Ruckelshaus also created the Office of Planning and Evaluation within the EPA to provide the agency with independent economic advice and to counter pressure from OMB.[21]

After Ruckelshaus departed in 1973 to take a high-level position at the Justice Department, Russell Train was named as EPA's new administrator. Train was unambiguously committed to the environmental movement. He had previously served as the chairman of the Council on Environmental Quality (CEQ), created by the National Environmental Policy Act of 1970 (NEPA) to provide independent advice to the president on environmental matters. Train had also served as the president of the Conservation Foundation, a pro-environmental group. These credentials made his selection popular with environmentalists.

Train ran into immediate conflict with the Nixon White House. The Nixon administration attempted to prevent many of the EPA's regulations from taking effect and introduced legislation in Congress that would have greatly weakened the EPA's authority. The reforms would have forced EPA to become more cost-conscious, rather than environmentally cautious. Train vehemently opposed these White House initiatives. His opposition was so strident that the EPA became an active opponent of White House policy in the area of environmental protection. This situation led one of Train's subordinates to speculate that, as the EPA's administrator, Russell Train survived only "because Richard Nixon did not."[22] Train also survived under the administration of Gerald Ford. Ford, assuming the presidency under the most unusual of circumstances, was not in a position to replace an administrator who was popular with a very influential interest group. Consequently, Train served as EPA administrator throughout Ford's presidency.

Although Jimmy Carter is credited with the appointment of a large number of pro-environmental officials to the Environmental

Protection Agency, he also had a number of policy differences with the agency. Carter came under fire when he tried to relax auto emission standards as a means of reducing the regulatory costs facing the slumping automobile industry.[23] Later, Carter put pressure on his EPA administrator, Douglas Costle, to delay the implementation of controls on nonpoint sources of water pollution, again in an attempt to reduce the costs of federal regulation.

Following Gerald Ford's example, Jimmy Carter instituted the use of cost-benefit analysis as a means of controlling the costs of government regulation.[25] This move forced the EPA to consider the costs of environmental regulation to business and the economy and was a forerunner of the Reagan administration's more comprehensive efforts to control the costs of social regulation.[26]

The Carter administration's employment of cost-benefit analysis was uneven and often contradictory. With Executive Order #12044, Carter initiated a program that forced federal departments and agencies, with the exception of the independent regulatory agencies, to consider the costs and benefits of all new regulatory proposals. This new process was employed by such economists as Alfred Kahn, William Norhaus, and Charles Schultze as a means of promoting a more cost-conscious and thus more efficient regulatory climate. This objective fit in well with Carter's goal of constraining the size and cost of government. However, environmentalists argued that the employment of the procedure unfortunately prohibited the development of regulations required to protect the health and safety of workers and the environment. Carter, who was sympathetic to the environmentalists and considered them to be an important potential ally in any reelection bid, consequently followed the urging of his appointees to the social regulatory agencies — in particular, EPA administrator Douglas Costle — and created the Regulatory Analysis and Review Group (RARG). While RARG provided appointees at the social regulatory agencies with greater input in the cost-benefit process, it also undercut the authority of Carter's economists. Dealing with conflicting authorities in any particular case was left with the president.

The debate over cotton dust, and the role of the Occupational Safety and Health Administration (OSHA), was the first test of the new process. Carter listened to the intense, often heated debate on the issue and then rendered a decision on cotton dust. Following this formal decision, Carter rendered a second informal decision, one that would have a great impact on the future regulatory policy of his administration. Dissatisfied with the controversy and conflict surrounding the cotton dust issue, and very unhappy with his new role as arbitrator, Carter decided to avoid such conflict-ridden situations in the future. The arbitration process now lacked an arbitrator.

Although the EPA did not play an active role in the cotton dust debate, the president's decision to distance himself from further controversy had a major impact on policy development within the EPA. With the president having acknowledged that he would take a back seat in the process, and with a contradictory and conflicting institutional process in place, cost-benefit analysis played a less important role during the remainder of Carter's presidency. The results satisfied environmentalists but did little to advance Carter's goals of cost-effectiveness.[27]

The case of Carter and the use of cost-benefit analysis demonstrates that the president had conflicting goals that complicated his ability to extend his influence over environmental policy. Rather than promoting cost-effective policies or a pro-environmental agenda, Carter vacillated between the two, with the result that he was unable to control the environmental policy process and his appointees were uncertain over where they stood. This often had the effect of reducing their influence. The end result was that Carter did not have the firm control over the Environmental Protection Agency that he had over the Interstate Commerce Commission. (I will return to a discussion of the implications of President Carter's vacillation on this issue in chapter 7.)

As this brief review of the Nixon, Ford, and Carter presidencies has shown, all three Chief Executives prior to Ronald Reagan had opposed some of the goals of the Environmental Protection Agency. In the case of the Nixon administration, particularly during the second term, this opposition was intense. But even with this history of conflict between the president and the EPA, the Reagan administration's reform agenda represented a major break with past environmental policy.

Reagan and His Appointees

Richard Nixon's experiences with the Department of Housing and Urban Development demonstrate that in order to employ the techniques of the administrative presidency strategy, a president must have clearly articulated policy choices. Ronald Reagan came to the White House with a clearly delineated ideology for dealing with what he considered to be the excesses of federal social regulation. His objective was to reduce the federal government's role in environmental affairs, consumer protection, workplace safety, and health, and other targets of social regulatory activity. Following the success of the Carter administration in administratively deregulating the transportation industries, Reagan adopted a similar strategy in promoting social regulatory reform. Reform was initiated at the administrative level, before legislation was offered to Congress. In this way, Reagan's revolutionary agenda was promoted.[28]

The first step in promoting administrative deregulation was the appointment of loyal conservatives to head the social regulatory agencies, such as Thorne Auchter at OSHA and Raymond Peck at the National Highway Traffic and Safety Administration (NHTSA). In the area of environmental regulation, Reagan nominated a number of ideological conservatives, many of whom had publicly expressed opposition to the policies of the Environmental Protection Agency. The Reagan administration's decision to nominate individuals who opposed the policies of the EPA broke with the tradition, which had extended back to Richard Nixon, of naming individuals who were sympathetic to the environmentalist cause.

In no case was this more apparent than in the appointment of Anne Burford to be the Environmental Protection Agency's new administrator. Burford shared the president's anti-regulatory philosophy. In addition, she had been highly critical of the environmental movement and environmentalists in general. As administrator, she sought to exclude environmentalists from positions of influence within the EPA; of the individuals that she appointed to serve at the EPA none was from the environmentalist movement. Besides refusing to appoint environmentalists, Burford used other techniques to limit their input. For example, Burford denied environmental groups the right of pre-notification of upcoming rule changes, a right EPA willingly granted to the regulated industry. Burford also limited private contact with environmental groups, though she met extensively with industrial and business representatives. Still, at her confirmation hearings, Burford denied that she was anti-environmental:

I am confident that President Reagan did not ask me to serve because of any advocacy position I have taken. I have not made my living fighting for or against environmental laws and regulation.[29]

Despite this denial, Burford's testimony at her confirmation hearings deliberately skirted a number of serious questions. She refused to give definitive answers to such questions as whether she supported cost-benefit analysis for standard-setting (as opposed to regulations), whether she would support fundamental changes in the Clear Air Act, and whether she would retain EPA's right to designate "protected" waters under Section 404 of the Clean Water Act or delegate this authority to the less environmentally sympathetic Army Corps of Engineers. By refusing to provide clear answers to these questions, Burford left both senators and environmentalists outside the government with the clear impression that she would not be a staunch supporter of existing environmental regulation.

President Reagan's selection of Anne Burford raised other concerns. Unlike her predecessors, Burford lacked even a rudimentary amount of management experience. Neither did she have any experience working in Washington, D.C. Even though William Ruckelshaus had lacked environmental experience when he was first appointed by Richard Nixon—a fact that initially provoked the environmentalists' ire—he had served in the Justice Department. He also quickly demonstrated that he supported the EPA's pro-environmental goals. Russell Train's credentials, as chairman of the Council on Environmental Quality (CEQ) and the Conservation Foundation, were impeccable. Carter's nominee, Douglas Costle, had been the head of the state of Connecticut's Department of Environmental Protection. In contrast, Burford's experience consisted of having served two terms in the Colorado state legislature, where she was chairperson of a committee with jurisdiction over environmental matters. Her only previous Washington experience had consisted of a few visits to the city.[30]

Burford also lacked experience working in a large bureaucracy—experience that would have justified her appointment. Largely because of inexperience, Burford performed in office more like a political neophyte than a skilled politician. This inexperience was evident in her naive decision to withhold documents from Congress on the recommendation of the Justice Department, a decision that eventually resulted in her being found in contempt of Congress and that later led to her forced resignation.

Reagan's other environmental appointees also lacked sympathy for the EPA's prior goals. Many also lacked management experience, or were stridently pro-business in their backgrounds and beliefs. In terms of experience, Dr. John Hernandez, who was named the EPA's deputy administrator, was an exception; his background included a master's degree in environmental engineering and a doctorate in water resources management.[31] His views on environmental regulation, however, were consistent with those of the president: Hernandez believed that environmental regulation was overly burdensome on private interests. Acting on these beliefs, for approximately two years he blocked EPA action to clean up school yards and playgrouds in two Dallas neighborhoods that were located near lead smelters, despite growing evidence that the health of the children in the neighborhood was being imperiled.[32] Hernandez also permitted officials from the Dow Chemical Company to examine and make changes in a report prepared by EPA officials which had been highly critical of the Dow Company.[33] Revelations concerning these two events precipititated Hernandez's resignation shortly after Burford was forced to step down in the spring of 1983.

Most of Reagan's other appointees lacked experience and were also unsympathetic to the environmental cause. John P. Horton, the nominee for the important post of Assistant Administrator for Administration, had virtually no governmental experience. He had served only as the chairman on a citizen-member state Clean Air Council, where his input was purely advisory. Most of Horton's experience was in business.[34] Many other Reagan appointees likewise had most of their experience with business, often with industries that were directly regulated by the Environmental Protection Agency. Robert Perry, the EPA's General Council, had been an attorney for the Exxon Corporation. Kathleen Bennett, assistant administrator for Air, Noise, and Radiation, had been a lobbyist for the American Paper Institute.[35] Jim Sanderson, Anne Burford's closest adviser, had worked on several cases for the Mountain States Legal Foundation, which was founded by the ultra-conservative Colorado brewer Joseph Coors and which ardently opposed pro-environmental decisions by the Environmental Protection Agency. Sanderson also represented a number of firms regulated by the EPA. He continued to represent these firms, even after assuming office as an adviser to Anne Burford at EPA. When Reagan nominated Sanderson in late December 1981 to be the new administrator for Policy and Resource

Management, the number three position in the agency, allegations of conflict of interest were raised. Continuing investigations into the matter eventually forced Sanderson to remove his name from consideration in June 1982.[36]

Rita Lavelle, who was nominated to serve as the assistant administrator for Solid Waste and Emergency Response, the office that oversaw the Superfund program, had served as a public relations officer for Aerojet-General. Lavelle's lack of qualifications led Anne Burford to turn her down when she first interviewed for the position at the EPA. Shortly thereafter, the White House sent her résumé back to Burford and asked the administrator to give Lavelle a second chance. Burford took this not-so-subtle hint and supported Lavelle's nomination.[37] Because of Lavelle's prior close ties with Aerojet-General, her nomination was vigorously attacked by environmentalists. The Sierra Club argued that Lavelle's "only qualifications appear to be that she worked with President Reagan while he was Governor of California and as the Chief Spokesperson for a company with a dismal environmental record."[38]

Lavelle's tenure at EPA was highly controversial. She often refused to provide Superfund money to clean up dangerous waste sites, even when there was evidence that the public was at risk. She justified her position by arguing that the EPA studies were overly pessimistic. To Lavelle, the only means of demonstrating that the public's health was actually at risk was to show clear evidence that an individual's health had already been impaired by the polluting source in question.[39] This type of epidemiological evidence is often difficult to derive.

Lavelle also made judgments concerning the release of Superfund money purely on the basis of political criteria. Funding for the Stringfellow acid pits dump site in California was held up until after the 1982 midterm elections for fear that it might promote the election of Jerry Brown, the Democratic senatorial candidate.[40] Such decision-making on Lavelle's part eventually led to an investigation of her activities by Congress. Later she was indicted and convicted for offering perjured testimony to congressional committees.

Reagan's EPA appointees contrast with Jimmy Carter's highly qualified ICC appointees. Whereas Carter's appointees had extensive management and Washington experience, Reagan's EPA appointees lacked experience in government, especially with Washington-level politics. Consequently, Reagan's appointees, who were no less committed to the president's program than were Carter's appointees, promoted change in a manner that provoked congressional objections regarding the administration's policies, exacerbated interest group opposition, and raised concerns that legal violations had occurred. These developments in turn helped to subvert the policy objectives of the Reagan administration and eventually threatened to reduce presidential influence over environmental politics.

Two conclusions, then, can be reached about the Reagan administration's appointment strategy. First, because Reagan came to office with consistent and well-articulated policy choices, he was able to make full use of the major component of the administrative presidency strategy, the appointment of loyal, like-minded individuals, as Richard Nathan had recommended.[41] Second, the appointment of individuals who support the president's program is not sufficient to influence bureaucratic behavior and thus to promote presidential objectives. Rather, presidents should select qualified individuals, especially those who have either prior management or Washington-level experience (or both). This finding is supported by a number of scholars who have been critical of the Reagan administration's appointment strategy. Chester Newland was highly critical of the practice of naming individuals with little Washington experience to top-level positions.[42] Nolan J. Argyle and Ryan J. Barilleaux, while generally supportive of Reagan's management style, note that the administration's reliance on "political loyalty over professional expertise" can lead to "amateurism in the policy-making process,"[43] the sort of amateurism exemplified in the EPA under Burford.

Removal Power

During the transition period in late 1980 and early 1981, Louis Cordia, a former staffer at the Heritage Foundation and a low-level EPA official, began putting together a list of agency employees. The list rated scientists and other employees on the basis of their skills. More importantly, it also rated them on the basis of their policy views. For example:

> Technically good, but should not be kept on the job, bad policy. . . .
> Interesting, once a protege of a reputable individual, bright and held
> in high esteem, now an environmentalist, should go. . . . Interesting

enigma, applied ecologist, excellent administrative background and experience, yet a follower, won't stand out in front, definitely keep.[44]

Approximately ninety scientests from advisory positions and the EPA staff plus a number of other top bureaucrats were included on Cordia's list. Burford's top adviser, Jim Sanderson, actively urged EPA appointees to get rid of career employees who had been identified by Cordia.[45] To accomplish this task, the Reagan administration borrowed many of the techniques used earlier by the Nixon administration. Now, however, due to changes in the civil service laws, the Reagan administration had greater leverage to actually extract recalcitrant civil servants from the bureaucracy.

Under the provisions of the Civil Service Reform Act of 1978, the Reagan administration was able to remove a number of civil servants from key positions. Many were offered the choice of resigning or being transferred from Washington to one of the field offices, usually in some remote location. Many employees who were committed to the EPA's prior goals chose to resign rather than to serve political appointees who did not share their pro-environmental views.[46] As a result, the number of EPA employees dropped dramatically: in 1980 there were 13,078 employees; by 1984, this number had shrunk to approximately 10,000.[47] During Fiscal Year 1981 alone, 4,129 employees (or approximately one-third of the staff) left the agency, though some new staff were also hired.[48] Among those who departed were a number of experts who would be difficult to replace.[49]

In addition to applying its appointment and removal strategies, the Reagan administration also left several key positions vacant for extended periods of time. The Office of Research and Development, a key office under previous presidents, did not have a permanent head during Burford's entire twenty-two-month tenure. Of another six assistant administrator positions, two were left open for seven months, one for ten months, and two others for fifteen months.[50] Without environmental advocates in these positions, it was easier to reduce the functions of these offices. This was particularly true of the Office of Research and Development, which suffered the most extreme personnel and budget cuts of any EPA office. Without opposition from a permanent head who could defend the office's record, it was easier for the Reagan administration and OMB to implement drastic budgetary reductions.

Reagan's removal strategy provided the administration with greater influence over the Environmental Protection Agency, but at a cost. Revelations that EPA had put together a hit list and that a large number of employees had departed as a result led to a series of highly critical congressional investigations. These investigations eventually helped focus media and public attention on the political excesses of Reagan's appointees,[51] which in turn promoted increased opposition to the Reagan administration's reform agenda. While putting into practice its plan to extend presidential influence over the EPA, the administration was also planting the seeds for a counterrevolution.

EPA and Its Budget

The decision to appoint loyal lieutenants to the Environmental Protection Agency was crucial to the implementation of a second arm of Reagan's administrative approach: large-scale budget reductions for a variety of social regulatory programs. By appointing individuals who supported his economic recovery program, Reagan removed a source of resistance to his proposed budget reductions. Reagan surrounded himself with appointees who would give his proposals credibility by testifying before Congress on their behalf rather than defending their agencies against the administration's budget cuts.

Another key to the administration's budget-cutting strategy was the decision to tie the issue of budget cuts to a discussion of the economy as a whole, rather than attacking the goals of the Environmental Protection Agency or any other social regulatory program. By adopting this approach, the administration could claim that reductions in a wide variety of governmental programs were needed to help spur the economy. This line of defense was extremely important, since most critics of the administration's proposed EPA budget cuts maintained that reductions would force the agency to severely curtail its regulatory functions, particularly in the areas of research and development and enforcement. The administration did not have to answer these charges. Instead, it was able to argue that the cuts were regrettable, but that all federal non-defense programs were going to have to sacrifice funds for the good of the economy.

A final component of the Reagan administration's budget reduction strategy consisted of centrally coordinating proposed reductions through the Office of Management and Budget. One means of cutting agency budgets could have been to allow each individual agency the opportunity to submit proposals. In this way the agencies could have determined how their budgets could best be reduced with minimal damage to their program goals. Instead of this strategy, OMB provided the agencies with detailed plans for cutting their agency budgets. These plans included not just the amount of money to be cut, but also suggestions as to the number of employees that should be fired and specific offices that should be abolished or reorganized.[52] The agencies were then responsible for formulating a budget that met OMB's guidelines.

This comprehensive strategy for budgetary reduction was widely successful. Cuts were made across the board in a wide variety of programs. The deepest cuts, however, were in programs such as environmental policy that the Reagan administration objected to on philosophical grounds.

The proposed cuts for the Environmental Protection Agency were deep.[53] The budget for research and development suffered particularly heavy reductions: from $250.5 million in Fiscal Year 1981 to $154 million in FY 1982, $121 million in FY 1983, and $111.7 million in FY 1984.[54] These cuts included large-scale reductions in epidemiological studies concerning criteria air pollution effects. They also forced EPA to terminate the Great Lakes and Chesapeake Bay research programs.[55] These budget reductions in R & D greatly impaired the ability of the Environmental Protection Agency to provide scientific studies and reliable data that could be used to defend existing regulations or justify new standards.[56]

Reductions in EPA's budget also had a significant and immediate impact on the agency's enforcement capability, as B. Dan Wood has demonstrated.[57] The actual number of EPA enforcement referrals to the Justice Department also decreased. In 1980, under President Jimmy Carter, EPA referred 252 cases to the Justice Department for further investigation; in 1981, EPA referred only 78 cases. In 1980, EPA's regional offices forwarded 313 cases for enforcement action to EPA's central office; in 1981, they forwarded only 66 cases.[58] The EPA Enforcement Counsel, William Sullivan, defended this drop in enforcement activity as did Administrator Anne Burford, who stressed voluntary compliance with pollution laws.[59]

It is not surprising that Sullivan supported the agency's diminished enforcement activity. In 1981, at a meeting of officials from EPA's ten regional offices, he stated that "every case you do refer [to EPA's enforcement office] will be a black mark against you."[60] Quite likely, Sullivan's threatening comments encouraged reductions in enforcement activity independent of the budgetary reductions.

Responding to this precipitous drop in EPA enforcement activity, the pro-environmental Conservation Foundation wrote in their mid-decade environmental assessment, "It appears that during the present dearth of government enforcement, private enforcement of traditional environmental laws is more frequent than EPA enforcement."[61] The Reagan budget-cutting strategy, and Sullivan's comments, had clearly helped the administration to achieve one of its primary goals: a reduction in the EPA's ability to enforce the existing environmental statutes.

In the budgetary process, Administrator Anne Burford was a strong advocate for the Reagan administration's proposed cuts. She defended the reductions before congressional committees, maintaining that EPA could perform its legal duties with a smaller budget by "focusing resources on statutory responsibilities; simplifying relations with the states and the regulated community; eliminating duplication of effort; and pursuing regulatory reform."[62] In defending the cuts in the area of research and development, Burford stated, "we have invested in research to a point where the additional investment could be wasted or where we now feel we are ahead of an industry's development."[63]

Burford's support for the administration's position enhanced the credibility of the budget reduction proposals. Perhaps more importantly, it removed a potential source of resistance to the reductions, a source that congressional critics of the president's program could have rallied around. Had Burford and other political appointees at EPA argued that the proposals would have seriously undercut their agency's ability to perform its legally mandated functions, Congress could then have more easily justified smaller reductions in EPA's budget. But Congress was not given this opportunity. Instead, Congress heard a united chorus of support for the president's economic recovery program. Accordingly, it was exceedingly difficult for Congress to resist the requested reductions in EPA's budget.

Reorganization at the EPA

The appointment of Reagan loyalists, coupled with deep cuts in EPA's budget, greatly increased the president's influence over environmental policy decisions in the short term. Even with these moves, however, there was still a possibility that bureaucratic resistance could bring the Reagan revolution to a halt. By 1982, *Automotive News* was reporting that the Environmental Protection Agency, "once a robust, dynamic entity [had] shriveled to a gray shadow of its former self, wracked by internal dissension, run by people with little experience in environmental issues, and dogged by a paranoia that [had] virtually brought it to a standstill."[64] Given the low level of morale within the agency, the possibility existed that career bureaucrats could appeal to more sympathetic congressional committees. Although the Reagan administration had already taken some steps to emasculate the influence of the career bureaucracy by reducing the number of employees within the agency and by transferring potentially recalcitrant employees away from Washington to regional offices, the possibility still existed that agency staff could subvert the Reagan administration's policy objectives. To further reduce the influence of EPA staff, Anne Burford used the administrator's reorganization authority to eliminate offices that could possible threaten the Reagan administration's agenda.

One of Burford's first acts was to centralize more authority in the Office of the Administrator by disbanding the Policy Office, which had previously played a major role in personnel and budgetary decisions. The reorganization guaranteed that no one subordinate would have the kind of power that Policy had exerted under EPA administrator Douglas Costle.[65]

Burford also abolished the Office of Enforcement (later reestablishing it within the agency's legal office). This move furthered the Reagan administration's goal of reducing the level of enforcement of environmental standards. It also provided a tangible demonstration to industry and EPA staff that the agency would move towards a policy of voluntary compliance. In addition, agency staff could no longer count on the Enforcement Office to argue the case for increased enforcement within the Environmental Protection Agency. This potential source of opposition had been eliminated.

Although the reorganization of the Enforcement Office helped Burford achieve a major goal of the administration, it also provoked intense external opposition, as well as opposition from the career bureaucracy. The initial deletion of the Office of Enforcement was followed by a chorus of complaints that the EPA would no longer properly enforce the environmental statutes. It was a clear signal to environmentalists and members of Congress that the Reagan administration did not have an objective plan for reducing the federal government's regulatory burden. Rather, the administration planned on eradicating the agency's ability to perform its legally mandated function, no matter what it had to do. Cuts in the agency's research and development budget were one indication. The removal of career bureaucrats and the failure to fill a number of assistant administrative positions was another. The abolition of the Enforcement Office was an added signal. Even after Enforcement was reconstituted within the Legal Office, critics continued to argue that the EPA had no intention of enforcing the legal statutes, a criticism supported by Wood's analysis of EPA enforcement activity.[66]

In addition to deleting the Enforcement Office, Burford also abolished other potential sources of bureaucratic resistance, such as the Special Pesticide Review Division, which was responsible for banning carcinogenic pesticides. Its functions were transferred to the EPA division responsible for pesticide registration.[67] Following this reorganization, a number of pesticides that had been considered carcinogenic were approved for distribution. The reorganizations of the Enforcement Office and the Special Pesticide Review Division promoted external opposition, as they were sending a clear signal that the Reagan administration was determined to emasculate existing environmental standards. Rather than building a basis for cooperation with members of Congress and environmentalists over environmental questions, these moves were intensifying opposition.

Presidential Reorganization

The Reagan White House also assured itself of direct supervision over the activities of EPA and other regulatory agencies by creating a series of cabinet councils with responsibility over specific policy areas. This idea was borrowed partly from the Nixon administration's practice of using work groups (established by John Ehrlichman's Domestic Council) to oversee various cabinet departments and regulatory agencies, partly from the Nixon administration's short-lived experiment with the Super Secretaries, and partly from the Ford administration's Economic Policy Board.

The Cabinet Council on Natural Resources and Environment, chaired by Interior Secretary James Watt, was responsible for keeping a close eye on all policy decisions emanating from EPA. An ardent critic of environmental regulation, Watt had previously served as the head of Joseph Coors' Mountain States Legal Foundation. Watt's Council played a particularly important role in attempting to weaken the Clean Air Act Amendments. Since Watt and Burford shared the same basic viewpoint on environmental policy matters, it is impossible to determine whether or how much the Cabinet Council influenced EPA policies.[68] Rather than providing EPA with set policy options, the Council's most important function may have been to give the administration's blessing to the policies that Burford and her subordinates were initiating.

Delegation of Authority to the States

Another technique used by the Reagan administration was the delegation of program authority from the EPA directly to the states. The administration's New Federalism proposals called for a "sorting out" of federal programs. Under this strategy, programs that can best be handled by the states should be returned to state jurisdiction. Programs best handled at the national level should remain the responsibility of the federal government.[69] Although this was the professed goal of the Reagan administration, its New Federalism proposals often seemed to be guided more by ideological considerations than by a rational sorting out of administrative functions.

Under the Carter administration there was a real hesitancy on the part of the EPA to delegate authority to the states. A state government had to demonstrate that in terms of planning, monitoring, record-keeping, inspections, and enforcement its program was equivalent to the federal program it would supersede. According to Michael Kraft, Bruce Clary, and Richard Tobin, under Burford, EPA greatly eased these requirements and "delegated responsibility with a vengeance."[70] Between December 1981 and December 1983, nineteen new states were given full authority to conduct the Clean Air Act's program for prevention of significant deterioration (PSD). In addition, between 1981 and 1984, twelve new states were delegated full authority to administer the program to control hazardous air pollutants.[71]

At the same time that the EPA was delegating greater authority to the states to administer environmental policies, the agency was also reducing the level of grants-in-aid to the states. These reductions left many state governments without the financial resources to properly perform their newly expanded responsibilities. A survey of state environmental programs conducted by the pro-environmental National Resources Defense Council in the fall of 1981 found that forty-four states expected to receive less funding from the federal government. Thirty-four states said they could not carry out additional responsibilities without increased funding; Idaho in fact announced that cuts in federal funding were forcing the state to return responsibility for its air quality program to the EPA.[72]

Even these figures do not demonstrate the magnitude of the states' dependency on federal funding. In 1982, federal funds to the states accounted for 45 percent of state air quality program budgets, 46 percent of state water quality budgets, 69 percent of state hazardous waste program budgets, and 48 percent of state water supply budgets.[73] Given this heavy reliance on federal funding, it is easy to see why so many states found the prospect of further funding decreases intolerable.

According to the Conservation Foundation, "Future dramatic reductions in funding for state programs [would] undermine the administrative structures and improvements carefully nurtured since the 1960s." The report went on to state that "It is not clear whether even environmentally sympathetic states will be willing or able to assume a substantially increased role in funding environmental programs."[74] By the time the Fiscal Year 1984 budget was presented by the Reagan administration, however, Congress had begun to reassert its presence in the budgetary process. As a result, further reductions were averted.[75]

To date, the effect of the delegation strategy is debatable. According to B. Dan Wood, the delegation of authority to the states did not have the expected effect of impeding the implementation and enforcement of the air pollution statutes.[76] Ann O'M. Bowman found mixed support for the conclusion that the delegation strategy had impeded the ability of states to deal with hazardous waste management.[77] James P. Lester discovered that program delegation had generally had a negative impact on the ability of states to deal with environmental matters.[78]

The delegation strategy also had unanticipated consequences, including an increase in some business support for federal regulation. Some businesses which had previously opposed federal standards (such as the chemical industry and automobile manufacturers), reversed their position on regulation and supported continued federal standard setting. The reason for this sudden reversal was the manner in which the states chose to regulate environmental matters. Some states chose to adopt more stringent standards than those imposed by the federal government. In addition, the wide variation among the standards of the various individual states (particularly standards having to do with noise abatement and the manufacture of automobiles), complicated interstate business ventures.[79] The uncertainty created by the transfer of authority to the states thus sparked a countermovement from industry to return authority for some environmental programs to the federal government. Thus, the move to delegate greater authority to the states, while advancing the Reagan administration's reform agenda, in some cases provoked opposition from the very constituency that the reforms were meant to assist.

Cost-Benefit Analysis

Another means by which the Reagan administration asserted its influence over the administrative state was through the use of cost-benefit analysis. Reagan's Executive Order #12291 required that the benefits of any new regulations would have to outweigh the expected costs if the regulation was to be promulgated.[80]

One of the Reagan administration's first acts was to single out regulations that it considered to be too costly. Vice-President George Bush's Task Force on Regulatory Reform wrote state and local governments, as well as businesses, asking them to identify those regulations they considered to be redundant or involving too much red tape. Of the offending regulations, more than half had been promulgated by the EPA.[81] These included all regulations dealing with the disposal of hazardous waste materials. While the Bush Task Force examined these regulations, EPA enforcement of hazardous waste violations came to a virtual halt.[82]

A number of economists urged the EPA to institute cost-benefit analysis as a means of restraining the runaway costs of regulation.[83] In an attempt to control costs, the Ford and Carter administrations had also employed cost-benefit analysis, although not so rigorously as the Reagan administration. Although the technique was thought useful in terms of making the EPA more cost-conscious, many agency personnel felt the estimates derived by the technique were not reliable enough to be used as a litmus test for new regulations.

With regard to the use of cost-benefit analysis, three EPA employees wrote:

> The agency is concerned that little thought has been given to the results of inserting cost-benefit analysis into the adversary process of rulemaking. It is predictable that both (or all) sides will be able to introduce analyses that support their points of view. Each will then bring forward analysts, of equivalent credentials, who will argue among themselves about the superiority of their particular analyses in a language all their own. Incomprehensible analysis may then drive out understandable argument.[84]

Ronald Reagan followed his predecessor's example by issuing Executive Order #12291, which established the process for conducting cost-benefit analyses. Unlike the somewhat schizophrenic institutional arrangement that Carter had created, Reagan's centralized control for cost-benefit analysis was firmly within the Office of Management and Budget. In addition, the Office of Information and Regulatory Affairs (OIRA) was established to ensure that agencies conducted cost-benefit analyses of major regulations. Under the Reagan administration, the task of determining which regulations would be classified as major was left to OMB and OIRA. This practice contrasted with that of the Ford and Carter administrations, where major regulations were defined as those costing in excess of $100 million. Given this definition, a large number of regulations managed to come in just under the $100 million level, thus avoiding the need for analysis. Under Reagan's system, agencies would not be able to employ this subterfuge.[85]

There was immediate criticism of Executive Order #12291. Douglas Costle, President Carter's EPA administrator, argued that the order was designed to delay environmental regulation. The order accomplished this in two ways. First, the regulatory impact analyses (RIAs) required of all new regulations "stack the deck against regulation because benefits are usually more difficult to quantify than are costs." Second, the mandatory review process allows "those who wish to fight regulation . . . an extra opportunity to kill or weaken a rule,"[86] because this review process takes place before OMB, rather than within an agency itself.

Others criticized cost-benefit analysis on the grounds that is is politically motivated.[87] According to this argument, there was never any intention of really determining the costs and benefits of environmental regulation. Rather, the technique was simply a means of removing old regulations from the books, while slowing the development of new regulations. Evidence for this point of view can be found in statements made by Jim Tozzi, an employee of OMB's Office of Information and Regulatory Affairs. Tozzi has maintained that, in the actual cost-benefit analyses conducted by OMB under Executive Order #12291, costs and benefits were never really compared: "Let's say you had a real bad environmental reg [*sic*] that didn't cost much. Maybe we should—all that good stuff—but we didn't. The cost was the alarm bell."[88] He acknowledged, however, "Of course, this isn't benefit-cost . . . we're just here to represent the President."[89]

Clearly, such statements suggest that cost-benefit analysis and the Reagan administration's Executive Order #12291 were merely means of extending presidential influence. There is, however, no consensus of scholarly opinion that Executive Order #12291 in fact expanded presidential influence or that it has radically delayed the promulgation of new regulations.[90] Still, it remains a potential roadblock to new environmental regulations.[91]

Administrative Central Clearance

A final means by which the Reagan administration attempted to extend its influence over the Environmental Protection Agency and other bureaucratic entities was through the use of administrative central clearance. On January 8, 1985, President Reagan signed Executive Order #12498,[92] which was designed to ensure that agency heads would become involved in the rule-making procedure at an early stage. Previously, civil servants had possessed the authority to formulate and to prepare regulations, often without the knowledge of appointed officials or OMB personnel. Since top-level appointees were often not involved in the decision-making process until the regulation was already formulated and ready for promulgation, they had limited input in the rule-making process. Executive Order #12498 mandated that agencies submit a written statement to OMB, providing a regulatory overview and a description of significant regulatory actions that were being planned or conducted; OMB then reviewed these statements to determine if they were consistent with the president's program.[93] Through this process the administration would be provided with greater control over the rule-making process.

OMB claimed that this added oversight did not interfere with agency discretion, since only federal agencies have the right to formulate rules and regulations. By requiring another level of oversight, however, the administration obviously intended to prevent rules and regulations inconsistent with its goals from being formulated in the first place. In this sense, then, the new procedure was clearly designed to control administrative discretion.

It is too early to determine conclusively whether the order provided the Reagan administration with greater control over agency regulatory initiatives. At a minimum, it should have provided the administration with better information regarding agency activities. This information then could have provided the basis for increased presidential influence. But the new procedure may also have had the effect of increasing external opposition to the administration's regulatory program. By the last year of Reagan's term of office, several key congressmen, including Senator Albert Gore (D-Tennessee), and such public interest groups as OMB Watch had expressed concern that the technique was being used to stifle regulatory creativity, thus preventing agencies from complying with congressional intent.

The best available evidence to determine whether Executive Order #12498 increased presidential influence is the number of prerule-stage activities reported by the various federal agencies and departments reporting to the Office of Management and Budget's *Regulatory Program of the United States*. Prerule-stage activities, which include the decision to create an agency task force or to study a particular problem, are the best means of evaluating the effect of the executive order, since these are the rule-makings most likely to be affected by the new administrative central clearance procedure. Proposed and Final Rules would have already been reviewed under the existing procedures delineated under Executive Order #12291. From 1985 through 1987 there was a reduction of prerule stage activities from 125 (23 percent) to 83 (15 percent) in the total number of reported significant regulatory actions. This decrease in the total number of prerule actions came at a time in which the number of federal agencies reporting to OMB increased: from 17 in 1985 to 26 in 1987.[94] Thus, with more agencies reporting, the reduction in prerule stage actions is likely even greater than the absolute figures suggest. From this limited evidence it appears that the new administrative central clearance technique did promote presidential influence over the regulatory environment.

Revolution and Counterrevolution

After two years in office, the Reagan administration had achieved many of its goals in the area of environmental regulation. The number of new regulations promulgated by EPA had diminished significantly, and many existing standards had been either relaxed or delayed. The level of enforcement activity had been greatly reduced, as EPA relied more heavily on a system of voluntary compliance with agency guidelines. Activity in the area of research and development had also been severely reduced. Finally, the EPA under Administrator Anne Burford had delegated a great deal of authority directly to the states, thus expanding the role of local and state governments in environmental affairs while simultaneously limiting the federal government's role. All of these had been major objectives of the Reagan administration when it came into office in 1981. The fact that the administration had gone so far in achieving these objectives by the end of Reagan's second year in office should therefore be indisputable proof of the efficacy of the administrative presidency strategy.

Unfortunately for the Reagan administration, environmental history does not end with the year 1982. Although the administration had achieved a great deal in its first two years in office, the very strategy that had propelled the Reagan environmental agenda forward would foment a new rebellion: a counterrevolution that would force the Reagan administration to abandon many of its spoils of war. What were the seeds of this counterrevolution?

The problem with the Reagan approach was not that Reagan's appointees were not sufficiently committed to the president's program, but that they were too committed. Unable to see the necessity of creating a balance in the policies they derived, Reagan's appointees alienated important and powerful interest groups. At the same time, in using environmental politics as a means of promoting what they felt was "the cause"— the conservative revolution in general — they committed a number of politically and legally questionable acts that seriously undermined their ability to implement the president's program.

The most important reason for the counterrevolution was the inexperience of Reagan's appointees. The zeal of these officials was not tempered by the considered reflection that goes with experience. Burford, Lavelle, and other appointees had been given a task to perform and perform it they would. The result was activity that promoted reform in the short term, but at a very high political cost.

The combination of the inexperience of the administration's environmental officials and such actions as the severe budget cuts, the delegations of authority to the states, and the elimination of the Enforcement Office provided environmentalists with a cause to rally their supporters around. The Reagan administration's frontal assault against environmental regulation helped the environmental lobby to build internal support, which made for a better unified front in arguing its case before Congress.

The Environmentalists' Resurgence

Prior to the election of Ronald Reagan as president, membership growth in the major environmental groups had stagnated. Some observers argued that the environmental movement was over and that the time was ripe for a new environmental agenda; this was clearly the argument advanced by Reagan and his followers. But shortly after Reagan's election, and the transformation of the EPA, environmental groups began to register large increases in new membership. Between 1981 and 1983, the membership of the eleven largest environmental groups increased by approximately 250,000 or 13 percent. The Wilderness Society doubled, and the Friends of the Earth increased by 38 percent.[95] The Sierra Club's membership increased from 243,317 in 1981 to 324,910 in 1982 and 362,564 by 1985. Membership income increased from $4,439,100 in 1981 to over $8 million in 1985. Likewise, gift income increased from $2,624,200 in 1981 to $6,691,300 in 1985.[96] The environmentalist lobby now had more members and greater resources with which to influence the political agenda. This it set out to do in the congressional elections of 1982 and the presidential election of 1984.

Both the Sierra Club and the Friends of the Earth donated money directly to congressional candidates through their Political Action Committees. The Sierra Club Committee on Political Education contributed $253,927 between 1983 and 1984 to 176 Democratic and 11 Republican candidates for House and Senate seats and the 1984 presidential election. During the same period, the Friends of the Earth Political Action Committee contributed over $56,000 to 70 Democratic candidates and 4 Republicans.[97] As these figures demonstrate, although the environmental movement prior to the Reagan administration was considered bipartisan, financial support following Reagan's election went overwhelmingly to Democratic candidates.

Public Opinion

At the same time that the environmental interest groups were gaining strength, the public was becoming less pleased with the Reagan approach to environmental issues. In October 1982, a Harris Poll asked respondents to rate the Reagan administration's performance on enforcing air and water environmental standards. Thirty-two percent said they approved, while a resounding 61 percent said they did not approve of the president's handling of these matters.[98] In December 1982, pollster Lou Harris reported to the Subcommittee on Environmental Pollution that 74 percent of the American people felt that it was "very important in improving the quality of life in this country to strictly adhere to clean air and clean water standards."[99] A number of scholars have similarly found that the public is strongly committed to an active government role in protecting the environment.[100] Everett Carll Ladd has argued that the American public is committed to environmental protection, but that they also seek economic growth;[101] in other words, the public prefers a balance between the two approaches.

An analysis of data from the University of Michigan's 1984 Continuous Monitoring Survey suggests that the public overwhelmingly supports a clean environment and that little support exists for President Reagan's environmental budget cuts. Forty-nine percent of the survey's respondents supported increases in environmental funding, while another 34 percent stated that the budget should remain at its present level. Only 5.4 percent of the respondents expressed the president's view that the environmental budget should be reduced. These conclusions, however, are tempered by the fact that even those who expressed pro-environmental views overwhelmingly voiced support for President Reagan's reelection. Even among those voters who called for increasing the budget for environmental programs, 58.6 percent stated that they approved of the job the president was doing. In addition, 56 percent stated that they would vote for President Reagan; this is only about 3 points less than the actual percentage of the vote Reagan received in the 1984 presidential election.[102]

Still, with opinion polls pointing towards increased public concern over the environment, and with membership proliferating in the major environmental organizations, congressional oversight of the EPA intensified.[103] With increased oversight came daily headlines charging EPA officials, mostly Reagan appointees, with a variety of offenses. In the end, Burford resigned and the Reagan administration was forced to moderate its environmental policy.

With the appointment of William Ruckelshaus and the subsequent termination of most of Burford's top lieutenants, the Reagan administration lost much of the control over EPA it had fought so hard to achieve. As a result, the Reagan administration was forced to restore funds to EPA's budget, including support for research and development. The large-scale delegation of authority to the states was also halted.[104] Ruckelshaus and his successor, Lee Thomas, also increased the administration's commitment to acid rain research, intensified EPA supervision and enforcement in the area of water pollution control,[105] placed toxic waste cleanup prominently on the agency's agenda,[106] and improved relations with the environmental lobby.[107] The total number of EPA employees also increased to a level commensurate with that of the 1980 pre-Reagan EPA.[108] These changes led the Conservation Foundation to announce that "William D. Ruckelshaus presides over a reinvigorated agency whose morale and integrity have been restored by one of the most impressive rescues on record."[109]

Although somewhat hyperbolic, this comment implied that Ruckelshaus had rescued EPA from the Reagan revolution. The ability of EPA to perform its regulatory duties had been impaired by the large-scale departure of many competent employees, and the agency still would not have been characterized as pro-environmental, but Reagan's administrative approach had indeed failed. This failure was largely the result of the administration's selection of inexperienced political appointees and the blind vigor with which they sought to achieve the president's program. Surely, a more experienced team would not have made many of the mistakes—or lacked the political tact—that Reagan's appointees did. The president's strategy would have been better served by appointees with prior Washington experience.

The fact that a counterrevolution forced the Reagan administration to abandon many of its goals in the area of environmental regulation does not indicate that the administrative presidency strategy could not have been successful. The major problem at the EPA was the heavy-handed manner in which the strategy was applied. Essentially, the strategy as implemented represented overkill. A more moderate approach, employing loyal but competent individuals, would have better served the Reagan administration.

Since environmental protection is such a high-profile policy area, one might legitimately ask whether it would have been possible to achieve the Reagan administration's goals under any strategy? It is to this question that I now turn.

Could Any Strategy Have Avoided Controversy?

Clearly, any strategy to alter the existing manner of administering the environmental statutes would have been controversial, for the Reagan administration's goals represented a major break with past policy. But then, so did Carter's motor carrier regulatory policies. While Carter's success was enduring, Reagan's was fleeting. The essential difference is that Carter chose a more moderate variation of the administrative presidency strategy, relying heavily on the appointment of competent loyalists. Reagan simply attempted to do too much and in too obvious a fashion. Reagan could have achieved more success by using a more limited model of the administrative presidency strategy—one that endeavored to build support for the administration's objectives, rather than attempting to steamroller the opposition.

The very fact that Reagan's variation of the administrative presidency strategy was able to accomplish so much in a two-year period suggests that a more moderate approach could have succeeded in achieving many of these same goals, while simultaneously building more enduring support. Confrontation had its limited success; cooperation could have promoted more permanent accomplishments.

One of the keystones of the Reagan approach to environmental politics was a strong reliance on voluntary compliance in meeting regulatory standards and a reduction in EPA's traditional enforcement program. Although this idea was controversial, it was not without merit. Academics such as Eugene Bardach and Robert A. Kagan had argued for a greater reliance on voluntary compliance.[110] Others had pointed out that strict enforcement involves very high costs.[111] In addition, enforcement is very difficult, since there are obviously many more sources of pollution than there are EPA personnel to oversee them. Even among ardent environmental supporters there has long been a realization that a strict enforcement program is beyond the present capabilities of the Environmental Protection Agency. Arguments like these could have been used by the Reagan administration as a basis for supporting a move toward voluntary compliance.[112]

Rather than arguing the merits of voluntary compliance over strict enforcement, Burford and the EPA took a heavy-handed approach that had immediately alienated environmentalists and many members of Congress. Perhaps even more importantly, this approach demonstrated that environmentalists would not get a fair hearing on issues before the EPA. The most obvious example was the repeated use of secret meetings between EPA administrators and industry officials to discuss specific regulations. Not only did these meetings lack such basic procedural requirements as public notice and public comment, but they specifically excluded environmental groups.

In testimony before Congress, environmental groups accused EPA's Deputy Administrator John Hernandez and Assistant Administrator for Pesticides and Toxic Substances John A. Todhunter of conducting a series of "science courts" in which industry was allowed to participate, while environmental groups and the public were excluded. After holding these meetings, the EPA decided not to proceed with the regulation of formaldehyde and diethylhexyl phthalate.[113]

Todhunter also advocated a plan for the testing of toxic substances by the chemical industry, rather than independent testing by the EPA. Environmentalists objected to this proposal, arguing that industry might agree to test substances and then not follow through with adequate testing. They also complained that small chemical manufacturers might not have the capacity to do rigorous testing.[114]

In addition to these actions, the abolition of the Enforcement Office and deep cuts in the agency's budget had undermined any basis for trust among environmentalists, members of Congress, and the administration. Rather than building support for the idea of voluntary compliance, the deletion of the Enforcement Office was a clear signal to the environmentalists that they would have to turn elsewhere for support.

Reagan's EPA appointees advanced the cause of voluntary compliance, but at the high political cost of increasing congressional and interest group opposition to the administration's policies. By holding meetings in secret and by excluding environmentalists and other members of the public, the strategy provoked cries of favoritism toward business. The abolition of the Enforcement Office and deep budget cuts added to this distrust. Thus, the worst fears of environmentalists were realized: under the Reagan administration, voluntary compliance would be a euphemism for government capitulation to business interests.

The administration's drive to delegate program authority to the states could also have benefited from wise use of scholarly support. David B. Walker had provided the intellectual basis for the idea of transferring many programs back to the states.[115] Since the states already played a major role in environmental affairs, it would have been easy to advance an argument that the delegation of some functions to the states could actually improve the management of environmental affairs. The Reagan administration could have argued that, with the limited resources available at the federal level, the state governments provide the most logical means of addressing environmental concerns. Moreover, had the Reagan administration accompanied the delegation of program authority to the states with increased funding, it is unlikely that the states would have complained as vociferously as they did. In addition, environmentalists would have had a much less convincing case against the administration, since the federal government would still have been providing the necessary funds for program implementation.

The Reagan administration did not adopt this more moderate approach, however. Instead, it further alienated environmentalists and many congressmen by delegating greater authority to the states while concurrently reducing grants-in-aid. Such actions, coupled with deep budget cuts, provided environmentalists with strong ammunition for arguing that the Reagan administration's real motive was to gut existing environmental standards and not to sort them out logically.

Even though a more moderate approach would not have achieved all of the administration's objectives, it could have achieved some of them, and these reforms would likely have been more enduring, as were Carter's trucking reforms. In the short term the extreme approach adopted by the Reagan team did slow down the environmental revolution; under Reagan, the EPA was never so active a regulator as it had been in the days of the Carter administration. But as Reagan's term of office progressed, many of his administration's achievements were abandoned. Even Reagan's own vice-president, George Bush, while campaigning for the presidency in 1988, stated, "I'm an environmentalist." Certainly, this statement signaled a move away from the Reagan environmental agenda, and a more pro-environmental Bush administration agenda.

Carter's regulatory revolution at the Interstate Commerce Commission, in contrast, has not been reversed, and for this reason: Carter was able to build support for his reforms within the agency itself and then promote reform legislatively. By employing a more cooperative approach, Carter was able to achieve his goals and to ensure that the policy change would endure. Furthermore, though using a more cooperative approach, Carter did not foreclose the possibility of resorting to a more confrontational style. If his initial strategy had failed, he still could have sought deep cuts in the agency's budget and attempted to remove recalcitrant employees.

In the case of Reagan and the Environmental Protection Agency, the administration, by commencing with a confrontational approach, had no credibility upon which later to base a more cooperative approach. By 1983, the Reagan variation of the administrative presidency strategy had created such distrust and hostility among interest groups and legislators that it would have been futile for the administration to suddenly adopt a more cooperative approach. If, on the other hand, the administration had started with a more cooperative approach, it could then have moved to a more confrontational style when necessary. If, for example, the administration had tried to build support for voluntary compliance and failed, it could then have employed the budget, reorganization, and removal powers of the president in an attempt to force compliance with its goals and objectives. These techniques then could have been justified on the grounds that conciliation had already been attempted and failed. The threat of more extreme measures could then have been seen as bargaining chips or inducements to environmentalists and other groups to compromise. Had they not agreed to compromise, the Reagan administration could then have proceeded with its administrative revolution with a stronger rationalization for moving unilaterally.

Although the Reagan administration sought a policy change that was controversial in nature, it was not justified in using all of the techniques of the administrative presidency strategy. A more moderate approach, emphasizing the appointment of competent and loyal individuals, along with an attempt to build support for reform, could have promoted a more enduring success. As it is, the Reagan revolution in environmental affairs will likely be viewed by scholars of the future as simply a temporary deviation from the policies of Reagan's predecessors.

Conclusions

What are the lessons of the Reagan administration's attempts to employ the administrative presidency strategy at the Environmental Protection Agency? First, although the administration's attempts to alter the goals of the EPA were largely abandoned after a tempestuous two-year fight, this policy reversal does not prove that the administrative presidency strategy had to fail. A more moderate approach, like the one adopted by Carter at the ICC, could have been more successful in promoting the Reagan administration's goals. The administration's initial success—dramatically altering the EPA's goals within a period of two short years—was a remarkable achievement. The oppressive manner in which the strategy was implemented, however, promoted increased political pressure on the Reagan administration and the EPA and eventually resulted in a loss of much of Reagan's influence over environmental policy.

Second, this case study demonstrates that the quality of appointees, and not simply their loyalty to the president, is important in promoting presidential influence. Reagan's appointees shared the president's political philosophy and wanted to implement his program. However, these qualities were insufficient. Appointees should not only share the president's philosophy, but they should also have the experience, both in management and in Washington-style politics, to implement the president's program effectively. Had more experienced individuals been selected to serve at the EPA, it is doubtful that they would have made the kinds of egregious mistakes that Burford and her team made—misjudgments that eventually sabotaged the president's program and forced the administration to back away from its environmental agenda.

Third, the Reagan administration's experience with the EPA demonstrates that one component of the administrative presidency strategy can be extremely effective: the president's budgetary authority. Through deep reductions in the EPA's research and development budget, the administration was able to reduce the agency's enforcement activities as well as retard the process of promulgating new regulations. The administration succeeded so well with the budgetary technique because it sold its budget reductions to Congress as a policy to restore the economy. If the administration had acknowledged that the reductions sprang from its desire to emasculate the EPA, the budgetary technique likely would have failed.

Fourth, this case study also demonstrates the interrelationship of the various techniques of the administrative presidency strategy. The appointment and budgetary strategies can be used in tandem to promote the president's objectives. The appointment of individuals at EPA who supported the president's budgetary reduction proposals before Congress was instrumental in gaining congressional acquiescence for the budget cuts.

Fifth, several of the administration's reform techniques had unanticipated consequences. The removal strategy actually increased congressional and media scrutiny of the EPA's activities. The delegation of program authority to the states created a countermovement for federal regulation within many of the industries the original Reagan reforms were meant to assist. The reorganization strategy also increased interest group and congressional resistance to the administration's environmental agenda.

Sixth, when the president's agenda ran contrary to public opinion, the administrative presidency strategy met with intense resistance. The Reagan administration badly misinterpreted the 1980 election result as a broad mandate to attack environmental regulation. Virtually every opinion poll unambiguously demonstrated that the general public supported strong environmental standards.

The case of the Reagan administration and the Environmental Protection Agency suggests that the administrative presidency strategy can be an effective means of promoting presidential influence, but not if implemented in the heavy-handed fashion of Burford and her team. A more moderate and more cooperative approach, building on the academic literature and other sources of existing support for Reagan's ideas, could have achieved more enduring success. The strategy of purposely excluding environmentalists and the public intensified the hostility that already existed. Had Reagan used an approach more like the one employed by Carter at the ICC, his influence over environmental policy might have been more enduring.

Chapter 6

Reagan and the
Nuclear Regulatory Commission:
The Limitations of the
Administrative Presidency Strategy

When Ronald Reagan assumed the office of president in January 1981, the Nuclear Regulatory Commission (NRC) was an agency under fire. In the aftermath of the accident at Three Mile Island (TMI), investigators charged that the Commission had been too lax in its enforcement of safety requirements. Two investigations of the Three Mile Island Accident called for fundamental changes in the NRC's organizational structure. The nuclear power industry itself was also in serious trouble. Not only had the TMI accident seriously undercut public confidence in the nuclear industry's ability to provide safe nuclear power, but economic forces were also making the nuclear power option less attractive as a future energy source. Demand for electricity had fallen far below original projections; at the same time, construction costs were escalating.

In this uncertain environment the Reagan administration decided to make expanded reliance on nuclear power one of the cornerstones of its energy policy. Reagan was committed to the idea that burdensome federal regulation was the primary reason for cost proliferation and construction delays. Accordingly, the administration came to office determined to reduce the level of government regulation wherever possible. At a time of increasing congressional and public concerns regarding the safety of the nuclear option, and with the NRC under intense criticism for the lax manner in which it had regulated safety, this approach was the wrong policy, in the wrong agency, at the wrong time. As such, Reagan's approach was a perfect example of a president ignoring the dictates of political and economic feasibility. At a time when public concerns about nuclear safety were escalating, Congress was unwilling to streamline the licensing process for nuclear power plants. Moreover, the highly decentralized organizational structure of the NRC made it difficult for the Commission to avoid responding to its own staff's concerns for safety. The Reagan program also ignored certain basic economic truths, such as the law of supply and demand. With demand for electricity falling, supply was also likely to diminish unless the government actively subsidized the industry, a proposal the Reagan administration was unwilling to offer. How this dilemma reflects the limitations of the administrative presidency strategy is the subject of this chapter.

The Atomic Energy Commission

The Atomic Energy Commission (AEC), the forerunner of the NRC, was established on January 1, 1947, to regulate non-military uses of nuclear energy. The AEC had two major and often contradictory goals: the regulation and promotion of the nuclear power industry. In order to accomplish one task, it was often necessary for the AEC to ignore the other. Usually, the AEC ignored its regulatory duties in favor of its promotional responsibility. The AEC's hearings process exemplified this tendency.

The hearings process, which involved a decision to grant a construction or an operating permit to a utility, was controlled largely by the nuclear power industry and the AEC. When a new plant was being considered, the industry and the AEC worked out the details for the construction of the proposed plant. The AEC would then assist the utility during the construction of the facility, which usually took several years. Only at the end of this period were public hearings held and intervenors (such as those opposing the proposed plant) allowed to introduce testimony. By this time, most of the major decisions had already been made and had received AEC support. According to a study of the AEC by Steven Ebbin and Raphael Kasper, the licensing process was nothing more than a sham; the outcome was usually determined before the hearing commenced.[1]

The AEC hearing process was but one example of the Commission's lack of commitment to safety regulation. The AEC also had few regulations on the books. Prior to 1972, the AEC seldom used generic rule-making as a means of setting standards. Rather, such questions as the permissible level of radiation and the adequacy of emergency core cooling systems (ECCS) were handled on an ad hoc basis. The AEC's first major contested rule-making proceeding, the ECCS hearings, did not occur until 1972.[2]

During the 1950s and 1960s, criticism of the AEC's hearing and rule-making procedures was limited. Nuclear energy was generally considered a safe and cost-effective means of providing electricity. By the early 1970s, however, the conjunction of a series of mishaps and the publication of scholarly reports concerning the likelihood of a major nuclear accident created a somewhat different atmosphere in which there was an increased public concern regarding nuclear safety.[3]

An Organizational Shakeup

The Atomic Energy Commission was viewed by its critics as an ineffective regulator and a biased promoter of nuclear power. Such criticism, coupled with increasing concern that a major nuclear accident was possible, forced the AEC to intensify its regulatory oversight function during the early 1970s.

In 1970 the AEC had less than a dozen active regulations dealing with nuclear power. By 1972, the number of regulations increased to several dozen, and by 1977, under the NRC, there were several hundred.[4] Even with this increased regulatory activity, critics argued that the AEC was incapable of performing its regulatory duties in an unbiased manner. Regulation, they felt, would always come into conflict with the AEC's promotional activities.

Congress responded to the growing dissatisfaction with the AEC's performance by passing the Energy Reorganization Act of 1974, which abolished the AEC and established the Nuclear Regulatory Commission. The Energy Reorganization Act had several immediate consequences. First, it divided the reponsibility for nuclear regulatory policy between two agencies. The Nuclear Regulatory Commission was assigned the task of regulating the nuclear power industry, and the Energy Research and Development Administration (ERDA) was established to handle the promotional aspects of nuclear power. As the functions of ERDA were later transferred to the Department of Energy (DOE) by the Carter administration, there are now two competing bureaucratic units which influence the nuclear power industry.

Second, the act indirectly led to the replacement of the Joint Committee on Atomic Energy (JCAE), the long-time congressional protector of the AEC and the nuclear power industry. Since the JCAE had originally been established to be the congressional watchdog over the AEC, the elimination of the AEC was followed by an increase in congressional support for the replacement of the JCAE by a new committee structure. In addition, a rapid turnover on the JCAE left it vulnerable to the congressional reform movement of the late 1970s. Because of these factors, the joint committee was eliminated and replaced by three congressional committees which share jurisdiction over nuclear power issues.

This congressional committee structure proved to be less sympathetic to the goal of nuclear power than the JCAE had been. Even though the House Appropriations Committee was chaired by Thomas Bevill (D-Alabama), who strongly advocated streamlining the licensing process,[5] other committees took more divergent approaches. The House Interior Committee, chaired by the staunchly pro-environmental Morris K. Udall (D-Arizona), was likely to be more critical of proposals to ease the regulatory burden. The clear implication of the demise of the JCAE was that nuclear power would no longer retain a special protected status in Congress. Rather, the NRC would now have to deal with a number of different committees, each with its own goals and objectives. Often faced with contradictory goals, the NRC was forced to try to serve two different masters. The tendency toward increased congressional supervision would make an administrative approach more attractive to policymakers in the executive branch than the traditional legislative approach.

NRC's Organizational Structure

Unlike the Environmental Protection Agency and the Interstate Commerce Commission, the Nuclear Regulatory Commission is a highly decentralized agency. It consists of five commissioners who are both geographically and organizationally separated from the NRC staff. It was thought that this separation of commissioners and staff would protect the staff from the influence of politics; thus, they would be capable of acting impartially on the basis of scientific evidence. In practice, however, this division of authority has contributed to communication problems between the commission and its staff.

Following the Three Mile Island accident, this highly decentralized organizational structure was criticized by a number of presidentially appointed commissions. The Kemeny and Rogovin Reports recommended a total reorganization of the NRC, with the five-member commission replaced by a single administrator, such as is the case with the Environmental Protection Agency.[6] The reports argued that this move would centralize control in one individual and thus reduce the possibility of communication problems between management and staff.

In 1983, President Reagan's Private Sector Survey on Cost Control (also known as the Grace Commission), while conceding that the authority of the NRC chairman had been strengthened after the recommendations of the Kemeny and Rogovin reports, argued that the position "still lacks the executive and administrative authority provided by law to the Chairman of the other Federal regulatory agencies."[7] The report was also highly critical of the restrictions on communication between the NRC commissioners and the staff, concluding that "this vestige of a need to separate the promotional and regulatory functions . . . impedes the Commission's ready access to the most knowledgable sources of staff technical advice and impairs the Chairman's ability to exercise effective staff oversight."[8] The Grace Commission called for the consolidation of the NRC's Washington staff in one location, rather than the existing process of locating various NRC staff in twelve separate sites.[9]

The decentralized nature of the NRC had the effect of making an administrative approach to policymaking less feasible. Whereas a president could appoint commissioners according to personal political philosophy, these appointees had limited means for ensuring that the NRC staff obsequiously followed the Commission's lead. Thus, the administrative presidency strategy was a less powerful alternative than it was in the areas of motor carrier or environmental regulation.

Escalating Costs

At the same time that the nuclear regulatory agencies were experiencing an organizational shakeup, the nuclear power industry was going through an upheaval of its own because of changing economic factors. The early promise of low-cost nuclear power dissipated quickly. From the middle of 1974 through the spring of 1976, 23 nuclear power plant orders were cancelled and another 143 deferred. The principal reason for these cancellations and deferrals was a sudden and dramatic contraction in the demand for electricity.[10] Early projections had indicated that the demand for electricity would continue to grow well into the future. This precipitous decline in orders for new power plants reflected a recognition that these early projections for a continued demand for electricity had been in error. The contraction in the demand for electricity had a further impact in the climate of economic uncertainty it created among investors and utility companies. Investors now had to consider the possibility that after spending over a billion dollars for a nuclear power plant, there might not be enough demand to make the enterprise profitable.

Other factors beyond the demand for electricity were also imperiling the economic vitality of the industry. Even by the 1980s, the nuclear industry was still technologically in its infancy. Because there were few precedents for building designs, construction costs rose, as utilities were often forced to alter the design of partially completed plants. Labor problems also led to increased construction costs.

Adding to these costs was the increased regulatory vigor of the NRC. To the nuclear power industry the most easily avoidable of these various problems was the growing number of government regulations. Whereas demand for electricity and labor problems could not easily be avoided, the scope of government regulation could be reduced. Consequently, the nuclear power industry charged that government regulations—such as those requiring backfitting or design changes to meet newly derived governmental standards, not to mention the lugubrious hearings process—were too costly and did not promote public safety.[11]

When Jimmy Carter assumed the presidency, he was sympathetic to this point of view. Carter believed that nuclear power had a place in America's future and that current regulatory standards were too strict. At the same time, Carter also wanted the continued support of environmentalists, most of whom argued that nuclear power was too dangerous and had not been effectively regulated. These contradictory ideas had a major impact on the manner in which the Nuclear Regulatory Commission conducted business during the Carter years.

Carter and the NRC

Jimmy Carter purposely appointed individuals to the NRC who held diverse views on the subject of nuclear power. Carter's choice for the chairman of the NRC, Joseph Hendrie, was generally considered pro-nuclear. Two of Carter's other appointees, Peter A. Bradford and John Ahearne, exhibited a greater concern for nuclear safety. Carter also reappointed Victor Gilinsky, originally appointed by Gerald Ford, to a second term as commissioner.[12] Gilinsky was an outspoken critic of the nuclear industry and a strong supporter of strict safety requirements.[13]

Why did Carter appoint individuals who held varied perspectives on nuclear power? Carter wanted the Commission to be representative of society in general and its lack of unanimity on the subject of nuclear power. The appointments also reflected the ambivalence of Carter's own views toward nuclear power. On the one hand, Carter was a strong proponent of nuclear energy, a self-professed nuclear engineer. On the other hand, he was concerned about the potential safety hazards associated with nuclear energy, particularly nuclear fission.[14] In addition, he was aware of the vigorous antinuclear movement and its strong associaton with the environmental movement which had helped elect him to office.[15] With these concerns in mind, Carter characterized nuclear energy as the energy source of "last resort with the strictest possible safety precautions."[16]

Carter's ambivalence was also reflected in the policy style of the Nuclear Regulatory Commission during his tenure. In William Lanouette's opinion, the Commission was less of a "deliberative body" and more of a "debating society," unable to deal conclusively with many of the issues that came before it.[17] As a result, neither the nuclear power industry nor the environmental movement was satisfied with the NRC during this period.

Because Carter's views on the issue of nuclear power were ambiguous, it was impossible for him to take advantage of the typical techniques of the administrative presidency strategy to promote his policy preferences. Unlike the case of the deregulation of the motor carrier industry, where Carter's views were clearly and concisely articulated, Carter's ambivalence regarding nuclear power left him unable to appoint individuals who represented his viewpoint. By selecting individuals who represented varied perspectives on the issue, Carter unfortunately produced a "debating society" that made it impossible for him to initiate change directly at the administrative level, as he had done at the ICC. Consequently, he was forced to rely on the traditional legislative approach.

The Carter administration's legislative initiatives on nuclear power further underscore the administration's vacillation on the issue. According to John Reynolds and Leonard Champney, these proposals were designed to "accelerate the licensing process by eliminating a number of procedural safeguards and limiting public participation."[18] The same proposals also called for government financing for intervenors, designed to assist the anti-nuclear movement and environmentalists. The legislation, which succeeded in alienating both the nuclear power industry and environmentalists, died in committee.

While Congress did not act on Carter's bill, two congressional research bodies attacked it. Both the General Accounting Office (GAO) and the Congressional Budget Office (CBO) released reports which concluded that Carter's legislation would not greatly reduce the costs of constructing nuclear power plants. The CBO report concluded that the real problem was not regulatory but economic. Two-thirds of the delays in construction were not the results of regulation but rather of such factors as interest rates, the effects of the various recessions of the 1970s, and a decline in demand for electricity.[19]

At 4 A.M. on March 28, 1979, the Carter administration's attempts at a balanced nuclear policy ended abruptly. Three Mile Island quickly altered the political equation. For the next two years, the Nuclear Regulatory Commission was the subject of congressional, presidential, and in-house investigations. Allegations surfaced that NRC chairman Joseph Hendrie was aware of serious safety problems at a number of plants, yet refused to act because it would have slowed down the licensing process.[20] In response to these allegations, President Carter removed Hendrie as head of the NRC, though he continued to serve as an NRC commissioner until his term expired. Thus, for most of the next two years, the NRC was an agency without a chairman. Furthermore, because a vacancy on the Commission was left unfilled, only four active commissioners were available to deal with a multitude of problems.

Besides these administrative difficulties, the accident at Three Mile Island shook public confidence in nuclear power. Within a year of the TMI accident, only a slight majority favored more nuclear power plant construction. By the early 1980s, Gallup and Roper polls indicated that only about 30 percent of the public still favored increased construction. In several polls a majority favored an immediate moratorium on construction.[21] Not only had public confidence in nuclear power failed to rebound following the accident, but public opposition was actually increasing.

It was in this turbulent atmosphere that Ronald Reagan was elected to the presidency. The NRC was an agency whose legitimacy had been severely threatened. The nuclear power industry was suffering through an economic crisis as well as a serious loss of public confidence. To this uncertain environment President Reagan brought his philosophy of limited government and streamlined regulation, a philosophy that both the GAO and CBO reports had recently attacked as ignoring the real problems facing the nuclear power industry. It was a clear case of the wrong policy at the wrong time.

Reagan and His Appointees

When Reagan entered the White House in January 1981, the Nuclear Regulatory Commission had one vacancy. In addition, Joseph Hendrie was departing. This provided Ronald Reagan with the opportunity to name two new members to the Commission at the very beginning of his term.

The administration's first task was to name a new chairman. Reagan's first choice for this position was Thomas Roberts, formerly the chief executive officer and owner of Southern Boiler and Tank Works, a company which produced components for nuclear power plants. Roberts' views were consistent with those of the administration. At his confirmation hearings Roberts testified that his first priority would be to "pay particular attention to developing new ways of streamlining the [licensing] process consistent with the goals of environmental protection and public health and safety."[22] Despite the fact that he was the administration's first choice, Senate opposition developed over Roberts' nomination because of his previous close political ties to George Bush (during the 1980 presidential primaries, Roberts had served as George Bush's treasurer). Because of this opposition, Reagan decided to nominate Roberts as a commissioner only and to select someone else to serve as chairman of the NRC.[23] As a nominee for commissioner, Roberts was easily confirmed.

Unable to secure their first choice for chairman of the NRC, the administration nominated Nunzio Palladino for the post. Palladino was well qualified for the position, even if much of his experience, like Roberts', had come within the nuclear industry. Palladino had served ten years on the Advisory Committee on Reactor Safety, worked twenty years with the Westinghouse Corporation designing and building reactor cores, and was dean of the college of engineering at Penn State. He was also a member of Pennsylvania Governor Richard Thornburgh's Commission on Three-Mile Island and on the NRC Citizen Advisory Panel on the TMI cleanup.[24] Unlike Reagan's appointments to the Environmental Protection Agency, neither Roberts nor Palladino could be attacked on the basis of a lack of qualifications.

Like Roberts, Palladino was staunchly pro-nuclear. At his confirmation hearings, Palladino advocated increasing the evidentiary burden on intervenors in the hearings process.[25] This reform, which had been advocated by the NRC before Palladino was confirmed, would have limited public participation in the licensing process by forcing intervenors to support each fact they disagreed with prior to the publication by the NRC of the documents reviewing the licensing application. This reform would have provided the nuclear industry with a clear tactical advantage over intervenors.

Further evidence of Palladino's support for the nuclear industry had appeared in several articles he had written. In one, Palladino argued that the escalating financial crisis in the nuclear power industry was largely the result of increased uncertainty created by anti-nuclear groups. He also argued that the continually changing regulatory requirements were contributing to the industry's financial burden.[26]

Although Palladino clearly supported the industry's point of view, he also argued that the nuclear industry had to have a better record on safety. At a speech on December 1, 1981, before the Atomic Industrial Forum's Annual Conference, Palladino criticized the nuclear industry's record, arguing that the industry must do its part or no level of regulatory reform would be sufficient to save it. Palladino's statement, which followed revelations concerning serious safety and quality control problems at the Diablo Canyon nuclear power plant, took the industry by surprise.[27] Faced with the lingering reality of the Three Mile Island cleanup, and its rising costs, Palladino realized that without a sound record of safety, the nuclear industry could not regain its credibility with the public and with financial institutions. Unfortunately, his public statements were not matched by action at the NRC.

Following the appointment of Roberts and Palladino, the Commission remained seriously divided over such questions as whether and to what extent the hearings process should be reformed. Palladino could count on only Roberts' vote and his own. Commissioners Victor Gilinsky and Peter Bradford were opposed to accelerating the licensing process. Commissioner John Ahearne thus became the swing vote.[28] Although he tended to align himself with Roberts and Palladino by voting to reform the licensing process, Ahearne did not vote with Reagan's appointees on every issue. For example, he voted with Gilinsky and Bradford on the controversial issue of whether to provide an early start for construction of the Clinch River Breeder Reactor, one of the major components of Reagan's nuclear power program. Thus, the president's gaining control of the Commission would have to wait until Bradford's term expired in early 1982. Because the president lacked a solid majority, the administrative presidency strategy was not a feasible alternative during this period.

In 1982 the Reagan administration nominated Willie J. Nunnery to replace Bradford on the Commission. Senatorial opponents of the Clinch River Breeder Reactor, realizing that Nunnery would provide Reagan with a majority on the Commission, tied up his nomination in committee. Faced with this opposition, Reagan withdrew Nunnery's name and instead nominated James K. Asselstine, who had served as the Minority and Majority Counsel for the Republicans on the Subcommittee on Nuclear Regulation (for the Committee on Environment and Public Works). Asselstine's nomination was much less controversial. After Congress assured itself that the new nominee had not worked out a deal with the White House to support the Clinch River project, Asselstine was easily confirmed.[29] Asselstine's appointment came to represent a thorn in the side of the Reagan administration's pro-nuclear power program, for he proved to be an outspoken critic of the NRC's policies.

With Asselstine's appointment, Reagan still lacked a clear majority on the Commission. In August 1983, Reagan appointed Frederick Bernthal, a chief legislative aide to Howard Baker (one of the strongest senatorial advocates for the Clinch River project). In 1985, Reagan appointed the fifth and final member of the NRC, Lando W. Zech, a retired vice admiral. Zech later became the chairman of the NRC when Palladino's term ended. To replace Palladino on the

Commission, Reagan then appointed another former vice admiral, Kenneth M. Carr, who had extensive service in the Navy's nuclear program.

By 1985 all of the members of the Nuclear Regulatory Commission were Reagan's appointees. With the exception of Asselstine, Reagan had selected individuals who represented his policy views. These appointments made an administrative approach to policy-making feasible. However, other factors, such as the unwillingness of the administration to subsidize the nuclear power industry, the decentralized organizational structure of the NRC, and strong public and congressional opposition to the president's program, greatly constrained efforts by the Reagan administration to implement the administrative presidency strategy.

The NRC and Its Budget

During the Reagan administration's first three years in office, federal expenditures for research and development of solar energy, energy conservation, and conservation information were slashed by more than 90 percent. Among all of the research and development programs run by the Department of Energy, only the one dealing with nuclear energy received a budget increase during this period.[30] Funding for the Clinch River Breeder Reactor was retained and was listed by OMB as one of the few untouchables, despite David Stockman's own personal reservations about the program.[31]

Likewise, the budget for the Nuclear Regulatory Commission was increased during this period. Total appropriations increased from Fiscal Year 1981 to FY 1983 by approximately $25 million. Actual outlays, or funds expended by the NRC, increased during this same period from $416 million to $514 million.[32] These increases reflected the high-priority status which nuclear power had been assigned by the Reagan administration.

Further evidence of this high priority is that the NRC was one of the few agencies to experience an increase in its number of employees. While agencies like the EPA were absorbing deep reductions in their budgets and personnel levels, the NRC was adding new employees. In a time of severe financial belt-tightening, the administration justified these increases by arguing that its economic recovery program required a reliable source of energy.[33] After the cutbacks in solar and other alternative energy sources, nuclear power was one of the few remaining options.

Despite its strong commitment to nuclear power, the Reagan administration refused to subsidize the industry in spite of expert opinions that government subsidies were necessary for resuscitation.[34] In addition, the administration did ultimately reduce the NRC's budget. In Fiscal Year 1985 total appropriations were reduced to $448 million, while actual outlays were reduced to $467.5 million. Even with these reductions (without adjusting for inflation), funding levels were still higher than they had been in 1981.

Reorganization at the NRC

After the accident at Three Mile Island, both the Rogovin and Kemeny Reports recommended that the five-member Nuclear Regulatory Commission be replaced by a single administrator. Although this idea was rejected, Congress did act to consolidate the commissioners and the NRC staff. By early 1981, the search was underway for a building that could house the five commissioners and the staff. One plan called for locating the NRC in the Matomic Building in downtown Washington. When this plan fell through, the General Services Administration (GSA) began the search for another building.[35] Another proposal called for moving the commissioners to Bethesda, Maryland, and splitting the Office of Nuclear Reactor Regulation between its Washington and Bethesda offices.[36] Problems soon developed with this proposal. Finally, the General Services Administration secured a lease on a building in Rockville, Maryland.[37]

Despite the difficulties in securing a central location for the commission and its staff, several changes were made to provide greater centralized control over the agency. The Office of Standards Development was combined with the Office of Nuclear Reactor Research. Several support offices were merged, including the Offices of Equal Employment Opportunity, Women's Programs, and Small and Disadvantaged Business Utilization.[38]

In addition, several organizational changes were made to help implement the president's program. On October 16, 1981, Chairman Palladino announced the creation of the Committee to Review Generic Requirements (CRGR). This committee, which makes recommendations to the Executive Director of Operations (EDO) on proposed reactor requirements, was designed to assist the EDO in bringing greater centralized management control over the number and nature of the requirements the NRC places on licensees.[39] It was also designed to determine whether NRC regulations contribute to the public's health and safety or whether they place an unnecessary burden on licensees or NRC resources.[40] In performing this task, the CRGR provided the organizational framework for implementing President Reagan's Executive Order #12291 on cost-benefit analysis (see ch. 5). The immediate impact of CRGR activity was a 47 percent reduction in the number of new reactor licensing actions from 1981 to 1982.[41] This effect led Commissioner Asselstine to attack the use of cost-benefit analysis by the CRGR. Asselstine argued that the technique was biased in favor of cost considerations and ignored the benefits of nuclear safety.[42] Regardless of Asselstine's criticisms, the results of the new review process were clearly in line with the goals of the Reagan administration.

A second move designed to implement the president's program was initiated in April 1982 when the NRC established the Office of Investigation. The office was given the responsibility for investigating all allegations of wrongdoing by organizations or individuals except those made by the NRC staff.[43] The creation of this new office underscored the Reagan administration's desire to rely on less coercive means of achieving compliance than traditional enforcement. Still, the NRC did not relax its efforts to enforce existing regulations. In the safety-conscious public mood following Three Mile Island, the NRC found it untenable to cut back on enforcement activity.[44] The method of retribution for safety violations, however, was altered. Under Reagan, the nuclear industry convinced the NRC to impose fines for safety violations rather than shutting plants down.[45]

In October 1986, under the new chairman, Lando Zeck, a major reorganization abolished the Office of Inspection and Enforcement. The inspection functions were divided between the Office of Nuclear Reactor Regulation and the Office of Nuclear Material Safety and Safeguards. At the same time, a new office of Enforcement was established which reported directly to the Deputy Executive Director for Operations. Other reforms were also adopted, such as the establishment of a new Office of Governmental and Public Affairs. In addition, the "scope of operations" of the Office of Research and the Office for Analysis and Evaluation of Operating Data were expanded.[46] These reforms suggest that the NRC under Zech would take a more active role in regulatory enforcement and in research and development. Zeck's justification for the massive reorganization was based on the changing nature of the NRC's role:

> Our mission is far different today than it was in 1975 when the NRC was created. . . . As the plants presently in the final stages of construction are completed, we will have progressively less regulatory actions with large complex construction facilities and much more involvement with plant operations, maintenance, life extension and other operational issues. The new organization will focus NRC's major program offices on day-to-day safety of operational facilities and make them more accountable for our safety programs.[47]

Along with these changes designed to centralize greater control within the NRC, a third major organizational change, which was instituted by Chairman Palladino, decentralized authority by giving regional offices more autonomy. The objective was to improve licensing, inspection, and enforcement by bringing the NRC nearer to state and local governments and the public.[48] This goal, consistent with the administration's New Federalism proposals, had the effect of returning some of the influence over nuclear policy to the states and away from the NRC. Thus, at the same time that the Commission was attempting to centralize greater control over policy implementation, it was also decentralizing its control over enforcement and other functions. This process was similar to the Reagan strategy within the EPA, which also centralized greater internal authority while delegating greater program authority to the states. Both reorganizations suggest that these reforms were not agency-specific, but rather part of an overall administration strategy to gain greater control over the bureaucracy, while simultaneously delegating greater responsibility to the states.

The combined effect of the NRC reorganizations under Chairman Palladino was to ease the regulatory burden on the nuclear power industry, an effect consistent with the goals of the Reagan administration. The reorganization under Zeck suggests a somewhat greater emphasis on nuclear safety, which may reflect changes in the NRC's regulatory philosophy over the period of the Reagan presidency. Considering the political fallout following the Chernobyl nuclear accident, a move toward a greater emphasis on nuclear safety may be a necessity, even in the Reagan era of regulatory reform.

Although the reorganization proposals, particularly those under

Palladino, were consistent with the president's philosophy, they did little to solve the problems identified in the Kemeny and Rogovin Reports. The NRC still remains an agency with divided responsibility and divided authority. As such, it is still susceptible to the same criticisms as those articulated in the Kemeny and Rogovin reports.

Reagan's Statement on Nuclear Power

Even though Reagan appointed a number of individuals to the NRC who were staunchly pro-nuclear, increased the number of NRC employees, and increased the Commission's budget, his personal commitment to regulatory reform was less active than many proponents of nuclear power had hoped for. In the summer of 1981, Reagan's new NRC chairman, Nunzio Palladino, called on the president to make a strong statement on nuclear power. The chairman maintained that "a strong [presidential] statement would reestablish that the nation is on course with the development of nuclear power, which would allay some of the debate on that issue."[49] The nuclear power industry, which also wanted the president to endorse nuclear power forcefully and unambiguously, was concerned by the president's delay in issuing such a statement.

President Reagan finally did offer his support for nuclear power, but not until October 8, 1981. In his statement Reagan called nuclear power "one of the best potential sources of new electricial energy." He also expressed his view that burdensome government regulation was the cause of the industry's problems:

> Unfortunately, the Federal Government has created a regulatory environment that is forcing many utilities to rule out nuclear power as a source of new generating capacity. Nuclear power has become entangled in a morass of regulations that do not enhance safety but do cause extensive licensing delays and economic uncertainty.[50]

Reagan went on to state, "I anticipate that the Chairman of the Nuclear Regulatory Commission will take steps to facilitate the licensing of plants under construction and those awaiting licenses."[51] On November 18, 1981, Palladino announced the formation of a Regulatory Reform Task Force to make a detailed evaluation of the commission's licensing process. The task force evaluated various methods of streamlining the licensing process, by both legislative and administrative means.[52]

Reagan's address also included an admission that other problems, beyond the licensing process, may also be responsible for the nuclear power industry's severe economic problems. In particular, Reagan addressed the need to deal with the nuclear waste disposal problem.[53] He also stated that further study would be required to determine how other problems facing the industry (e.g., construction and labor costs, diminishing demand for electricity) could best be approached. These issues, however, were not the major focus of the address. Rather, Reagan's emphasis was on streamlining the nuclear licensing process and removing other regulatory barriers to economic growth.

Although Reagan's address provided supporters of nuclear power with a clear statement of his intent, the presence of a number of pro-environmental Carter appointees still on the Commission meant that the administrative presidency strategy was not a feasible alternative at that time. As a result, the first reform initiatives were handled through the traditional legislative approach.

The Legislative Approach

Following Reagan's address, Secretary of Energy James B. Edwards established his own Nuclear Licensing Reform Task Force as a means of formulating specific policy initiatives for reform. The task force consulted frequently with the nuclear power industry, which argued that the NRC would not approve licensing reforms unless it were forced to do so. The DOE task force concurred, and Edwards launched a legislative initiative designed to streamline the licensing process.[54]

The DOE legislative proposal called for major reforms designed to exclude intervenors from the hearings process and to expedite the licensing process. Unlike Jimmy Carter, the Reagan administration made no attempt to assuage the concerns of environmental groups. Since the administration had been elected to office without the support of most major environmental groups, and since no attempts at reconciliation would likely prove successful anyway, the DOE bill ignored the environmentalists' concerns entirely.

The bill was not enthusiastically received by the NRC. The commission felt that the bill was too broad in its reform proposals and ignored legitimate safety concerns. The NRC also objected to proposals calling for a reduction in the NRC's decision-making authority. After several meetings between DOE and NRC staff failed to settle differences of opinion, the NRC decided to offer its own legislative proposal. Although this proposal proved more moderate than the DOE bill, the NRC proposal was likewise condemned by environmental groups.[55]

In mid-1983, the two proposals were submitted to Congress. Between strong environmentalist opposition and the presence of competing proposals, the two bills calling for substantial regulatory relief—and thus a weaker commitment to regualtory safety—had little realistic chance for adoption. Eventually, both proposals died in committee.

Since the licensing issue was addressed by two competing agencies and then referred to congressional committees where environmental groups had significant influence, the traditional legislative approach was doomed to failure. If reform was going to be achieved, it would have to come at the administrative level. But even at the administrative level, the probability for success was severely constrained by the decentralized organizational structure of the NRC. Still, it was the Reagan administration's only real hope for promoting its regulatory reform proposals.

The Administrative Approach

While debating the legislative alternative, some NRC commissioners had argued that the most effective means of promoting reform would be at the administrative level. Some staff members, who were responsible for preparing the legislative proposal, also agreed that the NRC could unilaterally adopt all of the reforms encompassed in the draft legislation.[56] With the failure of the DOE and NRC legislative initiatives, no other realistic alternative existed for reforming the licensing process.

Administratively, the NRC had made some progress in easing the regulatory burden on the nuclear power industry, particularly with regard to the hearings process. On May 28, 1981, the NRC struck down the requirement that nuclear power companies needed to present detailed plans for an alternate site location along with their operating license application.[57] The NRC also voted to prevent intervenors from raising the alternative site issue.[58] This decision was controversial, for it eliminated an important criterion which intervenors could raise against a proposed nuclear power facility.

In 1981 the NRC also attempted to prevent intervenors from participating in the formal discovery process against NRC staff. Most commentators before the NRC opposed the proposal because it would have severely impeded the participation of intervenors in licensing proceedings. Intervenors would have lost a valuable means of obtaining relevant information prior to a formal licensing hearing. Because a majority of commissioners opposed the rule, it was not adopted in 1981.[59] By 1985, however, the Commission consisted of five Reagan appointees. Administrative reform was now a more realistic policy-making option. As a result, a number of administrative decisions were rendered which streamlined the licensing process.

On May 16, 1985, for example, the Commission voted by a narrow 3-2 majority to hold staff briefings and discussions in private with no official transcript of the proceedings. This vote not only eliminated public participation from such proceedings but it also removed the transcripts of these proceedings that had been regularly used by environmentalists and other intervenors as the basis for lawsuits regarding the licensing of plants.[60]

Other reforms included a limitation on the number of questions (50) that intervenors could raise. Since challenges to a particular nuclear facility's license often involve thousands of pages of information, the requirement that intervenors limit themselves to fifty questions was an effective means of emasculating outside criticism. Intervenors were also forced to testify on the probability of a nuclear accident rather than to determine this information through cross-examination. The effect of this change was to force intervenors to prove their case before they were allowed access to the very information they needed.[61]

These reforms limiting the role of intervenors ran contrary to the recommendations of the Rogovin and Kemeny Reports. Both reports recommeded that the NRC encourage public access to the licensing process. The Rogovin Report also recommended the establishment of an Office of Public Counsel as a means of providing greater assistance to intervenors.[62]

These moves to limit the role of intervenors in the licensing process were not accompanied by a move to promote nuclear safety. According to then Commissioner Peter Bradford in testimony on

November 19, 1981, before a House committee investigating the Diablo Canyon nuclear power plant,

> We've [the Commission] had close to twenty meetings on expediting licensing since last Winter. I would be surprised if we've had more than one or two dealing with quality assurance for specific plants.[63]

This comment suggests that the NRC's concern with nuclear safety diminished at the same time the Commission was acting to limit the rights of intervenors. The exclusion of intervenors from the licensing process became the major goal of the NRC.

Besides limiting intervenor participation, other decisions sought to ease the industry's regulatory burden. During February 1985 the NRC promulgated a new rule on the decommissioning of nuclear power plants. The rule-making proceeding had commenced in 1977 as anti-nuclear groups advocated that utilities operating nuclear power plants set aside funds for the express purpose of decommissioning aging plants. This would avoid the possibility that the public might have to pay for the costs. The NRC under Carter was sympathetic to this point of view. By 1985, however, the Commission had altered its view after protracted negotiations with the nuclear industry. The new rule gave utilities considerable flexibility with respect to methods for financing plant decommissioning, thus basically sanctioning existing industry practices.[64]

The NRC also relaxed standards on the long-term carcinogenic effects of nuclear power and on the probability of a core meltdown during the lifetime of a plant.[65] In June 1984 the NRC proposed the elimination of some interim requirements for safeguarding the shipment of spent fuel. Eliminated would be requirements for armed guards in cities, NRC approval of routes, and coordination of shipments with local agencies.[66]

Each of these reforms was designed to ease the nuclear industry's regulatory burden. They were also meant to encourage the construction of more nuclear power plants. As of 1982, there were 72 nuclear power plants producing electricity and another 72 under construction. Twenty-two plants had been cancelled in the last two years.[67] By April 28, 1986, there were 101 nuclear power plants operating in the United States and 27 under construction. These plants produced 17 percent of the total U.S. electricity.[68]

Although these figures seem to suggest that the Reagan program was working, one other statistic indicates that the Reagan administration was unable to make nuclear power a viable energy alternative: no new nuclear power plant was ordered during Reagan's tenure in office. The NRC had succeeded in moving some plants already under construction on-line, but it had not been able to reduce the costs of nuclear power plant construction to the point where any utility in the United States was willing to gamble on the future of nuclear power. Despite the optimistic numbers cited above, the trend was still moving away from nuclear power.

Despite the highly decentralized nature of the NRC, the Commission was able to successfully ease a number of regulatory standards, expedite the hearings process, and streamline the licensing process. That the administrative presidency strategy apparently can be implemented even when an organization's structure does not permit strict hierarchical control could be extremely important for future presidents who decide to adopt the administrative approach to policymaking.

Even with the Reagan administration's successful adoption of a number of regulatory reforms, the NRC could not ignore the problems of nuclear safety. Concerns with safety led the NRC to make several decisions which undercut the effect of their other reforms by increasing uncertainty over the economic viability of the nuclear option. For example, the NRC vacillated over the issue of whether to grant the Diablo Canyon nuclear power plant a license to begin low-level operations. This plant was particularly controversial because it was located on an earthquake fault line. On September 21, 1981, the NRC unanimously approved a license for the Diablo plant. But after revelations that engineers at the Diablo Canyon site had inverted the blueprints, thus installing important safety equipment on the wrong reactor, the NRC revoked Diablo Canyon's license. This was the first time the NRC had suspended a utility's operating license. The official reason for this action was that the power plant had a poor management record. Yet in addition to revoking the Diablo Canyon license, the NRC announced that it was considering similar action against the Zimmer and South Texas nuclear power plants. Such reversals undercut the confidence of investors in nuclear power plants. They also demonstrated that the Commission could not ignore strong public, congressional, and staff support for the goal of nuclear safety.

In January 1984, in a much more significant decision, the NRC denied a Commonwealth Edison plant an operating license. As a direct result, Cincinati Gas and Electric decided to convert a plant that was 97 percent completed from nuclear power plant to coal. This was the first such plant conversion in U.S. history.[69] The combined effect of these decisions was a major blow to the development of a viable nuclear power industry. Another blow was the $1.2 billion default of the Washington Public Power Supply System.[70] Such incidents led the Edison Electric Institute (EEI), the electric utilities lobby, to conclude in 1985 that despite the future need for nuclear power, it was no longer a "viable option" to construct a nuclear power plant. The costs of construction were prohibitive.[71] A Department of Energy report, finding that costs for nuclear power plants were at least double the amount of preconstruction estimates, blamed rising costs on interest rates and increased construction costs.[72] A report by the Office of Technology Assessment blamed rising costs on uncertainty about the demand for electricity, growing public opposition, escalating regulatory requirements, and the immaturity of present nuclear technology.[73]

To counter resistance to nuclear power, the industry spent between $30 million and $40 million in 1983 in an attempt to alter public opinion. A number of utilities also formed the U.S. Committee on Energy Awareness to make the public more aware of the need for nuclear power.[74] Following the Chernobyl nuclear accident in the Soviet Union, however, public confidence in nuclear power diminished further. Almost half of all Americans surveyed stated that they opposed nuclear power, while only 34 percent stated that they favored it. Further, a resounding 70 percent said they opposed construction of a plant within five miles of their home. This level of opposition is significantly higher than the 60 percent opposition in April 1979 at the time of the Three Mile Island accident and the 45 percent opposition in June 1976.[75] As a result of these factors, nuclear power remained a moribund industry. The Reagan administration's prescription for the ailing industry simply did not work.

Alternatives For A Moribund Industry

Richard Lester, a professor of nuclear engineering at the Massachusetts Institute of Technology, has proposed a number of methods by which the nuclear power industry could be made more profitable. Lester has suggested that government subsidies, rather than Reagan's "hands-off" approach are vital; the government needs to return to the active promotionalism of the 1950s and 1960s. The government also needs to help the nuclear industry find a solution to the nuclear waste problem (which the government is attempting since the passage of the 1982 Nuclear Waste Policy Act). Most of Lester's prescriptions, however, are not aimed at government activity, but rather call for unilateral industry action. Plants should be centered in rural settings away from heavily populated metropolitan areas, and experts should always be on hand. Nuclear plants should be smaller than the present 1,000 to 1,300 megawatt plants and of a standardized design. These changes would reduce construction costs.[76]

Ex–NRC Commissioner Victor Gilinsky has stated that the nuclear power industry controls its own destiny. If nuclear power plants have poor performance records over the next several years, he feels that "there is little future for nuclear power." On the other hand, if the nuclear power industry's record is commendable, the industry will be in a much stronger position to develop and expand.[77] Along a similar line, Susan J. Tolchin and Martin Tolchin have argued.:

> Once the public loses confidence in the regulators—as in the case of the NRC's ability to regulate the domestic nuclear power industry—the industry itself appears all but doomed. Its only hope for survival is the emergence of a strong, independent NRC.[78]

The Reagan era reforms weakened the NRC's ability to effectively regulate the nuclear power industry. With the public concerned more than ever with the problems of nuclear safety, this strategy proved counterproductive. Rather than advancing the economic viability of the nuclear industry, it threatened to further reduce the industry's chances of survival. In order for the nuclear industry to reemerge as a viable energy alternative, reforms will have to be made along the lines of those proposed by Lester and others. The NRC will have to become more concerned with regulating safety than with promoting the nuclear power industry at all costs.

Conclusions

The Reagan strategy for promoting nuclear power ignored the very real problems the industry faces. The administration unrealistically argued that government regulation was the primary source of the nuclear industry's problems. Yet the escalation of construction costs is only partially attributable to government regulation; interest rates, labor problems, and the immaturity of nuclear technology have had a greater effect on cost overruns. The decreasing demand for electricity and the growing public opposition to nuclear power have also added to the industry's economic woes. If the nuclear power industry is to be brought back from the precipice, it will take a realistic program that deals with these problems.

Besides failing to deal with the basic problems that confront the nuclear power industry, the Reagan program also ignored political reality. Given the mood in Congress and among the electorate following the Three Mile Island accident, and given the recommendations of a number of investigators, it was not politically realistic to seek regulatory reform that weakened existing safety requirements. Congressional and environmental opposition limited the likelihood that the traditional legislative approach would be successful. The fact that the legislative approach involved a much more decentralized political environment also reduced the probability that legislation would be adopted. The administrative presidency strategy was not feasible as an alternative during much of Reagan's first term in office because the president lacked a solid majority on the Commission. Later, however, the strategy was able to promote a number of reforms which streamlined the licensing process and reduced the industry's regulatory burden; even in a highly decentralized organizational setting the tools of the administrative presidency strategy can be employed. Yet, even with these achievements, the NRC could not ignore its legal responsibility to oversee questions of nuclear safety. NRC decisions in this regard reinforced the trend away from investment in new nuclear power plants.

Concerning the administrative and legislative approaches to public policy-making, this case study is an example of the failure of the legislative alternative leading to the employment of an administrative option. In this example, unlike that of the Interstate Commerce Commission, the two approaches were not compatible in promoting the Reagan administration's nuclear energy goals; the administrative approach did not facilitate a legislative approach. As in the case of the ICC, however, the administrative approach was employed after the legislative approach failed to promote the president's objectives. The handling of the NRC demonstrates a major point with regard to the administrative presidency strategy: future presidents will be more likely to adopt this approach if the policy involved is not amenable to legislation. Since Congress is often concerned with public opinion, presidents may be more likely to employ the administrative approach, than the traditional legislative approach when dealing with more controversial policy initiatives.

Finally, Reagan's handling of the NRC has important implications for the appointment process. President Carter's lack of a clearly articulated program made it difficult for him to appoint individuals who supported his views. Thus, he ended up appointing a Commission that was badly divided. The "debating society" that resulted was unable to promote presidential objectives. Reagan's more consistent ideology allowed him to appoint a number of individuals who supported his goals. Thus, the Carter and Reagan experiences indicate that a clear and consistent policy is a necessary prerequisite to the employment of the various tools of the administrative presidency strategy.

Chapter 7

Analyzing the Administrative
Presidency Strategy

Richard Nathan has argued that presidents should play an active role in managing the bureaucracy.[1] The degree to which that dictum has been followed in four cases is the subject of this book. This chapter will examine the experiences of the Nixon, Carter, and Reagan presidencies to determine which tools of the administrative presidency strategy have advanced presidential control over the bureaucracy and which have led to reduced presidential influence. My argument here is that although some of the techniques of the administrative presidency strategy have actually promoted presidential influence, the employment of a strategy that stresses command and control cannot succeed when the president does not have the constitutional authority to do so.

The various tools of the administrative presidency strategy are premised on the somewhat misleading assumption that presidents can control the bureaucracy. This assumption grants insufficient consideration to the dynamic nature of the American political system. For example, it does not adequately deal with the fact that since many of the tools of the strategy were delegated to the president by Congress, presidents share this authority with the legislative branch. It also pays insufficient attention to the fact that interest groups are powerful policy actors and that public opinion plays an important role in the American political system. The four case studies in this book demonstrate that these factors play a critically important role in presidential-administrative relations.

When President Nixon attempted to use his impoundment authority to freeze funds appropriated for public housing construction, Congress and the courts responded. When Nixon proposed his strategy for reorganizing the domestic departments and agencies, Congress rebelled. When Nixon's appointees removed career civil servants from the social service agencies, Congress again reacted (although in this case belatedly).

Likewise, when Anne Burford abolished EPA's Office of Enforcement, environmental groups cried foul. When a hit list was devised as a means of eliminating career civil servants who did not agree with administration policy, the press and Congress responded with front-page stories and congressional investigations. Although Congress initially agreed to deep reductions in EPA's budget, it later forced the administration to accept slight increases in environmental funding.

Presidents cannot ignore Congress, the courts, interest groups, bureaucrats, the public, and the press if they are to increase their influence over the administrative state. To do so is to invite failure. In the cases of the Nixon administration and HUD and the Reagan administration and EPA, presidential failure to consider these constraints led to a serious reduction in presidential influence.

What then is the alternative? How can presidents increase their influence over the administrative state? The best way is to work with the bureaucracy and not against it.

This approach to presidential-administrative relations is no less political than the one suggested by Nathan. By *political*, however, I mean that presidents must be willing to deal with key elements of the bureaucracy in much the same way as they deal with key members of Congress: presidents must bargain and compromise in order to increase their influence over the bureaucracy.[2] This is so because presidents share authority with their subordinates within the Executive Branch; they do not control them.

This point at first seems to be so obvious that it does not even deserve mention. Yet the experiences of the Nixon and Reagan administrations suggest otherwise. Presidents in recent years have attempted to centralize greater control over the bureaucracy as a means of increasing their influence, but rather than working with the bureaucracy, they have tried to work against it.

Analyzing the Tools
of the Administrative Presidency Strategy

In the pages that follow I analyze each of the tools of the administrative presidency strategy in order to show the utility, as well as the limitations, of each of these techniques. Clearly, presidents cannot succeed in increasing their influence by totally ignoring the tools of the administrative presidency strategy. But presidents must also be aware that these tools are not a panacea and do not guarantee influence. If they are to promote their influence, presidents must be aware of when and how they can best employ these tools and when they should seek other means of extending their influence.

Appointment Power

Presidents Nixon, Carter, and Reagan each made careful use of their power of appointment. Richard Nixon used his appointment power as a means of selecting individuals who were personally loyal to him and committed to his programs. Ronald Reagan also went to extraordinary lengths to ensure that his appointees reflected his policy choices. In the case of the Interstate Commerce Commission, the power of appointment was Jimmy Carter's major source of presidential influence. Mainly through the use of this power, Carter was able to radically alter the ICC's position on the issue of deregulation. In fact, Carter was so successful in employing this approach with the ICC that it beckons the obvious question: why didn't he make greater use of the strategy in other policy areas?

One reason is that Carter lacked coherent policy choices in many other policy areas. On the issue of nuclear power, for example, Carter vacillated between support for nuclear energy and support for the environmentalists' position. Unable to clearly state his views on the issue, Carter resorted to an appointment strategy that left the Nuclear Regulatory Commission seriously divided over the basic issues of nuclear power. As constituted under Jimmy Carter, the NRC devolved into a "debating society" which was unable to advance clear and coherent policies. This lack of clarity and consistency emanated directly from Carter's own ambivalence regarding the issue of nuclear energy.

Carter also showed ambivalence with regard to environmental issues. Although he appointed a pro-environmental administrator,

Douglas Costle, Carter also relied on the advice of conservative economists like Charles Schultze and William Nordhaus. Carter's inability to place control over environmental policy in either Costle or the economists' hands during his first two years in office created confusion within the administration and resentment from both environmentalists and the regulated industry.

The treatment of the issue of nuclear power was not an exception in Carter's approach to administrative regulation. Carter had been elected in 1976 as a Washington outsider and came to office without a large cadre of supporters. Many of those who supported Carter in the 1976 campaign were more than a little confused about what exactly the new president would stand for once in office. Carter's ability to make broad generalizations and to avoid specifics had been extremely useful during the campaign. Unfortunately, it left him without a clearly articulated set of programs that others could follow. Since Carter lacked a clear message, his ability to appoint like-minded individuals to the executive branch agencies was severely limited.

On the subject of economic regulation, however, Carter's views were much more clearly stated. He supported the view espoused by many economists that the free market, rather than government regulation, was the most efficient means of providing goods and services. With a clear policy choice, Carter was able to appoint economists Alfred Kahn and Darius Gaskins, as well as a number of other individuals who supported his deregulation policy. As a result, the Carter administration was able to pursue deregulation with a vigor that was sadly lacking in many of the administration's other policy initiatives. Carter's clarity regarding the deregulation policy allowed the administration to adopt an administrative strategy in the area of motor carrier deregulation, but the same approach was unfeasible in such other policy areas as nuclear regulation.

The Nixon administration similarly lacked a clear and consistent domestic policy. Although Nixon assumed office in January 1969 with clearly articulated views on foreign policy, he did not have well-developed or consistent policy choices for domestic affairs. This lack of a consistent policy perspective led to Nixon's initial decision to select a highly decentralized cabinet-style government, with much authority delegated directly to subordinates. Many of these, like George Romney at HUD, were individuals who came to the cabinet with their own policies and programs in hand. Rather than supporting the administration's programs, they often recommended and endorsed their own ideas. The case of the Model Cities Program is but one example. As severe economic problems forced Nixon to develop more consistent views, he was able to use his power of appointment to name individuals who were sympathetic to his more conservative philosophy. These individuals were willing to support the administration's policies and programs rather than endorsing programs of their own.

Unlike Nixon and Carter, Ronald Reagan came to office with clearly articulated policy choices. Reagan's issue stances were well known and well publicized; he had long been a supporter of nuclear power, for example. As a candidate for president, Reagan had attacked the regulatory excesses of the Nuclear Regulatory Commission and the Environmental Protection Agency. Coming to office with this clearly stated view, Reagan was able to begin appointing individuals who supported his anti-regulatory program at the outset, rather than waiting until well into his term, as was the case with Nixon and Carter.

During the 1980 campaign, Reagan had also spoken out harshly against what he considered to be environmental extremists. There was little doubt among environmentalists and conservatives that Reagan intended to radically alter the policies of the Environmental Protection Agency. Upon assuming office, his administration adopted the administrative presidency strategy as a means of promoting his regulatory reform agenda. A large number of conservatives, mostly businessmen, were nominated to important posts in the Environmental Protection Agency, the Department of Interior, and the Council on Environmental Quality. This appointment strategy permitted Reagan to adopt an administrative approach as a means of enacting a wide series of changes in environmental practices. There was, however, a major limitation to Reagan's employment of the administrative presidency strategy: the quality of Reagan's appointees.

Carter's ICC appointees had impeccable credentials. Most had either extensive Washington experience or had served in positions that gave them broad knowledge of motor carrier regulatory issues. In addition, many of them had previous management experience at the federal level. On the other hand, many of Reagan's appointees had only limited experience in Washington. Anne Burford, Reagan's choice for EPA Administrator, for example, had no experience working at the federal level and had no management experience. Other appointees, such as Rita Lavelle and John P. Horton, also lacked practical experience with the Washington establishment. This inexperience proved highly detrimental to the Reagan administration's agenda for reforming environmental policy. Burford and Lavelle were guilty of serious errors of judgment. More experienced individuals probably would not have listened to the Justice Department's argument that they should claim executive privilege and refuse to release documents to congressional committees. Anne Burford listened and followed Justice's advice without regard to the potentially serious consequences. And why not? Without prior experience in Washington, Burford had no reason to doubt that Justice was representing the best interests of the president. An experienced Washington insider would have considered the possibility that compliance with Justice's demands could lead to serious political repercussions. Anne Burford did not. The resulting fiasco focused critical national attention on the EPA. This led to further revelations, including reports that EPA had a hit list of agency employees, that Superfund money had been used to influence congressional and gubernatorial elections, and that high-ranking EPA officials had met in secret with representatives of the regulated industry to alter environmental reports and standards. These revelations rocked the agency, eventually forcing many of Reagan's appointees to resign in early 1983. From that point on, the Reagan environmental revolution was inexorably in retreat.

Two factors regarding appointments emerge from the case studies in this book. First, in order to employ the appointment strategy recommended by Nathan, presidents must have clearly articulated policy choices. Presidents without such well defined views cannot hope to locate and nominate individuals who will represent their views, for the simple reason that their views have not yet been precisely expressed. This fact limits the potential for wide use of the appointment technique. Presidents are responsible for over 1,500 appointments, of which approximately 600 are considered major. These appointments cover a wide range of policy areas. Most presidents will not have clearly expressed views in all or even most of these policy areas. As a result, they will be forced to appoint individuals on the basis of considerations other than loyalty. Presidents like Ronald Reagan, who came to office with an ideology (stressing limited government intervention in the marketplace) which allowed him to appoint individuals to a wide range of governmental agencies, are the exception rather than the rule. Most presidents are interested in a few specific policies or programs. It would be unrealistic to expect all presidents to be able to employ the broad appointment strategy that Ronald Reagan adopted. Thus, the recommendation that future presidents should appoint loyalists will likely be limited to only those programs with which the president is most concerned, such as deregulation during the Carter administration.

A second factor that emerges from these case studies is that the appointment of loyal, like-minded individuals is not a sufficient means of promoting presidential influence at the administrative level. Presidents should be concerned with the quality of their appointees, not simply with their ideology or personal loyalty to the president.[3] Presidents who appoint individuals on the basis of loyalty, but without regard to whether they are experienced or whether they are capable of managing a major bureaucracy, will have an increased probability of failing in their attempts to influence administrative behavior. Again, considering the fact that presidents are now responsible for approximately 600 major appointments, it is not likely that they will be able to locate loyal and competent individuals in every policy area. Tradeoffs may have to be made which will further constrain the employment of the appointment technique on a broad scale.

Even with these constraining factors, it is clear that the appointment of loyal and competent individuals can be of great assistance to a president who wishes to convince a bureaucratic entity that a particular program is in the public interest. Presidents who seek to bargain and compromise within the executive branch are at a distinct advantage when they have loyal appointees arguing their case. Thus, although the conclusions derived from the analysis in this book do not suggest that the appointment technique can or should be used on the scope that Nathan counsels, it does suggest that the appointment of loyal individuals can increase presidential influence when the policy involved is one with which the president is personally concerned. Clearly, the appointment of loyalists is as compatible with the bargaining approach as it is with the administrative presidency strategy.

Removal Power

Presidential use of the removal power can be a costly strategy at best. The Nixon and Reagan administrations made extensive use of this approach. In both cases, the strategy resulted in congressional investigations and highly critical media exposure.

The Nixon administration's attempts to remove Democrats and liberals from the Department of Housing and Urban Development, the Department of Health Education and Welfare, and the Office of Economic Opportunity provided only limited benefits. Even though the number of Democrats and liberals diminished slightly and the number of Republicans increased somewhat, the limited benefits that the Nixon administration achieved by adopting the removal strategy were more than offset by its high costs. These costs included increased congressional scrutiny of the Nixon administration's activities and an eventual change in the Civil Service statutes. (Some of this increased oversight, however, likely resulted from the expanded scrutiny of the executive branch following the Watergate revelations.)

The Reagan administration likewise paid heavily for the few benefits its removal strategy provided. Although the evidence indicates that a large number of career civil servants departed from the Environmental Protection Agency following the election of Ronald Reagan and the appointment of Anne Burford, the record also shows that the number of agency employees eventually returned to a level commensurate with that under President Jimmy Carter in 1980. The Reagan administration also paid a high price for the temporary reduction in agency personnel. In particular, the revelation that an EPA official had put together a hit list of agency scientists and other career civil servants severely damaged the agency's credibility. It also focused congressional attention on the EPA's other activities, many of which were not popular with Congress. In addition, a series of front-page headlines proved highly embarrassing to the administration. Thus, although a large number of employees did depart, the removal strategy did not serve the best interests of the Reagan administration. Rather, it helped fuel the counterrevolution which forced the administration to retreat from its environmental agenda.

As the Carter administration's experience with the ICC indicates, it is not necessary to employ the removal strategy in order to alter administrative behavior. The ICC substantially altered its goals without the removal of recalcitrant individuals from the bureaucracy. All Carter did with regard to the removal strategy was to wait for the terms of pro-regulatory commissioners to run out. Thus, his strategy was passive, not active. Had Carter adopted an active removal strategy, he might have provoked deep opposition within the agency. By avoiding this risk, Carter was able to use his appointment power as a means of developing support for his policies, instead of using removal as a means of inviting confrontation.

It appears that the president's removal power does not promote presidential influence. Although there may be short-term benefits, the long-term costs indicate that presidents can lose substantial influence by adopting the removal strategy.

Budgetary Power

Both Richard Nixon and Ronald Reagan made extensive use of their budgetary authority. Nixon impounded billions of dollars in appropriated funds from a variety of governmental institutions, including the Department of Housing and Urban Development and the Environmental Protection Agency. Although the impoundment strategy was somewhat effective with HUD, it promoted court challenges and increased congressional scrutiny with regard to both HUD and the EPA. Ultimately, Congress reacted by permanently limiting presidential influence with the passage of the Budget and Impoundment Control Act of 1974, which constrained future presidential attempts to impound appropriated funds. This action also led to congressional consideration of an Article of Impeachment charging Richard Nixon with "high crimes and misdemeanors" for unconstitutionally refusing to release congressionally appropriated funds. The costs of the Nixon impoundment strategy were indeed prohibitive. Again, as with the Nixon administration and its employment of the removal power, a caveat must be appended; for it is impossible to distinguish the opposition aroused by the administration's adoption of the various techniques of the administrative presidency strategy from the controversy surrounding Watergate. Had Watergate not occurred, it is possible that opposition to the president's impoundment authority would have been less extreme. The fact that the courts acted in most cases to reverse the president's impoundment of funds, however, suggests that even without Watergate there would have been some opposition and that presidential influence would have been constrained.

Ronald Reagan was more successful in employing his budgetary authority. He was able to drastically reduce the budgets of a number of social regulatory and social welfare agencies. The reductions in the budget for the Environmental Protection Agency, for example, seriously impaired the agency's ability to enforce the law; draconian cuts in the EPA's research and development budget likewise constrained the development of new regulations. That Reagan's use of his budgetary authority increased presidential influence by impairing the bureaucracy's ability to act suggests that the budgetary device can be an effective means of promoting presidential influence. This is particularly true when a president is able to frame the budgetary issue in terms of a policy choice. When the budget is used solely as a management technique — that is, budget cuts are used to emasculate a particular agency or function — then its potential for controversy increases. With this controversy can come increased opposition from Congress and other external sources.

When Nixon attempted to impound funds as a means of fighting inflation, his confrontational approach antagonized members of Congress rather than winning converts. Nixon's actions raised congressional concerns regarding the president's ultimate objectives. It also increased fears that the presidency had grown too powerful and that it was ignoring Congress' constitutional role in the budgetary process. Reagan, in contrast, framed the issue of budget cuts as necessary to reduce the deficit, to cut the inflation rate, and to spur economic growth. Even members of Congress who supported such programs as environmental protection were forced to support the president's efforts to restore economic growth. By turning the call for reductions in EPA's budget into a call for economic stability, rather than attempting to justify the cuts on the idea that EPA's enforcement capability should be reduced, Reagan was able to secure deep reductions in EPA's budget. Thus, Reagan's budgetary strategy built congressional support rather than provoking congressional wrath. Still, it should be remembered that even in the case of Reagan's successful employment of the budgetary power, Congress did restore funds to the EPA within a matter of a few years. The initial success was only transitory.

What is important for presidents to remember is that while they have the authority to submit a budget to Congress, they still share budgetary power with the legislative branch. Presidents who try to ignore this fact, as Nixon did, will likely fail in their attempts to influence bureaucratic behavior. Presidents who are aware of this limitation will be in a stronger position to achieve their policy objectives.

One means by which presidents can increase their influence over the budgetary process is by appointing individuals who will support their budget in hearings before Congress. A loyal appointee who supports the president's budget can provide the president's requests with a sense of legitimacy. In addition, if the appointee supports the president's budget, rather than opposing it, there is one less obstacle in the president's path. Clearly, Anne Burford's support for President Reagan's funding cuts was beneficial in attaining congressional approbation for the Reagan administration's EPA budget. The fact that the appointment process can assist presidents in the employment of budgetary authority is significant. It means that each of the sources of presidential influence should not be seen in isolation from others. They are and should be compatible.

Although the budgetary option can increase presidential influence, it may not be an effective tool under all circumstances. When a president desires a reduction in governmental activity, the budgetary option may not be so amenable to presidential influence in the future as it was for Nixon or Reagan. Since many of the various techniques used by the Nixon administration have already been severely constrained, presidents have less flexibility to invoke the impoundment technique. Neither may furture presidents be able to count on the types of deep budgetary reductions that the Reagan administration induced Congress to adopt. A number of unusual circumstances, such as a 10 percent inflation rate and a 20 percent interest rate, coalesced to promote the Reagan administration's budgetary strategy. There was also strong sentiment that cuts would be needed to reduce the budget deficit. Congress was accordingly much more sympathetic to reductions in the EPA's budget than they were before or have been since. In fact, within two years Congress reverted to its previous policy of increasing the agency's budget, rather than agreeing with the Reagan administration that further cuts were necessary. Consequently, although the evidence from these case studies demonstrates that the president's budgetary power can be an impressive means of extending presidential influence, future presidents may not be able to make equal use of this authority. Whether they can will largely depend on a variety of factors, such as the state of the economy and the mood of Congress at the time.

It should be emphasized that the case studies in this book, with the exception of the one on the Reagan administration and the NRC, represent the budgetary politics of retrenchment. When future presidents attempt to influence administrative behavior by increasing an agency's budget, they may face an entirely different set of congressional concerns from those expressed here. Again, the incentives and constraints that presidents face will come largely in the form of external economic factors. If large budget deficits persist, a strategy of increasing appropriations may not be feasible. If the program is popular with the public, presidents may have greater discretion. Other research will have to provide evidence on this point.

One other matter deserves mention. Although presidents can increase their influence by using their budgetary authority, it is possible for them to increase their influence without resorting to the budgetary strategy. Jimmy Carter was able to fundamentally alter the goals of the Interstate Commerce Commission without resorting to deep reductions in the Commission's budget. In this case, strong bureaucratic support already existed for the president's program. With strong staff-level support already in evidence, presidential use of the budgetary strategy would have been a risky undertaking. Rather than promoting the president's program, budget cuts might have increased bureaucratic resistance, thus undermining the president's program. Under circumstances in which strong bureaucratic support is already in evidence, presidents may find it in their best interest to forego the budgetary option.

Reorganization Power

Another means of extending presidential influence is through the employment of the president's power to reorganize the bureaucracy. This strategy was indispensable in altering the goals of the Interstate Commerce Commission. The Nixon administration's Reorganization Plan No. 1 of 1969 greatly increased the president's direct influence over the ICC by granting the president the power to appoint the Commission's chairman. In addition, the reorganization delegated greater authority to the chairman. These changes provided the Carter administration with the necessary means to alter the ICC's position on the issue of deregulation. Had the previous system for appointing the ICC's chairman still been in place in 1977, it is highly unlikely that Jimmy Carter would have been able to successfully promote the policy of deregulation. Rather, he would have been forced to rely on the strategy employed unsuccessfully by each of his predecessors: the traditional legislative approach. The presence of powerful division chiefs would have prevented the Carter administration from initiating its reform agenda. Thus, the removal of these powerful sources of opposition from within the ICC was a prerequisite to the Commission's active promotion of the administration's pro-reform policy.

Whereas the reorganization technique can advance a president's policy objectives, it can also seriously undercut presidential influence. The reorganization strategy was an important component of the Reagan administration's environmental program. Administrator Anne Burford emasculated the enforcement capability of the agency by abolishing the Enforcement Office. This action promoted the administration's policy of voluntary compliance with EPA standards, rather than strict reliance on enforcement, but it also increased external opposition from interest groups and Congress as well as exacerbating internal disagreement among career civil servants. Consequently, although the reorganization strategy promoted presidential objectives in the short term, in the long term it reduced presidential influence by increasing opposition to the president's program.

As I suggested in chapter 5, the president might have been better served on the question of enforcement by directly addressing the limitations of the EPA's enforcement policy. There was support for voluntary compliance in the academic literature, in business, and even within the EPA itself. But instead of attempting to justify their policy choice, Reagan's EPA appointees adopted the heavy-handed approach of abolishing the Enforcement Office. In focusing critical attention on the enforcement issue, this action increased opposition.

Reorganization also proved highly controversial in the case of the Nixon administration. The attempt to create a system of Super Secretaries was seen by many of the administration's critics as a crude attempt to centralize power directly in the White House and to exclude the career civil service and other legitimate participants from the decision-making process. The Nixon administration's 1971 comprehensive reorganization proposals were also controversial. Had the Nixon reorganization been adopted by Congress, a restructuring of congressional committee jurisdiction would surely have been required. Thus, the Nixon reorganization proposals led to opposition in Congress as well as among interest groups.

The failure of the comprehensive Nixon reform proposals can be contrasted with the success of the Reorganization Plan No. 1 of 1969. Because that program was neither controversial nor a threat to congressional structure, it passed easily. The lack of controversy surrounding the ICC reorganization suggests an important conclusion regarding the use of presidential reorganization authority. When a reorganization threatens entrenched interests—be they career civil servants, congressional committees, or interest groups—the president's reorganization authority will stimulate opposition and thus may actually constrain presidential power. Because most reorganization proposals will threaten some entrenched interest, presidents must accordingly weigh with considerable skill the potential benefits of a reorganization proposal. Such conclusions regarding the costs and benefits of the reorganization strategy are likely to be highly subjective and surrounded by a great deal of uncertainty. One means of reducing uncertainty would be for presidents to attempt to build a broader base of support for their reorganization proposals. In the case of the Nixon administration, this could have been accomplished by involving Congress early, while reorganization proposals were still being formulated, rather than presenting proposals to Congress as a fait accompli.

The analysis of the four case studies in this book also indicates that administrative reorganizations can involve serious risks. Anne Burford's radical reforms within the EPA exacerbated tensions between the Reagan administration and environmentalists, thus threatening to reduce presidential influence.

Still, not all administrative reorganization involves high risk-taking. A. Daniel O'Neal's reorganizations within the ICC created the Office of Policy Analysis, which became an active proponent of deregulation. O'Neal also did away with the power of the divisional units, which could have threatened Carter's policies. Unlike Burford's elimination of the Enforcement Office, these important reorganization moves were made without stirring up controversy. Neither the public nor Congress was aroused. The relevant interest groups did not react.

Similarly, with the exception of the establishment of the Committee to Review Generic Requirements (CRGR), administrative reforms at the NRC were not controversial. The experience with administrative reorganization thus suggests that it can be a useful tool in promoting presidential influence. As the Burford case demonstrates, however, it is not risk-free. Presidents and their subordinates should be aware of the potential risks before adopting this approach.

Delegation of Program Authority to the States

The delegation of program authority by the Environmental Protection Agency returned the responsibility for a number of federal regulatory programs to the state level. At the same time, though, reductions in grants-in-aid to the states limited the states' ability to vigorously regulate the environment. Few programs, however, were actually abandoned by the states. The departure of Anne Burford and the arrival of William Ruckelshaus ended the practice of massive delegation and, with it, diverted the potential long-term effects the administration desired.

There were, however, unanticipated consequences to the Reagan administration's delegation strategy. By returning program authority to the states, the strategy was initially designed to limit the Environmental Protection Agency's ability to regulate the environment. Because states would receive less federal funding, it was also anticipated that they would not be able to vigorously enforce their own environmental standards and thus the burden on the regulated industry would be reduced.

Contrary to expectations, many states continued to vigorously regulate the environment. In some cases, such as with noise regulation, some states had standards which were stricter than the previously existing federal standards. Moreover, the wide variation among the different state standards complicated interstate commerce. As a result, many businesses that had initially supported the reforms began to advocate a return of regulatory responsibility to the federal level. Indeed, many of the very interests that the Reagan program was designed to assist eventually resisted the Reagan administration's reform proposals.

The Reagan administration's experience with the EPA suggests that presidents must pay more attention to the potential impact of their delegation authority. The actual impact, as opposed to the expected impact, increased opposition to the president's program and thus undercut his influence. Had policy analysts in the White House or within the Environmental Protection Agency examined the various existing regulatory standards in the states, the Reagan administration might have realized that the delegation strategy would produce unwanted consequences. The administration's failure to examine the possible repercussions of its actions increased opposition and threatened to reduce presidential influence in the long term.

The delegation strategy also increased opposition to the Reagan administration's program from state governments, environmental groups, and congressional critics. As I argued in chapter 5, if the administration had followed the logic of its own rhetoric and attempted to logically sort out various responsibilities that could best be handled at the state level, rather than attempting to delegate as a means of gutting the environmental standards, it likely would have been much more successful. And, if the administration included appropriate funding to the states for environmental programs, it could have reduced the level of opposition in Congress and from various interest groups. The administration's failure to adopt either of these alternatives further increased resistance to its program and thus reduced presidential influence.

Central Clearance

Central clearance, which has traditionally been accepted by scholars as one of the primary techniques for increasing presidential influence over the bureaucracy, did not play a major role in any of the four case studies included in this book. This can be explained by the nature of the policy change described in these studies. In each case, presidents decided to forego the traditional legislative approach in favor of an adminstrative approach. Since central clearance is primarily a means of keeping track of agency legislative proposals, its lack of prominence in these four case studies is not particularly surprising.

That central clearance played so small a role in these cases does not mean that it should be ignored by future studies of administrative action. The Reagan administration's decision to create a means for administrative central clearance indicates that this technique may play a prominent role in the future by constraining the ability of agencies and executive departments to formulate their own rules and regulations without administration knowledge or approval. As such, the technique could be extraordinarily beneficial to future presidents. It could make the administrative approach a much more feasible option by limiting an agency's ability to ignore or circumvent a president's policy objectives. This would centralize greater decision-making authority directly in the White House and increase presidential influence over the administrative state.

It is also possible that the strategy could increase opposition from interest groups, congressional committees, and particularly career bureaucrats. Since the strategy involves a further centralization of control within the White House, external groups may feel that their influence over regulatory policy has been diminished. Under the Reagan administration the employment of the administrative central clearance procedure was centralized within the Office of Information and Regulatory Affairs (OIRA) within the Office of Management and Budget. Attempts to limit bureaucratic discretion at the formulation stage, rather than at the promulgation stage, led to increased hostility between agency officials and OMB. In addition, several members of Congress, and such interest groups as OMB Watch, condemned the technique as preventing regulators from obeying their legal mandate. OMB denied this charge, arguing that the federal regulatory agencies were still responsible for the development of regulations. Still, OMB oversight provides another barrier to the development of agency initiatives.

Cost-Benefit Analysis

The Carter administration's use of cost-benefit analysis was symptomatic of the lack of clarity that characterized his appointment strategy within the NRC. Carter first used the technique as a means of restraining costs. When confronted by opposition from environmental groups and his own appointees, Carter altered the structure by which cost-benefit analyses were conducted. This weakened the influence of the technique. Carter's lack of consistency with regard to cost-benefit analysis can be explained by his desire to win support from both environmentalists and cost-conscious economists. The strategy eventually satisfied neither and, like his contradictory appointments to the NRC, undercut his ability to control the bureaucracy.

The Reagan administration's use of the technique was clear and focused much more on costs than on benefits. The evidence also suggests that the administration employed the technique as a means of promoting its policy objectives, rather than objectively determining whether a particular regulation should be promulgated. Even so, most regulations were not altered as a result of Reagan's Executive Order #12291.

It is possible, however, that the EPA and other social regulatory agencies may have held back regulations that they would otherwise have proposed, simply because they knew the regulations would not meet the Reagan administration's strict new standards with regard to cost. If this was the case, then the use of cost-benefit analysis, along with the administrative central clearance technique, may have had a much more significant effect than is suggested by the available data. This is not an unreasonable assumption. It is quite likely that the very fact that agency rules and regulations had to undergo a review by OMB constrained agency rule-making activity— a result which would clearly have been consistent with the Reagan administration's policy objectives.

Appraising the Strategy

My analysis above suggests that future presidents should not turn their backs on all of the tools of the administrative presidency strategy. Presidents should certainly appoint competent and loyal individuals. Presidents should also use their budgetary authority to advance their programs, but only when the budgetary request can be justified on the basis of a policy choice. Neither is the selective use of the president's reorganization authority ruled out, especially when a reorganization proposal does not threaten entrenched interests. Administrative reorganization can also promote presidential influence, though again it is not risk-free. Thus, even if a president seeks to work with the bureaucracy, careful use of these techniques can promote presidential influence. By *careful*, I mean that presidents should not invite confrontation. Rather, presidents must at all times be aware of the various factors that constrain their influence at the bureaucratic level. By understanding the limitations of their authority, presidents will be in a better position to advance their objectives.

The analysis also indicates that a relationship exists between the administrative approach and the traditional legislative approach. The former calls for the promotion of policy at the bureaucratic level, while the latter is an attempt to enact legislation through congressional action. In the cases of the Interstate Commerce Commission and the Nuclear Regulatory Commission, the administrative approach was undertaken only after the traditional legislative approach had failed. In these cases, administrative action was employed because other alternatives had already been attempted and had not succeeded. It would have been fruitless for Presidents Carter and Reagan to perpetuate the failed policy of their predecessors and to continue to propose legislation to a hostile Congress. In the case of Reagan and the EPA, an administrative approach was employed because the traditional legislative approach offered no real hope of success. Thus, the administrative approach offers presidents an alternative means of advancing their policy objectives when Congress is not amenable to their goals.

The case of the Carter administration and the Interstate Commerce Commission also demonstrates that one strategy can be employed to advance the likelihood of the success of the other. Carter adopted the administrative approach to policymaking with the motor carrier and airline issues. Having achieved success administratively, he then turned to Congress to adopt the same measures legislatively. Carter was able to use his administrative successes, and the threat of further unilateral administrative action, as a means of promoting legislative activity. Congress had been previously unsympathetic to the idea of adopting comprehensive legislation deregulating the trucking industry. The most powerful interest groups, such as the American Trucking Associations and the Teamsters, had successfully kept Congress from giving the issue serious consideration. After reform was adopted administratively, the interest groups had only one place to turn, the legislature, and Congress was no longer confronted with the potential blame should the legislation prove to have unsatisfactory long-term consequences. Congress could now put the blame squarely on the ICC and the Carter administration. Thus, administrative action promoted legislation.

Such was not the case with the NRC or the EPA. In both cases, strong public opposition to the Reagan administration's agenda likely played a major role in constraining congressional action. About the ICC and trucking deregulation, the public was decidedly neutral. But about questions of the environment, there was strong public opinion. Public opinion and strong organized opposition to the Reagan administration's environmental and nuclear regulatory proposals provided a major constraint which limited the ability of Reagan and his subordinates to use administrative achievements as a means of promoting legislation.

One further point derives from the analysis. As the case of the Nuclear Regulatory Commission demonstrates, presidents cannot expect the administrative presidency strategy to perform miracles. It is not a panacea for the all of a president's problems. Presidents must be keenly aware of the feasibility of a certain policy or course of action. If they ignore the very real factors that promote a particular policy outcome—such as the role of economic factors and public opinion in the development of a policy—use of the administrative presidency strategy will not increase presidential influence.

In the case of the NRC, the successful appointment of competent Reagan loyalists, increased in the Commission's budget, and successful administrative reorganizations did not achieve the president's policy objective of promoting the viability of the nuclear power industry. This failure resulted largely from the president's decision to ignore the fact that the demand for electricity had fallen, and thus the demand for nuclear power. He also ignored other problems that contributed to the nuclear industry's decline, such as the high costs of construction and the public demand for safety regulations. Without dealing with these types of problems, the administrative presidency strategy never had a real chance of achieving the president's objectives.

Given the experiences of the Nixon, Carter, and Reagan presidencies with the administrative presidency strategy, what then can be said about the central question of this book: how can presidents increase their influence over the administrative state?

Presidential Power

Presidential power is not a commodity that comes in unlimited supplies. Presidents have only so much of it. For this reason, Richard Neustadt recommended that presidents should constantly guard and protect their power so that they will have it when they need it.[4] Presidents thus should weigh each decision they make carefully. They should consider not only the possible short-term benefits of a particular alternative but also its long-term costs. Many options promise increased presidential influence in the short term. In the long term, however, they may threaten to significantly reduce presidential power. According to Neustadt, presidents should avoid such options.

The tools of the administrative presidency strategy offer great short-term benefits. Nixon's use of the impoundment technique brought an abrupt halt to federal funding for public housing construction, a result clearly consistent with Nixon's policy preferences. This short-term benefit, however, produced a long-term cost:

the impoundment technique eventually increased congressional oversight and eventually led to the passage of legislation designed to permanently constrain presidential budgetary authority. Although the
impoundment authority increased presidential influence in the short
term, it reduced presidential influence in the long term. Thus, Nixon,
in his use of impoundment, is an example of a president who did
not properly guard his power.

　　Ronald Reagan's strategy for altering the policies of the Environmental Protection Agency had tremendous short-term benefits.
Reagan was able to reduce the agency's budget, severely restrict
environmental enforcement activity, remove a large number of pro-
environmental scientists and career officials from the bureaucracy,
and delegate environmental program authority back to the states.
But these short-term benefits had long-term costs. Congressional
investigations focused attention on the administration's activities.
Front-page headlines chronicled the legally questionable activities
of Reagan's appointees. Interest group membership and income increased tremendously. In the 1982 congressional elections, a number of pro-environmental legislators were elected to Congress. Each
of these factors served to reduce presidential influence over environmental policy in the long term. Thus, Reagan's use of the administrative presidency strategy also did not properly guard his power.

　　Clearly, if presidents are to guard their power, they must consider
the potential risks of the administrative presidency strategy. The appointment strategy can reduce presidential influence when the appointees lack adequate managerial and Washington experience. The
budgetary strategy can reduce presidential influence when it directly
challenges Congress's authority. The reorganization authority can
reduce presidential influence when it threatens entrenched interests.
Each of the other tools of the administrative presidency strategy can
also involve significant risks. Presidents who do not guard their
long-term power by considering these risks endanger their influence
and thus their power.

　　Presidents who consider using any of the techniques of the administrative presidency strategy must be aware that presidents share
power. This realization will help them to use the various tools of
the strategy in a way that builds support, rather than inviting confrontation. By working with Congress and the bureaucracy, instead
of attempting to limit their input, presidents can reduce the risks
that can threaten long-term presidential power.

How then can president's increase their influence over the administrative state? Neustadt has listed five factors that promote compliance with presidential orders.[5] These factors are directly relevant to presidential-administrative relations and can help to increase presidential influence.

First, it is important for individuals to know that the president has spoken. It is crucial that appointive officials know that they are carrying out the will of the president and that career civil servants know in which programs the president is personally interested. Knowledge of presidential interest makes it much easier for presidential appointees to convince bureaucrats that they should implement the president's program.[6] Of course, the best way that a president can ensure that career civil servants know that they are following presidential policy is for the president personally to work with key elements within the bureaucracy.

The case of the Carter administration and the ICC is instructional in this regard. Carter made it well known that he personally supported the goals of deregulation. Career civil servants within the ICC who already supported the policy were in essence given a green light to pursue the deregulation policy enthusiastically. Along with Carter's appointment strategy, the personal interest he displayed in the issue was instrumental in the administrative and later legislative adoption of the trucking deregulation proposals.

Reagan, despite his clear support for nuclear regulatory reform during the campaign, did not endorse the policy as president until October 1981. Until that time his appointees were unable to move forward on the issue. Without a clear statement of presidential intent, there was no progress on the administration's reform proposals. Only after Reagan had spoken did his appointees move forward.

Along with a clear statement of presidential intent, the appointment of people who unambiguously represent the president's point of view can also advance presidential influence. Thus, presidents should appoint like-minded individuals to do their bidding at the bureaucratic level. But this penchant for loyalty must be counterbalanced by a commitment to competence. Moreover, although the appointment of loyal and competent individuals can be of immeasurable assistance to the president, it is not a substitute for a strong, active presidential role in bureaucratic politics. As the Iran-Contra case demonstrated, a president must play an active role to ensure that his subordinates are following presidential intent.

Second, the president's message should be clearly transmitted. Without clarity of enunciation there is plenty of room for bureaucrats to avoid compliance. The goal of clarity of purpose again suggests that presidents should appoint individuals who share their programmatic goals. If presidents lack clarity of intent, their influence is severely constrained. Presidents also need to know what is on the minds of their subordinates. The best way to do this is to ensure that policies are reviewed regularly for conformance to the president's intent.

Third, publicity not only can help reduce confusion over whether a directive comes directly from the president but also can reinforce presidential intent. It is not enough for a president to announce a program, as Reagan did with his pro–nuclear power speech. An announcement must be followed up with a further display of presidential interest. One means by which presidents can publicize issues at the administrative level is to become personally involved in the development of policy. A president's personal involvement is the best type of publicity because it demonstrates that the president is both concerned and knowledgeable about the issue at hand. This makes it more difficult for bureaucrats to avoid complying with presidential orders. Again, Carter's personal involvement with the deregulation issue is instructive. Transportation experts gave Carter the credit for increasing the issue's visibility. By placing it on the agenda and then following it up with a personal interest that his predecessors had never demonstrated, Carter was able to advance the deregulation issue, making its administrative adoption more feasible.

Fourth, a president must make sure that his subordinates have the authority and resources to carry out presidential orders. This is particularly important since presidents often are not aware of the nuance of bureaucratic politics. As Heclo and Lynn have noted, presidential directives are often transmitted to executives within the bureaucracy without any sense of whether or not they actually have the ability to implement the president's program.[7] Presidents who are attentive to the details of administrative politics will have a better sense of what their appointees can and cannot do. They will thus be in a better position to avoid the pitfall of ordering appointees to comply with directives that cannot be enforced.

Presidents should also be certain that their subordinates are not exceeding their authority in advancing a particular presidential program. As the Iran-Contra affair and the case of Burford and the

EPA demonstrated, when subordinates exceed their legal authority, or even when a perception exists that they have done so, the president's influence can be put at risk. The more familiar presidents are with the constraints facing their subordinates, the better able they will be to get results.

Finally, presidents must be sure that what they request is theirs by right. This point is particularly relevant to presidential-administrative relations, since the president has so little direct constitutional authority over the bureaucracy. As I have argued, the fact that the president shares power over the bureaucracy with Congress means that presidents cannot bully and control the administrative state. Presidents must be keenly aware of the limitations of their authority or they run the serious risk of losing presidential power.

Neustadt's recommendations are as applicable to presidential-administrative relations as to other areas of presidential politics. Presidential power is the power to persuade. Presidents must seek to work with the bureaucracy if they are to increase their influence. By understanding their limitations and working with Congress and the bureaucracy, presidents have a greater probability of advancing their policy objectives than they do if they employ the techniques of the administrative presidency strategy without regard to such constraints. The tools of that strategy entail risks that can curtail presidential influence in the long run. Presidents who understand this reality are in a better position to advance their policies and programs.

This does not mean that presidents should never employ the techniques of the administrative presidency strategy. Several of these techniques, particularly the power of appointment and the president's budgetary authority, can promote presidential influence. Presidents, however, must be aware of the circumstances under which these techniques are most likely to promote presidential influence and when they are likely to risk reducing presidential power. This analysis has endeavored to provide greater information regarding when, and under which circumstances, the tools of the administrative presidency strategy can be employed to increase presidential influence.

Leadership of the bureaucracy is one of the president's most important responsibilities. Presidents who can extend their influence over the bureaucracy have a good change of successfully promoting their policy objectives; those who cannot, however, face frustration and failure. The notion that presidents can command the bureaucracy is a sure prescription for failure. Instead, presidents should work with the bureaucracy to fashion support for presidential initiatives. As Dwight Ink has stated,

> One of the best investments the political leadership of a new administration can make is to explain to career employees the objectives of the new administration, its philosophy, and specifically what it will be asking of the bureaucracy in meeting the challenges as perceived by the new president.[8]

Such advice would be considered thoughtful if applied to presidential/congressional relations; it is no less so for presidential/administrative relations.

Presidents must summon all of their political skills to increase their influence with the bureaucracy. The astute president will keep the techniques of command in reserve, in case other less confrontational methods fail. But, in order to be successful, presidents must realize that the bureaucracy is their ally and that the bureaucracy will be a better ally to one who leads by persuasion than to one who leads by command.

Notes

Introduction

1. See Louis Fisher, *The Constitution Among Friends: Congress, the President, and the Law* (New York: St. Martin's, 1978) and *The Politics of Shared Power: Congress and the Executive* (Washington, D.C.: Congressional Quarterly, 1981); Nelson W. Polsby, *Congress and the Presidency* (Englewood Cliffs, N.J.: Prentice-Hall, 1976); George C. Edwards III, *Presidential Influence in Congress* (San Francisco: W. H. Freeman, 1980).
2. Hugh Helco, "OMB and the Presidency—The Problems of Neutral Competence," *The Public Interest* 38 (1975): 80–98.
3. Richard P. Nathan, *The Plot That Failed: Nixon and the Administrative Presidency* (New York: John Wiley, 1975); Nathan, *The Administrative Presidency* (New York: John Wiley, 1983); Nathan, "Political Administration Is Legitimate," in *The Reagan Presidency and the Governing of America*, ed. Lester M. Salamon and Michael S. Lund (Washington, D.C.: Urban Institute, 1984), 375–79.
4. Terry M. Moe, "The Politicized Presidency," in *The New Direction in American Politics*, ed. John E. Chubb and Paul E. Peterson (Washington, D.C.: Brookings Institution, 1985), 235–71.
5. Nathan, *The Plot That Failed* and *The Administrative Presidency*. The administrative presidency strategy is an approach by which presidents have attempted to alter the goals and objectives of federal agencies by seeking change directly at the administrative level. An alternative approach to policy development is the traditional legislative approach, whereby presidents make recommendations to Congress and seek to effect change by the passage of legislation. Although this book is primarily concerned with the administrative

strategy, it is also necessary to discuss the role of the legislative approach. Over the past twenty years, presidents have found that Congress has become less responsive to their demands. As the power of the congressional leadership has diminished and more independent minded members have been elected to office, the legislative approach has become more untenable. Facing stiffer opposition from Congress, as well as a more decentralized leadership, presidents have looked increasingly toward the bureaucracies of their own executive branch for a means of promoting their goals and objectives. This does not mean, however, that they have come to totally ignore the legislative approach. In some cases the two strategies have been used simultaneously. For example, chapter 4 delineates how Jimmy Carter utilized the administrative approach as a means of facilitating the legislative approach (the passage of the Motor Carrier Act of 1980). In this case, the two approaches were compatible; the achievement of the legislative approach depended on the successful adoption of the administrative approach.

6. Dwight Waldo, *The Administrative State* (New York: Ronald Press, 1948).
7. James L. Sundquist, *The Deline and Resurgence of Congress. (Washington, D.C.: Brookings Institution, 1981).*
8. Peri E. Arnold, *Making the Managerial Presidency: Comprehensive Reorganization Planning 1905–1980* (Princeton, N.J.: Princeton Univ. Press, 1986); John Hart, *The Presidential Branch* (New York: Pergamon, 1987).
9. Stanley L. Falk, "The National Security Council under Truman, Eisenhower, and Kennedy," *Political Science Quarterly* 79 (1964): 403–34; Lester G. Seligman, "Presidential Leadership: The Inner Circle and Institutionalization," *Journal of Politics* 18 (1956): 410–26.
10. Clinton Rossiter, *The American Presidency* (New York: Harcourt, Brace, and World 1960), 15–16.
11. Herman Finer, *The Presidency: Crisis and Regeneration* (Chicago: Univ. of Chicago Press, 1960), 119.
12. James MacGregor Burns, *Presidential Government: The Crucible of Leadership* (Boston: Houghton Mifflin, 1965), 330.
13. Richard E. Neustadt, *Presidential Power: The Politics of Leadership from FDR to Carter* (New York: John Wiley, 1980), 7.
14. Thomas Cronin, *The State of the Presidency* (Boston: Little, Brown, 1980), 9.
15. Charles Walcott and Karen M. Hult, "Organizing the White House: Structure, Environment, and Organizational Governance," *American Journal of Political Science* 31 (1987): 109–25.
16. Richard W. Waterman, "The Presidential Conundrum: The Benefits

and Risks of the New Strategies of Presidential Leadership," paper presented at the annual meeting of the Midwest Political Science Association, April 1988.

17. Arthur M. Schlesinger, Jr., *The Imperial Presidency* (Boston: Houghton Mifflin, 1973), x.

18. Stephen Hess, *Organizing the Presidency* (Washington, D.C.: Brookings Institution, 1976); Dom Bonafede, "White House Staffing: The Nixon-Ford Era," in *The Presidency Reappraised*, ed. Thomas E. Cronin and Rexford G. Tugwell (New York: Praeger, 1977), 151–73.

19. George Reedy, *The Twilight of the Presidency* (New York: New American Library, 1970).

20. Charles M. Hardin, *Presidential Power & Accountability; Toward a New Constitution.* (Chicago: Univ. of Chicago Press, 1974), 1.

21. Hess, *Organizing the Presidency*, 151–52.

22. I. M. Destler, "National Security II: The Rise of the Assistant (1961–1981)," in *The Illusion of Presidential Government*, ed. Hugh Heclo, and Lester M. Salamon (Boulder, Colo.: Westview, 1981), 280.

23. Fred I. Greenstein, *The Hidden Hand Presidency: Eisenhower as Leader* (New York: Basic Books, 1982).

24. Bradley D. Nash, Milton S. Eisenhower, R. Gordon Hoxie, and William C. Spragens, *Organizing and Staffing the Presidency* (Washington, D.C.: Center for the Study of the Presidency, 1980), 174–80.

25. Bruce Buchanan, *The Presidential Experience: What the Office Does to the Man* (Englewood Cliffs, N.J.: Prentice-Hall, 1978).

26. Richard Neustadt, *Presidential Power*, 2nd ed. (New York: John Wiley, 1980).

27. Daniel P. Moynihan, *Maximum Feasible Misunderstanding: Community Action in the War on Poverty* (New York: Free Press, 1969); Jeffrey L. Pressman and Aaron B. Wildavsky, *Implementation* (Los Angeles: Univ. of California Press, 1973).

28. Erwin Hargrove and Michael Nelson, *Presidents, Politics, and Policy* (New York: Knopf, 1984), 180.

29. Richard Nathan, *The Plot That Failed* (New York: John Wiley, 1975).

30. Richard Nathan, *The Administrative Presidency* (New York: John Wiley, 1983), vii.

31. Richard F. Fenno, Jr., *The President's Cabinet* (New York: Vintage Books, 1959).

32. Nathan, *The Administrative Presidency*, 78.

33. Ibid., 76.

34. Richard P. Nathan, Institutional Change under Reagan," in *Perspectives on the Reagan Years*, ed. John L. Palmer (Washington, D.C.: Urban Institute, 1986), 130–31.

35. Colin Campbell, *Managing the Presidency: Carter, Reagan, and the*

Search for Executive Harmony (Pittsburgh: Univ. of Pittsburgh Press, 1986); Gordon R. Hoxie, "Staffing the Ford and Carter Presidencies," in *Organizing and Staffing the Presidency*, ed. Nash et al.; Laurence E. Lynn, Sr., *Managing the Public's Business: The Job of the Government Executive* (New York: Basic Books, 1981).

36. David M. Hedge and Donald C. Menzel, "Loosing the Regulatory Ratchet: A Grassroots View of Environmental Deregulation," *Policy Studies Journal* 13 (1985): 599–606.

37. Frank J. Thompson and Michael J. Scicchitano, "State Enforcement of Federal Regulatory Policy: The Lessons of OSHA," *Policy Studies Journal* 13 (1985): 591–98.

38. Elizabeth Sanders, "The Presidency and the Bureaucratic State," in *The Presidency and the Political System*, ed. Michael Nelson (Washington, D.C.: Congressional Quarterly, 1988), 400.

Chapter 1

1. Robert Dahl has defined influence as the ability of an individual or group to get someone else to do something they would not otherwise do. In this book I will adhere to this definition. Robert A. Dahl, *Who Governs?* (New Haven: Yale Univ. Press, 1961): Introduction.

2. Nelson Polsby, "Presidential Cabinet Making: Lessons for the Political System," *Political Science Quarterly* 93 (1978): 18.

3. Ibid., 25.

4. William M. Goldsmith, *The Growth of Presidential Power: A Documented History: Volume I: The Formative Years* (New York: Confucian Press, 1980), 208–29.

5. Edward S. Corwin, *The President: Office and Powers* (New York: New York Univ. Press, 1957).

6. Hargrove and Nelson, *Presidents, Politics, and Policy*, 46.

7. Goldsmith, *The Growth of Presidential Power*, 184.

8. Louis Fisher, "The Administrative State: What's Next After *Chadha* and *Bowsher*," paper presented at the annual meeting of the American Political Science Association, Washington, D.C., 1986.

9. As Rohr points out, the Constitution does not mention political parties or judicial review either. Yet political parties have real influence, and the Supreme Court practices judicial review. The mere fact that the bureaucracy is not specifically enumerated in the Constitution does not in any sense undercut its legitimacy as an institution. John A. Rohr, *To Run a Constitution: The Legitimacy of the Administrative State* (Lawrence: Univ. Press of Kansas, 1986).

10. Arnold, *Making the Managerial Presidency*, 7.

11. R. Douglas Arnold, *Congress and the Bureaucracy: A Theory of Influence* (New Haven: Yale Univ. Press, 1979).

12. Emmette S. Redford and Marlan Blissett, *Organizing the Executive Branch: The Johnson Presidency* (Chicago: Univ. of Chicago Press, 1981), 2.

13. Woodrow Wilson, *Congressional Government: A Study in American Politics* (Baltimore: John Hopkins Univ. Press, 1981), 206; Sundquist, *The Decline and Resurgence of Congress*, ch. 7.

14. Sundquist, *The Decline and Resurgence of Congress,* chs. 11–12.

15. A number of scholars have argued that congressional oversight is merely a perfunctory process and that Congress does not take this responsibility seriously enough. See, for example, William J. Keefe and Morris S. Ogul, *The American Legislative Process* (Englewood Cliffs, N.J.: Prentice-Hall, 1981); Morris S. Ogul, "Congressional Oversight: Structures and Incentives," in *Congress Reconsidered*, ed. Lawrence C. Dodd and Bruce I. Oppenheimer (Washington, D.C.: Congressional Quarterly, 1981), 317–31; Lawrence C. Dodd and Richard L. Schott, *Congress and the Administrative State* (New York: John Wiley, 1979); Robert A. Katzmann, *Regulatory Bureaucracy: The Federal Trade Commission and Antitrust Policy* (Cambridge, Mass.: MIT Press, 1980); Robert A. Katzmann, "The Federal Trade Commission," in *The Politics of Regulation,* ed. James Q. Wilson (New York: Basic Books, 1980); John F. Bibby and Roger H. Davidson, *On Capitol Hill: Studies in the Legislative Process* (Hinsdale, Ill.: Dryden Press, 1972); J. W. Davis, *The National Executive Branch* (New York: Free Press, 170). Alternatively, a few scholars have argued that congressional oversight is a credible process and that it is an effective constraint on executive branch activity. See Barry R. Weingast, "Regulation, Reregulation, and Deregulation: The Political Foundations of Agency Clientele Relationships," *Law and Contemporary Society* 44 (1981): 148–77; Barry R. Weingast and Mark J. Moran, "Bureaucratic Discretion or Congressional Control? Regulatory Policymaking by the Federal Trade Commission," *Journal of Political Economy* (1983): 765–800; Erwin G. Krasnow and Lawrence D. Longley, *The Politics of Broadcast Regulation* (New York: St. Martin's, 1978).

16. Rossiter, *The American Presidency*, 19–22.

17. Fenno, *The President's Cabinet.*

18. Louis W. Koenig, *The Chief Executive* (New York: Harcourt Brace Jovanovich, 1975), 184.

19. Cronin, *The State of the Presidency*, 333.

20. Roger G. Noll, *Reforming Regulation* (Washington, D.C.: Brookings, 1971), 36; see also James Q. Wilson, "The Politics of Regula-

tion," in *The Politics of Regulation*, ed. Wilson (New York: Basic Books, 1980), 389–90.

21. Bruce Yandle, "FTC Activity and Presidential Effects," *Presidential Studies Quarterly* 15 (1985): 128–35; Jeffrey E. Cohen, "Presidential Control of Independent Regulatory Commissions Through Appointment: The Case of the ICC," *Administration and Society* 17 (1985), 61–71; Nathaniel Beck, "Presidential Influence on the Federal Reserve in the 1970's," *American Journal of Political Science* 3 (1982): 415–45.

22. Douglass Cater, *Power in Washington: A Critical Look at Today's Struggle to Govern in the Nation's Capitol* (New York: Random House, 1964); J. Leiper Freeman, *The Political Process: Executive Bureau-Legislative Committee Relations* (New York: Random House, 1965); Grant McConnell, *Private Power and American Democracy* (New York: Vintage Books, 1966).

23. Richard W. Waterman and Edward J. Ahern. "A Re-examination of the Capture Theory: The Cases of the Airline and Trucking Industries," paper presented at the annual meeting of the Southwest Social Science Association, Houston, Texas, March 1983.

24. Terry M. Moe, "Regulatory Performance and Presidential Administration," *American Journal of Political Science* 26 (1982): 197–225, "Control and Feedback in Economic Regulation: The Case of the NLRB," *American Political Science Review* 4 (1985) 1094–1116, and "Political Control and Professional Autonomy: The Institutional Politics of the NLRB," paper presented at the annual meeting of the American Political Science Association, Washington, D.C., Sept. 1986; B. Dan Wood, "Bureaucrats, Principals, and Responsiveness: The Case of the Clean Air Act," *American Political Science Review* 82: 213–34; and "Reagan's Environmental Policy and Federal Clean Air Enforcement Activities," paper presented at the annual meeting of the Southwest Social Science Association, Dallas, Texas, March 1987); Wenmouth Williams Jr., "Impact of Commissioner Background on FCC Decisions: 1962–1975," *Journal of Broadcasting* 20 (1976): 239–56; William E. Brigman, "The Executive Branch and the Independent Regulatory Agencies," *Presidential Studies Quarterly* 11 (1981): 244–61; Joseph Stewart, Jr., and James S. Cromartie, "Partisan Presidential Change and Regulatory Policy: The Case of the FTC and Deceptive Practices Enforcement, 1938–1974," *Presidential Studies Quarterly* 12 (1982): 568–73); Donald C. Menzel, "Redirecting the Implementation of a Law: The Reagan Administration and Coal Surface Mining Regulation." *Public Administration Review* 43 (1983): 411–20; Hedge and Menzel, "Loosing the Regulatory Ratchet"; Steven A. Shull, "President-Agency Relations in Civil Rights Policy," paper pre-

sented at the annual meeting of the American Political Science Association, Washington D.C., Sept., 1986.

25. Moe, "The Politicized Presidency"; Lester A. Salamon, "The Presidency and Domestic Policy Formulation," in *The Illusion of Presidential Government*, ed. Heclo and Salamon 177–201.

26. Cronin, *The State of the Presidency*, 333.

27. Moe, "The Politicized Presidency"; Waterman, "The Presidential Conundrum."

28. Nathan, *The Administrative Presidency.*

29. Ibid., 88.

30. Ibid., 7.

31. Ibid., 91.

32. Ibid., 94.

33. Neustadt, *Presidential Power*, 28–29.

34. Louis M. Kohlmeier, Jr., *The Regulators: Watchdog Agencies and the Public Interest* (New York: Harper and Row, 1969).

35. Hugh Heclo, *"A Government of Strangers: Executive Politics in Washington* (Washington, D.C.: Brookings Institution, 1977).

36. Lynn, *Managing the Public's Business.*

37. Neustadt, *Presidential Power*, 25.

Chapter 2

1. Nathan, *The Administrative Presidency; The Plot That Failed.*

2. G. Calvin Mackenzie, *The Politics of Presidential Appointments.* (New York: Free Press, 1981), 5.

5. James P. Pfiffner, "Political Appointees and Career Executives: Managing Change and Continuity," paper presented at the annual meeting of the American Political Science Association, Washington, D.C., Sept. 1986.

4. Paul C. Light, "When Worlds Collide: The Political-Career Nexus," in *The In-and-Outers: Presidential Appointees and Transient Government in Washington*, ed. G. Calvin Mackenzie (Baltimore: John Hopkins Univ. Press, 1987), 156–73.

5. Mackenzie, *The Politics of Presidential Appointments*, 11, 79; Bonafede, "White House Personnel Office from Roosevelt to Reagan," in *The In-and-Outers*, ed. Mackenzie, 30–59; Laurin L. Henry, "The Presidency, Executive Staffing, and the Federal Bureaucracy," in *The Presidency*, ed. Aaron Wildavsky (Boston: Little, Brown, 1969), 529–57.

6. Richard L. Schott and Dagmar S. Hamilton, *People, Positions, and*

Power: The Political Appointments of Lyndon Johnson (Chicago: Univ. of Chicago Press, 1983).

7. Jeffrey E. Cohen, "On the Tenure of Appointive Political Executives: The American Cabinet, 1952–1984," *American Journal of Political Science* 30 (1986): 507–16.

8. Linda L. Fisher, "Appointments and Presidential Control: The Importance of Role," paper presented at the annual meeting of the American Political Science Association, Washington, D.C., Sept. 1986, 21.

9. See also Laurence E. Lynn, Jr., "The Reagan Administration and the Renitent Bureaucracy," in *The Reagan Presidency and the Governing of America*, ed. Salamon and Lund 339–370.

10. Neustadt, *Presidential Power*, 31.

11. Fenno, *The President's Cabinet*, 225.

12. See also James P. Pfiffner, "Strangers in a Strange Land: Orienting New Presidential Appointees," in *The In-and-Outers*, ed Mackenzie, 141–55; Heclo, *A Government of Strangers*.

13. Carl Brauer, "Tenure, Turnover, and Postgovernment Trends of Presidential Appointees," in *The In-and-Outers*, ed. Mackenzie, 174–94.

14. G. Calvin Mackenzie, "'If You Want to Play, You've Got to Pay': Ethics Regulation and the Presidential Appointments System, 1964–1984," in *The In-and-Outers*, ed. Mackenzie, 77–89.

15. James D. King and James W. Riddlesperger, Jr., "Senate Confirmation of Appointments to the Cabinet and Executive Office of the President," paper presented at the annual meeting of the American Political Science Association, Chicago, Aug. 1987.

16. The practice of Senatorial Courtesy can also constrain presidential appointment power. Senatorial Courtesy allows a senator to object to a nominee if that individual comes from the senator's own state or if the nominee will serve in the senator's state. Usually the objecting senator is from the same party as the president, though this has not always been the case. The practice is non-binding; in other words, presidents do not have to reject a nominee simply because a particular senator objects. See Fisher, *The Constitution Between Friends,* 119, and *The Politics of Shared Power*, 122–23.

17. Christopher Deering, "Damned If You Do and Damned If You Don't: The Senate's Role in the Appointments Process," in *The In-and-Outers*, ed. Mackenzie, 100–19.

18. Kohlmeier, *The Regulators*, ch. 4.

19. Noll, *Reforming Regulation,* 43; U.S. Congress, *Appointments to the Regulatory Agencies*, Senate Committee on Commerce, 1976.

20. Goldsmith, *The Growth of Presidential Power*, 204.

21. Fisher, *The Constitution Between Friends*, 53.

22. Goldsmith, *The Growth of Presidential Power*, 182.

23. 272 U.S. 138 (1926); in *Shurleff v. United States* (189 U. S. 311 [1903] the Supreme Court has upheld the president's right to remove officials from office. However, the Court also ruled that Congress could restrain presidential removal power if it so decided. In *Myers v. United States* (272 U. S. 52 [1926]) the Court granted the president the broadest power to remove executive branch officials. Later, in *United States v. Lovett* (328 U. S. 303 [1946]), the Court again reaffirmed the president's right to remove executive branch officers.

24. 295 U.S. 602 (1935); in the case of *Weiner v. United States* (357 U. S. 349 [1958]) reaffirmed the *Humphrey* decision.

25. Frederick C. Mosher, *Democracy and the Public Service* (New York: Oxford Univ. Press, 1982), 66–73.

26. Sanders, "The Presidency and the Bureaucratic State," 393.

27. Ibid., 392–93.

28. Gerald R. Ford, *A Time to Heal: The Autobiography of Gerald R. Ford* (New York: Harper and Row, 1979), 352.

29. Lance T. LeLoup, *Budgetary Politics* (Brunswick, Ohio: King's Court, 1980), 126.

30. In the case of a deferral, Congress must vote to override or the deferral is implemented. In the case of a rescission, congressional approval is necessary before the recission can be implemented. Consequently, since congressional approval is necessary for rescissions, most presidents have made more extensive use of deferrals as a means of slowing congressional spending.

31. Louis Fisher, *Presidential Spending Power* (Princeton, N.J.: Princeton Univ. Press, 1975).

32. LeLoup, *Budgetary Politics*, 149.

33. David A. Stockman, *The Triumph of Politics: Why the Reagan Revolution Failed* (New York: Harper and Row, 1986).

34. Allen Schick, "The Problem of Presidential Budgeting," in *The Illusion of Presidential Government*, ed. Heclo and Salamon, 85–111.

35. Heclo, "OMB and the Presidency—The Problems of Neutral Competence," 97–98; several budgetary scholars have asserted that the Reorganization Plan No. 2 of 1970 (implemented via Executive Order #11541 on July 1, 1970), which created the Office of Management and Budget, politicized the new budgetary office. According to this view, OMB became more of an agent of the president than had its predecessor, the old Bureau of the Budget. Also, the addition of four appointed Associate Directors provided the president with greater control over OMB and its career civil servants. This had diminished the once routine contact that had previously existed between civil servants and the Director of OMB. This in turn has re-

duced the influence of career civil servants. See Larry Berman, *The Office of Management and Budget and the Presidency, 1921–1979* (Princeton, N.J.: Princeton Univ. Press, 1979), 119–21; Schick, "The Problem of Presidential Budgeting," 104–5; Shelley Lynne Tomkin, "Playing Politics in OMB: Civil Servants Join the Game," *Presidential Studies Quarterly* 15 (1985): 158–59.

36. Harold Seidman, *Politics, Position, and Power: The Dynamics of Federal Organization* (Oxford: Oxford Univ. Press, 1980), 38.
37. Robert E. DeClerico, *The American President* (Englewood Cliffs, N.J.: Prentice Hall, 1979), 118.
38. Seidman, *Politics, Position, and Power*, 262.
39. 103 S. Ct. 715.
40. Hart, *The Presidential Branch*, 40–41.
41. A number of studies have examined presidential reorganization planning in historical perspective. Among these are Arnold, *Making the Managerial Presidency*; Seidman, *Politics, Position, and Power*; Herbert Emmerich, *Federal Organization and Administrative Management*, (University: Univ. of Alabama Press, 1971); Harvey C. Mansfield, "Federal Executive Reorganization: Thirty Years of Experience," *Public Administration Review* 29 (July/Aug. 1969): 332–45; Harvey C. Mansfield, "Reorganization the Federal Executive Branch: The Limits of Institutionalism," *Law and Contemporary Society* 35 (1970): 461–95.
42. Lester M. Salamon, "The Question of Goals," in *Federal Reorganization: What Have We Learned?* ed. Peter Szanton (Chatham, N.J.: Chatham House, 1981), 58–84.
43. U.S. Commission on Organization of the Executive Branch of the Government *The Independent Regulatory Agencies: A Report with Recommendations*. (Washington, D.C.: Government Printing Office, 1949).
44. Maes G. Benze, Jr., "Presidential Reorganization as a Tactical Weapon: Putting Politics Back into Administration," *Presidential Studies Quarterly* 15 (1985): 145–56.
45. Quoted in Arnold, *Making the Managerial Presidency*, 103.
46. DeClerico, *The American President*, 121.
47. Quoted in Douglas M. Fox, ed., "A Mini-Symposium: President Nixon's Proposals for Executive Reorganization," *Public Administration Review* 34 (1974): 489.
48. Louis Fisher and Ronald C. Moe, "Presidential Reorganization: Is It Worth the Cost?" *Political Science Quarterly* 96 (1981): 302.
49. David M. Welborn, *Governance of Federal Regulatory Agencies* (Knoxville: Univ. of Tennessee Press, 1977), 74–75.

50. Michael D. Reagan and John G. Sanzone, *The New Federalism* (New York: Oxford Univ. Press, 1981).

51. David B. Walker, *Toward a Functioning Federalism* (Boston: Little, Brown, 1981).

52. Richard E. Neustadt, "Presidency and Legislation: The Growth of Central Clearance," *American Political Science Review* 48 (1954): 641–71.

53. Robert Gilmour, "Policy Formulation in the Executive Branch: Central Legislative Clearance," in *Case Studies in Public Policy Making*, ed. James Anderson (New York: Holt, Rinehart, and Winston, 1976): 80–96,

54. Federal Register, 39, 231: 41501–41502.

55. Edward Paul Fuchs, *Presidents, Management, and Regulation* (Englewood Cliffs, N.J.: Prentice-Hall, 1988), ch. 2.

56. Executive Order #11949 (Federal Register, 42, 3: 1017).

57. Fuchs, *Presidents, Management, and Regulation*, xii.

58. Richard Zeckhauser, "Procedures for Valuing Lives," *Public Policy* 23 (1975): 419–64.

59. See Lawrence H. Tribe, "Policy Science: Analysis or Ideology?" *Philosophy and Public Affairs* 2 (1972): 66–110; Michael S. Baram, "Cost-Benefit Analysis: An Inadequate Basis for Health, Safety, and Environmental Regulatory Decisionmaking," in The Administrative Conference of the United States, *1979 Recommendations and Reports*, 377–435; House Committee on Interstate and Foreign Commerce, *Use of Cost-Benefit Analysis by Regulatory Agencies*, 96th Cong., 1st sess., 1979.

Chapter 3

1. Nathan, *The Plot That Failed*; Nathan, *The Administrative Presidency*.

2. DeClerico, *The American President*, 133; Polsby, "Presidential Cabinet Making," 15–16.

3. Rowland Evans, Jr., and Robert D. Novak, *Nixon in the White House: The Frustration of Power* (New York: Random House, 1971), 51–52.

4. Bernard J. Frieden and Marshall Kaplan, *The Politics of Neglect: Urban Aid from Model Cities to Revenue Sharing* (Cambridge, Mass.: MIT Press, 1975), 113.

5. Ibid., 88.

6. The Urban Affairs Council was the first organization responsible for domestic policy formulation. It was used during the period when

the Nixon administration relied on the decentralized cabinet style of government. Its membership included all of the domestic policy-related cabinet secretaries, along with the president and the vice-president, and was chaired by Daniel Patrick Moynihan. Most departmental proposals were first aired at meetings of the Urban Affairs Council. According to Stephen Hess, who served as an assistant to Moynihan, the Council "was a flawed instrument in that its jurisdiction did not emcompass all domestic policy." As such, it was not an effective means of coordinating administration policy. The Council was replaced by the Domestic Council in 1970. See Hess, *Organizing the Presidency*, 123.

7. Frieden and Kaplan, *The Politics of Neglect*, 114–15.
8. Evans and Novak, *Nixon in the White House*, 37–41.
9. President's Task Force on Model Cities, *Model Cities: A Step Toward the New Federalism* (1970).
10. Frieden and Kaplan, *The Politics of Neglect*, 122–23.
11. William Safire, *Before the Fall: An Insider's View of the Pre-Watergate White House* (New York: Doubleday, 1975), 248.
12. John Ehrlichman, *Witness to Power: The Nixon Years* (New York: Simon and Schuser, 1982), 106.
13. Ibid., 107–10.
14. House Committee on Government Operations, *Overview Hearing on Operations of the Department of Housing and Urban Development*, 92nd Cong., 1st sess., 1971; U.S. Congress, *HUD–Space–Science–Veterans*. House Committee on Appropriations (1972).
15. R. Allen Hays, *The Federal Government and Urban Housing: Ideology and Change in Public Policy* (Albany: State Univ. of New York Press, 1985), 120.
16. U.S. Department of Housing and Urban Affairs, *Housing in the Seventies: A Report on the National Policy Review* (Washington, D.C.: Government Printing Office, 1974).
17. Ehrlichman, *Witness to Power*, 101–2.
18. Evans and Novak, *Nixon in the White House*, 358–60.
19. Quoted in Seidman, *Politics, Position, and Power*, 113.
20. I. M. Destler, "National Security Advice to U.S. Presidents: Some Lessons from Thirty Years," *World Politics* 29 (1977): 143–76; Bert A. Rockman, "America's Departments of State: Irregular and Regular Syndromes of Policy Making," *American Political Science Review* 75 (1981): 911–27.
21. Emphasis added; quoted in Mackenzie, *The Politics of Presidential Appointments*, 47.
22. Ibid., 47–50.
23. Ibid.

24. Richard M. Nixon, *The Memoirs of Richard Nixon* (New York: Grosset and Dunlop, 1978), 768.

25. The appointments of Weinberger and Lynn are consistent with James Best's contention that in-term appointments are different from presidents' initial cabinet selections. In-term appointments generally tend to be more personally loyal to the president. Initial appointees are chosen for a variety of political reasons and thus tend to be less loyal and less responsive to the president. Best refers to this replacement process as replacing an "outsider" with an "insider." See James J. Best, "Presidential Cabinet Appointees: 1953–1976," *Presidential Studies Quarterly* 11 (1981): 66.

26. Polsby, "Presidential Cabinet Making," 15–16.

27. Hess, *Organizing the Presidency*, 123–24.

28. Arnold, *Making the Managerial Presidency*, 284.

29. The Domestic Council and the Office of Management and Budget were both created via Reorganization Plan No. 2 of 1970. According to Larry Berman, the original design of the two organizations was altered so that greater power went to the Domestic Council, rather than its originally intended destination, the Office of Management and Budget. This was done because John Ehrlichman wanted to increase his personal power base within the White House. Ehrlicman has flatly denied this allegation. See Larry Berman, "The Office of Management and Budget That Almost Wasn't," *Political Science Quarterly* 92 (1977): 298; Ehrlichman, *Witness to Power*.

30. Seidman, *Politics, Position, and Power*, 114. The Advisory Council on Government Organization, better known as the Ash Council, was established to provide the president with advise regarding the organization of the government. Chaired by Roy Ash, the former president of the Litton Corporation, the Council had three basic tasks. First, given the fact that public demands on government had changed substantially, Nixon directed the Council to reexamine the whole executive branch. Second, he directed the Council to examine the effects of the diffuse mixture of the executive branch on policymaking (some 150-plus different departments, offices, and agencies). Finally, Nixon ordered the Council to assess the organizational capability of the executive branch with regard to matters of intergovernmental relations. Arnold, *Making the Managerial Presidency*, 277.

31. Salamon, "The Question of Goals," 182–84. There are a number of excellent studies of the Domestic Council: for example, John Kessel, *The Domestic Presidency: Decision-Making in the White House* (North Scituate, Mass.: Duxbury, 1975); John Ehrlichman, "How It All Began . . . By a Man Who Was There," *National Journal*

(Dec. 13, 1975): 1690–91; Ronald C. Moe, "The Domestic Council in Perspective," *Bureaucrat* 5: 251–72; Raymond Waldmann, "The Domestic Council: Innovation in Presidential Government," *Public Administration Review* 36: 260–68.

32. Safire, *Before the Fall*, 260.
33. Ibid.
34. *Papers Relating to the President's Departmental Reorganization Program: A Reference Compilation* (Washington, D.C.: Government Printing Office, 1972): 3–4.
35. Ibid., 10.
36. Ibid., 14.
37. Arnold, *Making the Managerial Presidency*, 300–1; William Lilley III, "Hostile Committee Chairman, Lobbies Pledge Fight Against Reorganization Plan," *National Journal* (Oct. 10, 1971): 2072–81.
38. Arnold, *Making the Managerial Presidency*, 300–1.
39. Nixon, *The Memoirs of Richard Nixon*, 767.
40. Nathan, *The Plot That Failed*, 76.
41. H. R. Haldeman and Joseph DiMona, *The Ends of Power* (New York: New York Times Books, 1978), 181.
42. Polsby, "Presidential Cabinet Making," 51.
43. Ibid., 51.
44. Quoted in Joel D. Aberback and Bert A. Rockman, "Clashing Beliefs Within the Executive Branch: The Nixon Administration Bureaucracy." *American Political Science Review* 70 (1976): 457.
45. House Subcommittee on Manpower and Civil Service of the Committee on Post Office and Civil Service, *Final Report on Violations and Abuses of Merit Principles in Federal Employment*, 94th Cong., 2nd sess., 1976.
46. Mosher, *Democracy and the Public Service*, 104.
47. Aberback and Rockman, "Clashing Beliefs Within the Executive Branch," 459–63.
48. Richard L. Cole and David A. Caputo, "Presidential Control of the Senior Executive Service: Assessing the Strategies of the Nixon Years," *American Political Science Review* 73 (1979): 405–6.
49. Louis Fisher, *Presidential Spending Power* (Princeton, N.J.: Princeton Univ. Press, 1975), 194–97; Hays, *The Federal Government and Urban Housing*, 133–34.
50. Fisher, *Presidential Spending Power*, 194.
51. Ibid., 194–95; U.S. Department of Housing and Urban Development, *Housing in the Seventies: A Report on the National Policy Review* (Washington, D.C.: Government Printing Office, 1974); U.S. Department of Housing and Urban Development, *Housing in the*

Seventies: Working Papers Volumes 1 and *2* (Washington, D. C.: Government Printing Office, 1976).

52. Fisher, *Presidential Spending Power*, 197.
53. 420 U. S. 35 (1975).
54. Fisher, *Presidential Spending Power*, 193.
55. Hays, *The Federal Government and Urban Housing*, 201.
56. Fisher, *Presidential Spending Power*, 174.
57. Hays, *The Federal Government and Urban Housing*, 136.
58. Ibid., 145–46.

Chapter 4

1. Alan Stone, *Regulation and Its Alternatives* (Washington, D.C.: Congressional Quarterly, 1982), 250.
2. Ibid., 250.
3. Roger G. Noll and Bruce M. Owen, *The Political Economy of Deregulation: Interest Groups in the Regulatory Process* (Washington, D.C.: American Enterprise Institute, 1983).
4. All motor carriers that had been in operation in 1935, when the original Motor Carrier Act was adopted, were automatically "grandfathered" (granted certificates) into the regulated market (Section 206[a] 7 [A]).
5. American Trucking Associations, *The Case for Economic Regulation of the Motor Carrier Industry* (Washington, D.C.: American Trucking Associations, 1979), 18.
6. Ibid., 36.
7. Senate Committee on Commerce, Science, and Transportation, *Economic Regulation of the Trucking Industry,* 96th Cong., 1st and 2nd sess., 1979–1980, 168; many economists also argued that ICC entry restrictions were a major stimulus for higher consumer prices. See, for example, Almarin Phillips, ed., *Promoting Competition in Regulated Markets* (Washington, D.C.: Brookings Institution, 1975); Thomas Gale Moore, "The Beneficiaries of Trucking Regulation," *Journal of Law and Economics* 21 (1978): 327–42; Stephen Breyer, *Regulation and Its Reform* (Cambridge: Harvard Univ. Press, 1982), ch. 12. Martha Derthick and Paul J. Quirk state in *The Politics of Deregulation* (Washington, D.C.: Brookings Institution, 1985), 36–39, that economists were virtually "unanimous in their condemnation of anti-competitive government regulation. See also Paul L. Joskow and Roger G. Noll, "Regulation in Theory and Practice: An Overview," in *Studies in Public Regulation*, ed. Gary Fromm (Cam-

bridge, Mass.: MIT Press, 1981), 8. Conservative economists, however, were not the only ones to support deregulation. Liberal groups
such as Ralph Nader's Study Group condemned the ICC for creating a legalized cartel. See Robert Fellmeth, *The Interstate Commerce
Omission: The Public Interest and the ICC* (New York: Grossman,
1970). Thus, scholarly support for deregulation came from a broad
ideological spectrum.

8. Irving Kristol, "Some Doubts About De-Regulation," *Wall Street
Journal*, Oct. 20, 1975, 14; Martin T. Farris, "The Case Against Deregulation in Transportation, Power, and Communications," *I.C.C.
Practitioners' Journal* 45: 330–31; Paul Kamerschen, "Contract Carriage as a Solution to Service Stability in an Unregulated Motor
Carrier Industry," *Transportation Research Forum Proceedings* 20:
159–63.

9. The argument was advanced to me by an ICC official who deals predominantly with entry policy that a concentrated trucking market
is developing in the Less-Than-Truckload (LTL) market, small shipments in which a shipper does not use all of the space in a truck
but shares it with other shippers. Only a few companies now provide LTL service. The same pattern has not developed in the Truck-
load Market (TL).

10. American Trucking Associations, *The Case for Economic Regulation of the Motor Carrier Industry*, 25.

11. With joint line service, trucking service is shared among several
different companies. One company might provide service between
New York and Cleveland, another between Cleveland and Chicago,
and so on. With single line service, one trucking company provides
the entire service. The contention that an antitrust exemption be
permitted for joint line rates has always been more strongly supported by a variety of groups, including the ICC. The reason for this
is that all trucking firms providing joint line service have to sit down
together in order to determine a fair price for a particular shipper.
The case for single line service has been more tenuous. Rate setting
on single line rates enables competitors on the same route to set
prices.

12. Senate Committee on Commerce, Science, and Transportation, *Economic Regulation of the Trucking Industry*, 449.

13. Ibid., 442.

14. American Trucking Associations, *Small Town Blues* (Washington,
D.C.: American Trucking Associations, 1976).

15. James R. Snitzler and Robert J. Byrne, *Interstate Trucking of Fresh
and Frozen Fruits and Poultry under the Agricultural Exemption*,
U.S. Department of Agriculture (March 1958), and *Interstate Truck-*

ing of Frozen Fruits and Vegetables under the Agricultural Exemption, U.S. Department of Agriculture (March 1959); J. C. Winter and Ivan W. Ulrey, *Supplement to Interstate Trucking of Frozen Fruits and Vegetables under the Agricultural Exemption*, U.S. Department of Agriculture (July 1961).

16. Karen L. Borlaug and Laurence T. Phillips, *Trucking Service in Six Small Michigan Communities*, U.S. Department of Transportation (1980); Denis A. Breen and Benjamin Allen, *Common Carrier Obligations and the Provisions of Freight Transportation Service to Small Communities*, U.S. Department of Transportation (1979); Bruce W. Allen, *An Examination of the Unregulated Trucking Experience in New Jersey*, University of Pennsylvania under contract DOT-OS-70069 (1978); Alice E. Kidder and Harold G. Willis, *Shipper/Receiver Transportation Mode Choice*, North Carolina A & T University under contract DOT-OS-80007 (1980); M. Dennis Marvich and G. Cleveland Thornton, *Trucking Service in Two Small Alabama Communities*, U.S. Department of Transportation (March 1980); Charles G. Orvis, *Trucking Service to Two Small Kansas Communities*, U.S. Department of Transportation (1980); Michael W. Pustay, *The Impact of Federal Trucking Regulation on Service to Small Communities*, Purdue University under contract DOT-OS-70069 (March 1979); R. L. Banks and Associates, *Economic Analysis and Regulatory Implications of Motor Carrier Service to Predominantly Small Communities*, under contract DOT-OS-50095 (June 1976).

17. Breen and Allen, *Common Carrier Obligations*.

18. U. S. Department of Transportation, *The Impact of Federal Trucking Regulation on Service to Small Communities*, (March 15, 1979).

19. Prior to deregulation, certificates were often sold to other trucking firms. A company wishing to expand to a new market could buy another firm's certificate, with ICC approval. Certificates thus had a market value. Many certificates for rural routes that the ATA claimed were unprofitable retained a high market value, suggesting that these routes were indeed profitable.

20. Ann F. Friedlander and Richard Spady, "Equity, Efficiency and Resource Allocation in the Rail and Regulated Trucking Industries," CTS Report 79-4 (March 1979).

21. U.S. Congress, Congressional Budget Office, *The Impact of Trucking Deregulation on Small Communities* (Feb. 1980), 8.

22. House Subcommittee on Surface Transportation of the Committee on Public Works and Transportation, *Examining Current Conditions in the Trucking Industry and the Possible Necessity for Change in the Manner of its Regulation*, 96th Cong., 1st and 2nd sess., 1979–1980.

23. Senate Committee on Commerce, Science, and Transportation, *The Impact on Small Communities of Motor Carrier Regulatory Revision,* 95th Cong., 2nd sess., 1978.

24. John P. Frendreis and Richard W. Waterman, "PAC Contributions and Legislative Behavior: Senate Voting on Trucking Deregulation," *Social Science Quarterly* 66: 401–12.

25. Barry M. Mitnick, *The Political Economy of Regulation: Creating, Designing, and Removing Regulatory Forms* (New York: Columbia Univ. Press, 1980), 185–204.

26. Charles A. Taff, *Commercial Motor Transportation* (Homewood, Ill.: Richard D. Irwin, 1955).

27. U.S. Commission on Organization of the Executive Branch of the Government, *The Independent Regulatory Agencies.*

28. Kohlmeier, *The Regulators,* 46–47.

29. Welborn, *Governance of Federal Regulatory Agencies,* 117.

30. Ibid., 22.

31. Marcus Alexis, "The Political Economy of Federal Regulation of Surface Transportation," in *The Political Economy of Deregulation,* ed. Noll and Owen, 128.

32. U.S. Commission on Organization of the Executive Branch of the Government, *Legal Services and Procedures* (Washington, D.C.: Government Printing Office, 1955).

33. Mansfield, "Reorganizing the Federal Executive Branch."

34. Senate Subcommittee on Administrative Practice and Procedure of the Committee on Judiciary, *Report on Regulatory Agencies to the President-Elect,* 86th Cong., 2nd sess., 1960.

35. Senate Committee on Commerce, Special Study Group on Transportation Policies of the United States, *National Transportation Policy Report, Senate Report No. 445,* 87th Cong., 1st sess., 1961.

36. Robert J. Bernard, "The Truck in Perspective," *I.C.C. Practitioners' Journal* 28 (1961): 460.

37. When the Johnson administration was preparing its proposal for a new Department of Transportation, it also floated the idea that the president be granted the authority to appoint the chairman of the ICC. Although Johnson said he intended to send a reorganization plan to Congress, he never did. See Redford and Blissett, *Organizing the Executive Branch,* 163.

38. Charles R. Perry, *Deregulation and the Decline of the Unionized Trucking Industry* (Philadelphia: Industrial Research Unit, The Wharton School, University of Pennsylvania, 1986), 22–23.

39. Senate Subcommittee on Surface Transportation of the Committee on Commerce, *Surface Transport Legislation,* 92nd Cong., 2nd sess., 1972, 231.

40. DeClerico, *The American President*, 119.
41. President's Summit Conference on Inflation, *The Economists' Conference on Inflation* (1974) and *The Conference on Inflation* (1974).
42. Ted Vaden, "Truckers Fear Continued Deregulation Drive," *Congressional Quarterly Weekly Reports* 34 (1976): 3249–54.
43. Paul W. MacAvoy and John W. Snow, eds., *Regulation of Entry and Pricing in Truck Transportation* (Washington, D.C.: American Enterprise Institute, 1977), 73.
44. House Subcommittee on Surface Transportation of the Committee on Public Works and Transportation, *Regulation of Carriers Subject to the Interstate Commerce Commission,* 94th Cong., 2nd sess., 1976, 106.
45. Ibid., 107.
46. Derthick and Quirk, *The Politics of Deregulation*, 59.
47. Ibid., 71.
48. Senate Committee on Commerce, *Nominations—February-March*, 93rd Cong., 1st sess., 1973, 174.
49. A. Daniel O'Neal, "No Clamor for Deregulation: Should There Be?" in *Perspectives on Federal Transportation Policy,* ed. James C. Miller III (Washington, D.C.: American Enterprise Institute, 1975); House Subcommittee on Surface Transportation, *Regulation of Carriers Subject to the Interstate Commerce Commission*, 109–23.
50. Senate Committee on Commerce, Science, and Transportation, *Nominations to the Interstate Commerce Commission*, 96th Cong., 1st sess., 1979, 64.
51. "New ICC Chief." *Wall Street Journal*, June 3, 1977, 1.
52. Anthony E. Brown, *The Politics of Airline Deregulation* (Knoxville: Univ. of Tennessee Press, 1987).
53. *Nominations to the Interstate Commerce Commission*, 23.
54. Ibid., 2.
55. Ibid., 31.
56. Ibid., 54.
57. Ibid., 28–29.
58. Ibid., 85.
59. Richard E. Cohen, "Will Carter Be Able to Apply the Brakes to Trucking Regulation?" *National Journal* 9 (May 9, 1979): 752; Mark G. Aron, "Deregulation: The Peaceful Revolution," *Survey of Business* (Summer 1981): 4–13.
60. Lynn, *Managing the Public's Business*, 55.
61. Senate Committee on Commerce, Science, and Transportation, *Nomination—Secretary of Transportation*, 96th Cong., 1st sess., 1979, 10.
62. Interstate Commerce Commission, *Annual Report*. (1978), 45.
63. 551 F. 2d. 1326 (1977).

64. 129 M. C. C. 1 (1978).
65. Federal Register, 1978: 56978.
66. *Liberty Trucking Company, Extension — General Commodities*, (130 M. C. C. 243 [1978]).
67. 1 M. C. C. 190 (1936).
68. 131 M. C. C. 574 (1979).
69. Senate Committee on Commerce, Science, and Transportation, *Economic Regulation of the Trucking Industry,* 53.
70. Richard E. Cohen, "The Kennedy Staff — Putting the Senator Ahead," *National Journal* 15 (Dec. 15, 1979): 1880–83.
71. "Carter Names Antitrust Review Panel," *National Journal* 12 (Dec. 12, 1977): 1942.
72. "Kennedy Calls for End to Trucker's Exemption," *National Journal* 11 (Jan. 27, 1979): 153.
73. Interstate Commerce Commission, *Annual Report* (1978): 48.
74. Alexis, "The Political Economy of Federal Regulation of Surface Transportation," 126.
75. John W. Kingdon, *Agendas, Alternatives, and Public Policies* (Boston: Little, Brown, 1983), 25.
76. Senate Committee on Commerce, Science, and Transportation, *Economic Regulation of the Trucking Industry,* 80–81.
77. Ibid., 119.
78. Alexis, "The Political Economy of Federal Regulation of Surface Transportation," 127.
79. Frendreis and Waterman, "PAC Contributions and Legislative Behavior," 404.
80. Perry, *Deregulation and the Decline of the Unionized Trucking Industry,* ch. 6.
81. "Kennedy Yields on Trucking Jurisdiction," *National Journal,* March 31, 1979: 536.
82. Derthick and Quirk, *The Politics of Deregulation,* 114–15.
83. Interstate Commerce Commission, *Initial Report of the Motor Carrier Task Force* (Washington, D.C.: Government Printing Office, 1979), 36.
84. Senate Committee on Commerce, Science, and Transportation, *Report Together with Additional Minority Views on the Senate Committee on Commerce, Science, and Transportation,* 96th Cong., 2nd sess., 1980, 2.
85. Interstate Commerce Commission, *Annual Report* (Washington, D.C.: Government Printing Office, 1980 [1981]), 45.
86. 133 M. C. C. 941 (1980).
87. See Senate Committee on Commerce, Science, and Transportation, *Oversight of the Motor Carrier Act of 1980,* 97th Cong., 1st sess.,

1981; House Subcommittee on Surface Transportation of the Committee on Public Works and Transportation, 97th Cong., 1st sess., 1981.

Chapter 5

1. Murray L. Weidenbaum, "Free the Fortune Five Hundred," in *Taking Sides: Clashing Views of Controversial Issues,* ed. Theodore D. Goldfard (Guilford, Conn.: Dushkin, 1983).
2. J. Clarence Davies III, *The Politics of Pollution* (New York: Bobbs-Merrill, 1970), 38–43.
3. Ibid., ch. 2.
4. Hazel Erskine, "The Polls: Pollution and Its Costs," *Public Opinion Quarterly* 36: 121–23.
5. Charles O. Jones, *Clear Air: The Policies and Politics of Pollution Control* (Pittsburgh: Univ. of Pittsburgh Press, 1975), 175.
6. Ibid., 238.
7. Ackerman and Hassler have suggested that a New Deal–style regulatory commission would have better served the environmental movement than the independent EPA. First, under a commission form, it would have been "difficult for a momentary national impulse to affect agency policy." This would be the case because commissioners are more isolated from the impact of public opinion than is the administrator of the EPA. Second, a commission is a body of experts who would be less open to judicial intervention. Although the courts would have jurisdiction to intercede, they would be less likely to do so than they have under the liberal standing provisions of the Clear Air Act. Bruce A. Ackerman and William T. Hassler, *Clean Coal/Dirty Air* (New Haven, Conn.: Yale Univ. Press, 1981), 6.
8. Alfred Marcus, "Environmental Protection Agency," in *The Politics of Regulation*, ed. James Q. Wilson (New York: Basic Books, 1980), 267.
9. Throughout the remainder of this book Anne Gorsuch Burford will be referred to as simply Anne Burford, although she did not take this name until late in her tenure as administrator of the Environmental Protection Agency.
10. Walter A. Rosenbaum, *Environmental Politics and Policy* (Washington, D.C.: Congressional Quarterly, 1985), 96.
11. Prior to Ronald Reagan, all presidents, at least publicly, acknowledged support for the goals of the EPA. Reagan was the first president to suggest an entirely new EPA agenda, though previous presidents had clearly had major policy disagreements with the agency.

12. The fact that EPA has so many functional responsibilities tends to limit the ability of any one individual to effectively control the EPA. Since 1970, when the EPA was established, Congress made the agency responsibile for environmental protection over a wide number of new policy areas. Congress enacted the Clean Water Act, the Clean Air Act, the Noise Control Act, the Safe Drinking Water Act, the Resource Conservation and Recovery Act, the Toxic Substances Control Act, the Marine Protection, Research, and Sanctuaries Act, the Federal Insecticide, Fungicide, and Rodenticide Act, and the Comprehensive Environmental Response, Compensation, and Liability Act. Each of these acts increased the workload of the agency. Yet, while expanding EPA's role, Congress did not see fit to adequately increase the agency's level of funding or employees.

13. R. Shep Melnick, *Regulation and the Courts: The Case of the Clean Air Act* (Washington, D.C.: Brookings, 1983), chs. 5 and 6.

14. Ackerman and Hassler, *Clean Coal/Dirty Air.*

15. Robert F. Durant, Michael R. Fitzgerald, and Larry W. Thomas, "When Government Regulates Itself: The EPA/TVA Air Pollution Control Experience," *Public Administration Review* 43 (1983): 209–19; Stephen J. Rechichar and Michael R. Fitzgerald, *The Consequences of Administrative Decision: TVA's Economic Development Mission and Intragovernmental Regulation* (Knoxville: Bureau of Public Administration, Univ. of Tennessee, 1983).

16. Ann O'M. Bowman, "Intergovernmental and Intersectoral Tensions in Environmental Policy Implementation," *Policy Studies Review* 4 (1984): 230–44; Ann O'M. Bowman, "Hazardous Waste Cleanup and Superfund Implementation in the Southeast," *Policy Studies Journal* 14 (1985): 100–10.

17. Melnick, *Regulation and the Courts,* 34–35.

18. Fisher, *Presidential Spending Power,* 184–92.

19. Marcus, "Environmental Protection Agency," 286–90.

20. Edward J. Burger, *Science at the White House: A Political Liability* (Baltimore: John Hopkins Univ. Press, 1980), 91–94.

21. Marcus, "Environmental Protection Agency," 286–90.

22. Quoted in Melnick, *Regulation and the Courts,* 34.

23. Rosenbaum, *Environmental Politics and Policy,* 10.

24. Ibid., 166–67.

25. Executive Order #12044, Fed. Reg. 43 (March 24, 1977): 12661–65.

26. Susan J. Tolchin and Martin Tolchin, *Dismantling America: The Rush to Deregulate 2* (New York: Oxford Univ. Press, 1983), ch. 2; Edward Paul Fuchs, "The Politics of Economic Efficiency: Regulatory Reform During the Carter Presidency," paper presented at the

annual meeting of the Southwest Social Science Association, San Antonio, Texas, March 1986; Fuchs, *Presidents, Management, and Regulation.*

27. Fuchs, *Presidents, Management, and Regulation*, ch. 3.
28. Burt Schorr and Andy Pasztor, "Reaganites Make Sure That the Bureaucracy Toes the Line on Policy," *Wall Street Journal*, Feb. 10, 1982, 1, 25.
29. Senate Committee on Environment and Public Works, *Nominations of Anne M. Gorsuch and John W. Hernandez, Jr.*, 97th Cong., 1st sess., 1981, 34.
30. Anne M. Burford and John Greenya, *Are You Tough Enough?: An Insider's View of Washington Politics* (New York: McGraw-Hill, 1986), 7.
31. *Nominations of Anne M. Gorsuch and John W. Hernandez, Jr.*, 281.
32. Jonathan Lash, Katherine Gillman, and David Sheridan, *A Season of Spoils: The Reagan Administration's Attack on the Environment* (New York: Pantheon, 1984), 131–32.
33. Ibid., 33–36.
34. Senate Committee on Environment and Public Works, *Nominations of John P. Horton and Kathleen M. Bennett*, 97th Cong., 1st sess., 1981, 3–9.
35. Norman J. Vig, "The President and the Environment: Revolution or Retreat," in *Environmental Policy in the 1980's: Reagan's New Agenda*, ed. Norman J. Vig and Michael E. Kraft (Washington, D.C.: Congressional Quarterly), 87.
36. Lash, Gillman, and Sheridan, *A Season of Spoils,* 62–66.
37. Burford and Greenya, *Are You Tough Enough?*, 111–13.
38. Senate Committee on Environment and Public Works, *Nominations of Frederick A. Eidsness, Jr. and Rita M. Lavelle*, 97th Cong., 2nd sess., 1982, 71.
39. Lash, Gillman, and Sheridan, *A Season of Spoils,* 94.
40. Ibid., 83.
41. Nathan, *The Administrative Presidency.*
42. Chester A. Newland, "The Reagan Presidency: Limited Government and Political Administration," *Public Administration Review* 43 (1983): 1–21.
43. Nolan J. Argyle and Ryan J. Barilleaux, "Past Failures and Future Prescriptions for Presidential Management Reform," *Presidential Studies Quarterly* 16 (1986): 730.
44. Lash, Gillman, and Sheridan, *A Season of Spoils*, 37.
45. Ibid., 37.

46. J. Clarence Davies, "Environmental Institutions and the Reagan Administration," in *Environmental Policy in the 1980s*, ed. Vig and Kraft, 148.

47. Rosenbaum, *Environmental Politics and Policy*, 55.

48. Lash, Gillman, and Sheridan, *A Season of Spoils*, 60.

49. The Reagan administration also fired almost all of the professional staff of the Council on Environmental Quality (CEQ). Reagan then named a number of loyalists to the CEQ, such as its chairman, A. Alan Hill, and Ernest Minor. Under this new leadership the CEQ recommended the use of cost-benefit analysis, a reliance on the free market rather than traditional regulation, and a sorting out of environmental functions to the state governments. By appointing like-minded conservatives to the CEQ, Reagan removed a source of independent advice that could have presented alternative policy approaches to the president. Clearly, Reagan did not want to hear this alternative viewpoint. See Council on Environmental Quality, *Environmental Quality 1981*, ch. 1, and *Environmental Quality 1982*, 3–4.

50. Davies, "Environmental Institutions and the Reagan Administration," 146.

51. Stuart Taylor, Jr., "Ex-EPA Aide Says He Drew Up 'Pro and Con' Lists on Personnel," *New York Times*, March 17, 1983: B14; Eliot Marshall, "Hit List at EPA?" *Science* 219 (1983): 1303, and "Hit Lists Claim a Victim at EPA," *Science* 220 (1983): 38.

52. Burford and Greenya, *Are You Tough Enough?*, ch. 6.

53. Robert V. Bartlett, "The Budgetary Process and Environmental Policy," in *Environmental Policy in the 1980s*, ed. Vig and Kraft, 124–41.

54. The source for these figures is the Executive Office of the President, Office of Management and Budget, *The Budget of the United States Government*, Fiscal Years 1983–1986.

55. Senate Subcommittee on Toxic Substances and Environmental Oversight of the Committee on Environment and Public Works, *Reauthorizations*, 97th Cong., 1st sess., 1981, 13–16.

56. House Committee on Post Office and Civil Service, *Impact of Budget Cuts on Federal Statistical Programs*, 97th Cong., 2nd sess., 1982.

57. Wood, "Bureaucrats, Principals, and Responsiveness"; and "Reagan's Environmental Policy and Federal Clean Air Enforcement Activities."

58. Senate Committee on Environment and Public Works, *Fiscal Year 1983 Budget Review*, 97th Cong., 2nd sess., 1982, 51.

59. Ibid., 52.

60. Lash, Gillman, and Sheridan, *A Season of Spoils*, 47.

61. Conservation Foundation, *State of the Environment: An Assessment*

at Mid-Decade (Washington, D.C.: Conservation Foundation, 1984), 36.

62. *Fiscal Year 1983 Budget Review*, 138; improving relations with the states was meant to indicate that the EPA was reducing program requirements on the states. Simplifying relations with the regulated community meant more negotiated settlements and less direct enforcement to achieve compliance. Eliminating duplication meant that rules and regulations would be simplified. It also meant that research and development would be cut back. Pursuing regulatory reform meant increasing the agency's operating efficiency.

63. Ibid., 143. Burford did meet at the White House with Edwin Meese, James Baker, and David Stockman in an attempt to get some of the deep reductions in the research and development budget reinstated. At the meeting Meese defended the cuts by arguing that "if we give you all the money, all you'll do is go out and find more problems that need to be solved." Burford and Greenya, *Are You Tough Enough?*, 80.

64. Quoted in Robert W. Crandall, "The Environment," *Regulation* 6 (1982): 29.

65. Burford and Greenya, *Are You Tough Enough?* 93.

66. Wood, "Bureaucrats, Principals, and Responsiveness."

67. Davies, "Environmental Institutions and the Reagan Administration," 148.

68. Ibid., 149.

69. Walker, *Toward a Functioning Federalism*.

70. Michael E. Kraft, Bruce B. Clary, and Richard J. Tobin, "The Impact of New Federalism on State Environmental Policy: The Midwestern Great Lakes States," paper presented at the annual meeting of the Southwest Social Science Association, San Antonio, Texas, March 1986, 19.

71. Conservation Foundation, *State of the Environment*, 456. The delegation of program implementation to the states was one of the major cost-saving recommendations of the President's Private Sector Survey on Cost Control (better known as the Grace Commission), such as delegation of responsibility for the implementation of the construction grant program. The Commission also recommended the consolidation of categorical grants (such as grants-in-aid to the states). *President's Private Sector Survey on Cost Control: Report on the Environmental Protection Agency, the Small Business Administration and the Federal Emergency Management Agency* (1983), 14–15.

72. *Fiscal Year 1983 Budget Review*, 399.

73. Conservation Foundation, *State of the Environment*, 435.

74. Ibid., 424, 435.
75. Kraft, Clary, and Tobin, "The Impact of New Federalism on State Environmental Policy: The Midwestern Great Lakes States," 29.
76. Wood, "Reagan's Environmental Policy and Federal Clean Air Enforcement Activities."
77. Ann O'M. Bowman, "Hazardous Waste Management: An Emerging Policy Within an Emerging Federalism," *Publius* 15 (1985): 131–44.
78. James P. Lester, "New Federalism and Environmental Policy," *Publius* 16 (1986): 149–65.
79. A. Janell Anderson, "Tipping the Lid on Pandora's Box: Decentralization and Deregulation," in *Regulatory Reform Reconsidered,* ed. Gregory A. Daneke and David J. Lemak (Boulder: Westview Press, 1985); Rochelle L. Stanfield, "Resolving Disputes," *National Journal,* Nov. 15, 1986: 2767.
80. 46 Fed. Reg. (Feb. 19, 1981: 13193–98).
81. Burford and Greenya, *Are You Tough Enough?* 121.
82. Lash, Gillman, and Sheridan, *A Season of Spoils,* 103.
83. Robert L. Green, "Water Pollution Controls for the Iron and Steel Industry," in *Benefit-Cost Analyses of Social Regulation: Case Studies form the Council on Wage and Price Stability,* ed. James C. Miller III and Bruce Yandle (Washington, D.C.: American Enterprise Institute, 1979), 131–45; Roger J. Mallet, "Emission Standards for New Motorcycles," in *Benefit-Cost Analyses of Social Regulation,* ed. Miller and Yandle, 113–130; Talbot Page, Robert Harris, and Judith Bruser, "Waterborne Carcinogens: An Economist's View," in *The Scientific Basis of Health and Safety Regulation,* ed. Robert W. Crandall and Lester B. Lave (Washington, D.C.: Brookings Institution, 1981), 197–228.
84. Victor J. Kimm, Arnold M. Kuzmack, and David W. Schnare, "Waterborne Carcinogens: A Regulator's View," in *The Scientific Basis of Health and Safety Regulation*, ed. Crandall and Lave, 241–42.
85. Fuchs, *Presidents, Management, and Regulation*, ch. 4.
86. Douglas M. Costle, "Environmental Regulation and Regulatory Reform," *Washington Law Review* 57 (1982): 418.
87. Fuchs, *Presidents, Management, and Regulation*.
88. Quoted in Lash, Gillman, and Sheridan, *A Season of Spoils,* 25.
89. Ibid., 26.
90. For different interpretations regarding the effect of the executive order see the following: Fuchs, *Presidents, Management, and Regulation*; Robert A. Shanley, "Presidential Executive Orders and Environmental Policy," *Presidential Studies Quarterly* 12 (1983): 405–16; V. Kerry Smith, *Environmental Policy under Reagan's Executive Order* (Chapel Hill: Univ. of North Carolina Press, 1984).

91. In 1985, of the proposed rules submitted by agencies to the Office of Information and Regulatory Affairs (OIRA), which reviews rules under the provisions of Executive Order #12291 to determine if benefits outweigh the costs, 71 percent were found to be "consistent with the President's regulatory principles without change," 23 percent were consistent with change by the agency, and just over 3 percent were withdrawn. Only 1.5 percent were returned to the agency because they were inconsistent with the president's principles. James C. Miller III, Prepared Written Statement of the Director of the Office of Management and Budget before the Senate Subcommittee on Intergovernmental Relations of the Committee on Governmental Affairs (Jan. 28, 1986), 6–7.
92. 50 Fed. Reg. 1036.
93. Miller testimony before Senate Subcommittee on Intergovernmental Relations, 33.
94. Office of Management and Budget, *Regulatory Program of the United States Government, April 1, 1987–March 31, 1988* (Washington, D.C.: Government Printing Office, 1987), L.
95. Conservation Foundation, *State of the Environment*, 29–31.
96. Sierra Club, *Sierra Club Foundation 1984–1985 Annual Report* (San Francisco: Sierra Club, 1985), 25.
97. Data were supplied by the Federal Election Commission.
98. Senate Subcommittee on Environmental Pollution of the Committee on Environment and Public Works, *American Attitudes Toward Clean Air,* 97th Cong., 2nd sess., 1982, 5.
99. Ibid., 3.
100. Lester W. Milbrath, *Environmentalists: Vanguard for a New Society* (New York: State Univ. of New York Press, 1984); Robert Cameron Mitchell, "Public Opinion and Environmental Politics in the 1970's and 1980's," in *Environmental Policy in the 1980's,* ed. Vig and Kraft, 51–74; Laura M. Lake, "The Environmental Mandate: Activists and the Electorate," *Political Science Quarterly* 98 (1983): 215–33.
101. Everett Carll Ladd, "Clearing the Air: Public Opinion and Public Policy on the Environment," *Public Opinion* 5 (1982): 16–20.
102. One criticism of President Reagan was that he did not understand the issues; particularly environmental issues. Still, of those respondents who called for an increased budget, when asked the question, "Is President Reagan knowledgeable?", 80 percent answered either "a great deal" or "somewhat."
103. Henry C. Kenski and Margaret Corgan Kenski, "Congress Against the President: The Struggle Over the Environment," in *Environmental Policy in the 1980's,* ed. Vig and Kraft, 97–120.

104. Conservation Foundation, *State of the Environment,* 449.
105. Helen M. Ingram and Dean E. Mann, "Preserving the Clean Water Act: The Appearance of Environmental Victory," in *Environmental Policy in the 1980's,* ed. Vig and Kraft, 251–71.
106. Stephen Cohen, "Defusing the Toxic Time Bomb: Federal Hazardous Waste Programs," in *Environmental Policy in the 1980's,* ed. Vig and Kraft, 273–91; Richard J. Tobin, "Revising the Clean Air Act: Legislative Failure and Administrative Success," in *Environmental Policy in the 1980s,* ed. Vig and Kraft, 227–49.
107. Michael E. Kraft and Norman J. Vig, "Epilogue," in *Environmental Policy in the 1980s,* ed. Vig and Kraft, 359–74.
108. General Accounting Office, *Federal Employees: Trends in Career and Noncareer Employee Appointments in the Executive Branch* (Washington, D.C.: Government Printing Office, 1987), 28.
109. Conservation Foundation, *State of the Environment,* 8.
110. Eugene Bardach and Robert A. Kagan, *Going by The Book: The Problem of Regulatory Unreasonableness* (Philadelphia: Temple Univ. Press, 1981).
111. Two studies comparing regulation in the United States and Sweden also provide support for greater voluntary cooperation and less reliance on strict enforcement. Lundqvist, in his comparative study of environmental regulation, and Kelman, in his analysis of occupational safety and health regulation, found that the United States government is much more reliant on strict enforcement of standards than is Sweden. In Sweden there is an environment of cooperation between business and government in setting standards. This corporatist relationship has been recommended as a possible alternative to present-day U.S. enforcement policy. Lennart J. Lundqvist, *The Hare and the Tortoise: Clean Air Policies in the United States and Sweden* (Ann Arbor: Univ. of Michigan Press, 1980); Stephen Kelman, *Regulating America, Regulating Sweden: A Comparative Study of Occupational Safety and Health Policy* (Cambridge, Mass.: MIT Press, 1981).
112. Under Burford's successors, the EPA took a more balanced approach to the issue of negotiation. Although the process has not resulted in uniform agreement that negotiation is preferable to the more adversary regulatory process that had existed, environmental and industry groups have conceded that negotiation does reduce the costs of litigation and expedite the formulation of new regulations. Stanfield, "Resolving Disputes."
113. Senate Committee on Environment and Public Works, *Nominations of Matthew A. Novick and John A. Todhunter,* 97th Cong., 1st sess., 16–17, 33–34.

114. Senate Subcommittee on Toxic Substances and Environment of the Committee on Environment and Public Works, *Implementation of the Toxic Substances Control Act,* 97th Cong., 2nd sess., 1982.

115. Walker, *Toward a Functioning Federalism.*

Chapter 6

1. Steven Ebbin and Raphael Kasper, *Citizen Groups and the Nuclear Power Controversy* (Boston: MIT Press, 1974).

2. John E. Chubb, *Interest Groups and the Bureaucracy: The Politics of Energy* (Stanford, Calif.: Stanford Univ. Press, 1983), 95.

3. Walter C. Patterson, *Nuclear Power.* (New York: Penguin Books, 1983), ch. 6.

4. William R. Freudenburg and Rodney K. Baxter, "Nuclear Reactions: Public Attitudes and Policies Toward Nuclear Power," *Policy Studies Review* 5 (1985): 99.

5. According to former Commissioner Victor Gilinsky, the NRC considers the House Appropriations Committee and its Subcommittee on Public Works as "the legitimate source of power." The Committee's chairman during the early 1980s, Thomas Bevill, strongly advocated speeding up the licensing process. According to former commissioner Peter Bradford, the NRC's emphasis on speeding up licensing was "not so much a product of Reagan but of Tom Bevill." Tolchin and Tolchin, *Dismantling America,* 209.

6. U.S. Nuclear Regulatory Commission, *Staff Report to the President's Commission on the Accident at Three Mile Island* (1979), 61; U.S. Nuclear Regulatory Commission, *Three Mile Island: A Report to the Commissioners and to the Public* (1980); *The President's Commission on the Accident at Three Mile Island: The Need for Change — The Legacy of TMI* (1979), 21–22.

7. *The President's Private Sector Survey on Cost Control: Report on the Department of Energy, the Federal Energy Regulatory Commission, and the Nuclear Regulatory Commission* (1983), 155.

8. Ibid., 155.

9. Ibid., 157.

10. Chubb, *Interest Groups and the Bureaucracy,* 96.

11. Michael Golay, "How Prometheus Came To Be Bound," *Technology Review* 84 (1980): 29–39.

12. Carter had one nominee to the NRC, Kent F. Hanson, rejected by the Senate Environment and Public Works Committee in 1977 because of committee reservations that he lacked experience in dealing with the types of issues that the Commission is regularly asked to

address. Another individual that the Carter administration was considering for a possible appointment to the NRC in 1978, Goldie Watkins, provoked strident congressional opposition largely because she was perceived as too closely aligned with Energy Secretary James Schlesinger and shared his pro–nuclear power viewpoint. These examples demonstrate the active role that Congress played in constraining presidential power. They also suggest that Carter did not put the same effort into selecting the members of the NRC that he did with the ICC, where commitment to deregulation and prior experience were key criteria. See Mackenzie, *The Politics of Presidential Appointments*, 114, 226–27.

13. Victor Gilinsky, "Nuclear Reactors and Nuclear Bombs," *Chemical and Engineering News* 59 (1981): 87–90, and "Full Speed Ahead for Nuclear Power?" *Technology Review* 85 (1982): 10–11, 18.

14. Carter was an ardent opponent of nuclear fission (rather than nuclear fusion) as a means of generating nuclear power. As such, he opposed the construction of the Clinch River Breeder Reactor, an experimental (prototype) fission reactor. Although Carter several times attempted to convince Congress to deny funding for the reactor, he was unsuccessful. Later, when Ronald Reagan proposed a continuation of the project, the mood in Congress had changed. In late 1983, Congress voted to deny further funding for the reactor, thus bringing the project to an end. James E. Katz, "The Uses of Scientific Evidence in Congressional Policymaking: The Clinch River Breeder Reactor," *Science, Technology, and Human Values* 9 (1984): 51–62; Stephen R. Lefevre, "Trials and Termination: President Carter and the Breeder Reactor Program," *Presidential Studies Quarterly* 15 (1985): 330–42; Rosenbaum, *Environmental Politics and Policy*, 234.

15. Largely due to influence from the Carter administration, the NRC commenced a more open policy with environmental groups in 1977. The Sierra Club, the Friends of the Earth, and Critical Mass received prenotification of impending proceedings and decisions. The Sierra Club and the Friends of the Earth also had sporadic meetings with NRC commissioners to discuss policy questions. Chubb, *Interest Groups and the Bureaucracy*, 108–9.

16. Marshall R. Goodman and Margaret T. Wrightson, "Nuclear Energy and the Politics of Reform," paper presented at the annual meeting of the Midwest Political Science Association, Chicago, April 1986, 12.

17. William J. Lanouette, "Reagan's NRC—Seeking to Streamline the Regulation of Nuclear Energy." *National Journal*, Aug. 1, 1981: 1379.

18. John Reynolds and Leonard Champney, "Streams of Policy Change and the Altered Currents of Nuclear Regulation," paper presented

at the annual meeting of the Midwest Political Science Association, Chicago, April, 1986, 35.

19. Goodman and Wrightson, "Nuclear Energy and the Politics of Reform," 6.

20. Wendy Swallow, "Has the Freedom of Information Act Worked — Or Has It Worked Too Well?" *National Journal*, (Aug. 15, 1981): 1471.

21. Rosenbaum, *Environmental Politics and Policy*, 233; Freudenburg and Baxter, "Nuclear Reactions: Public Attitudes and Policies Toward Nuclear Power."

22. Senate Committee on Environment and Public Works, *Nominations of Nunzio J. Palladino and Thomas M. Roberts,* 97th Cong., 1st sess., 1981, 46.

23. Lanouette, "Reagan's NRC — Seeking to Streamline the Regulation of Nuclear Energy," 1381.

24. Senate Committee on Environment and Public Works, *Nominations of Nunzio J. Palladino and Thomas M. Roberts,* 10–11, 36–39.

25. Ibid., 34.

26. Ibid., 33.

27. William J. Lanouette, "Reagan's NRC Chairman: Nuclear Power Could Still Be a Viable Option," *National Journal* 15 (1983): 1457.

28. Lanouette, "Reagan's NRC — Seeking to Streamline the Regulation of Nuclear Energy," 1380.

29. Senate Committee on Environment and Public Works, *Nominations of James K. Asselstine,* 97th Cong., 2nd sess., 1982.

30. Rosenbaum, *Environmental Politics and Policy*, 225.

31. Stockman, *The Triumph of Politics,* 144–46.

32. The source for these figures is *The Budget of the United States Government,* Fiscal Years 1983–1986.

33. Regina S. Axelrod, "Energy Policy: Changing the Rules of the Game." in *Environmental Policy in the 1980s*, ed. Vig and Kraft, 209.

34. Richard K. Lester, "Is the Nuclear Industry Worth Saving?" *Technology Review* 85 (1982): 39–47.

35. U.S. Congress, *Fiscal Year 1983 Budget Review,* 32.

36. Senate Committee on Environment and Public Works, *Nominations of Nunzio J. Palladino and Thomas M. Roberts,* 26.

37. U.S. Nuclear Regulatory Commission, *NRC 1986 Annual Report* (1986); 8.

38. U.S. Congress, *Fiscal Year 1983 Budget Review,* 72.

39. Ibid., 73.

40. William B. Cottrell, "Recent Developments: General Administrative Activity," *Nuclear Safety* 23, no. 1 (March/April 1982): 104.

41. Goodman and Wrightson, "Nuclear Energy and the Politics of Reform," 26.

42. Ibid.
43. William B. Cottrell, "Recent Developments: General Administrative Activity," *Nuclear Safety* 23, no. 4 (July/Aug. 1982): 479–80.
44. Goodman and Wrightson, "Nuclear Energy and the Politics of Reform," 27.
45. "The Nuclear Bargain." *Newsweek*, May 12, 1986: 49.
46. U.S. Nuclear Regulatory Commission, *NRC 1986 Annual Report*, 8–10.
47. Ibid., 10.
48. William B. Cottrell, "Recent Developments: General Administrative Activity," *Nuclear Safety* 24, no. 4 (July/Aug. 1983): 561–62.
49. Lanouette, "Reagan's NRC—Seeking to Streamline the Regulation of Nuclear Energy," 1381.
50. "Statement Announcing a Series of Policy Initiatives on Nuclear Energy," in *Public Papers of the Presidents: Ronald Reagan, 1981* (1982), 903–4.
51. Ibid., 904.
52. William B. Cottrell, "Recent Developments: General Administrative Activity," *Nuclear Safety* 23, no. 2 (March/April 1982): 224.
53. The year after Reagan's statement, Congress passed the Nuclear Waste Policy Act of 1982. This was an unsuccessful attempt to provide for the safe disposal of some 12,000 metric tons of nuclear waste (which will remain active for thousands of years). The act made provisions for the selection of two disposal sites, one to open in the West in 1998 and one to open in the East several years later. A firestorm of criticism erupted when the Department of Energy, which was given responsibility for selecting the two sites, announced in May 1986 that it would select a site in the West (in Texas, Nevada, or Washington), but would indefinitely postpone the search for a site in the East. The resulting conflict promised further delay in the selection of a site in either region. In 1987 Congress updated the Nuclear Waste Policy Act in an attempt to get the program back on track. Rochelle L. Stanfield, "Nuclear Waste Politics," *National Journal* 18 (1986): 2371–73.
54. Marshall R. Goodman and Frederic P. Andes, "The Politics of Regulatory Reform and the Future Direction of Nuclear Energy Policy," *Policy Studies Journal* 5 (1985): 115.
55. Goodman and Wrightson, "Nuclear Energy and the Politics of Reform."
56. Ibid., 21.
57. 46 Fed. Reg. (May 28, 1981): 28630.
58. Tolchin and Tolchin, *Dismantling America,* 224.
59. 46 Fed. Reg. (June 8, 1981): 30329.

60. Goodman and Wrightson, "Nuclear Energy and the Politics of Reform," 26.

61. Tolchin and Tolchin, *Dismantling America,* 223–35.

62. U.S. Nuclear Regulatory Commission, *Staff Report to the President's Commission on the Accident at Three Mile Island* (1979), and *Three Mile Island: A Report to the Commissioners and to the Public* (1980); *The President's Commission on the Accident at Three Mile Island: The Need for Change—The Legacy of TMI* (1979).

63. Quoted in Tolchin and Tolchin, *Dismantling America,* 200.

64. "Nuclear Decommissioning: Revenge of the Tortoise," *Regulation* (July/Aug. 1985), 10–11, 52.

65. Axelrod, "Energy Policy," 210.

66. E. G. Silver, "Recent Developments: General Administrative Activity," *Nuclear Safety* 25, no. 5 (Sept./Oct. 1984): 723.

67. Lester, "Is the Nuclear Industry Worth Saving?", 39.

68. "The Nuclear Bargain," *Newsweek,* May 12, 1986: 44.

69. "At a Glance," *National Journal,* Jan. 28, 1984: 188.

70. Peter Bernstein, "A Nuclear Fiasco Shakes the Bond Market," *Fortune,* Feb. 22, 1982: 100–18.

71. "At a Glance." *National Journal,* March 2, 1985: 504.

72. U.S. Department of Energy, *1983 Survey of Nuclear Power Plant Construction Costs* (Washington, D.C.: Government Printing Office, 1984).

73. Office of Technology Assessment, *Nuclear Power in an Age of Uncertainty* (1984); Steve Thomas and John Surrey, "What Makes Nuclear Power Plants Break Down?" *Technology Review* 83 (1981): 57–66.

74. Axelrod, "Energy Policy," 210.

75. "The Chernobyl Syndrome," *Newsweek,* May 12, 1986: 30.

76. Lester, "Is the Nuclear Industry Worth Saving?"

77. Quoted in William B. Cottrell, "Recent Developments: General Administrative Activity," *Nuclear Safety* 23, no. 5 (Sept./Oct. 1982): 610.

78. Tolchin and Tolchin, *Dismantling America,* 235.

Chapter 7

1. Nathan, *The Administrative Presidency,* 10.

2. Samuel Kernell has argued that the political conditions which allowed presidents to employ a bargaining approach have changed dramatically in recent years. Political parties have experienced declining influence. Congressional leadership is much more dispersed. Special interest groups have created new demands on politicians, especially with the development of powerful single-issue groups.

Election reforms have produced independent candidates who, once elected, are more comfortable using rhetoric to achieve their goals. Because of all of these factors, plus advances in communications and technology, presidents have employed a strategy of going public, rather than bargaining. Although Kernell's argument is meant to apply to presidential-congressional relations, the question could be raised: Is the strategy of going public applicable to presidential-administrative relations? The answer is no. It is much easier for bureaucrats to go behind the scenes to avoid presidential grandstanding than it is for members of Congress. After all, much of the business of the bureaucracy is not done in public. This fact would thus diminish the utility of a going-public strategy. Also, a strategy of going public against unelected, career bureaucrats would clearly not be so successful as a strategy of going public against elected members of Congress, because there would be no threat of electoral sanction against bureaucrats. Finally, Congress is an easily identifiable institution. On the other hand, the bureaucracy is a seamless web. Criticisms against the bureaucracy in general would have to apply to everything from the local police department to the giant Department of Defense. Although there may be some limited circumstances under which a strategy of going public might be useful as a means of influencing administrative behavior, in most instances it would not promote presidential influence. Samuel Kernell, *Going Public: New Strategies of Presidential Leadership* (Washington, D.C.: Congressional Quarterly, 1986).

3. This finding is consistent with a recommendation of the National Academy of Public Administration (NAPA) that "to exercise effective political management, Presidents need a reliable base of nonpartisan, unbiased advice. The institutional staffs reporting to the President should have a highly professional ability to supply objective and factual information." National Academy of Public Administration, *A Presidency for the Eighties* (Washington, D.C.: National Academy of Public Administration, 1980), 4.

4. Neustadt, *Presidential Power.*

5. Ibid., 16–25.

6. Heclo, *A Government of Strangers*; Herbert Kaufman, *The Administrative Behavior of Federal Bureau Chiefs* (Washington, D.C.: Brookings Institution, 1981).

7. Heclo, *A Government of Strangers:* Lynn, *Managing the Public's Business.*

8. Dwight A. Ink, "The President As Manager," in *Analyzing the Presidency,* ed. Robert E. DeClerico (Guilford, Conn.: Duskin, 1985), 138.

References

Books and Articles

Aberback, Joel D., and Bert A. Rockman. "Clashing Beliefs Within the Executive Branch: The Nixon Administration Bureaucracy." *American Political Science Review* 70 (June 1976): 456–68.

Ackerman Bruce A., and William T. Hassler. *Clean Coal/Dirty Air: or How the Clear Air Act Became a Multibillion-Dollar Bail-Out for High-Sulfur Coal Producers and What Should Be Done About It.* New Haven, Conn.: Yale Univ. Press, 1981.

Alexis, Marcus. "The Political Economy of Federal Regulation of Surface Transportation." In *The Political Economy of Deregulation: Interest Groups in the Regulatory Process,* ed. Roger C. Noll and Bruce M. Owen, 115–31. Washington, D.C.: American Enterprise Institute, 1983.

Allen, W. Bruce. *An Examination of the Unregulated Trucking Experience in New Jersey.* University of Pennsylvania under contract DOT-OS-70069. 1978.

American Trucking Associations. *The Case for Economic Regulation of the Motor Carrier Industry.* Washington, D.C.: American Trucking Associations, 1979.

———.*Small Town Blues.* Washington, D.C.: American Trucking Associations, 1976.

Anderson, A. Janell. "Tipping the Lie on Pandora's Box: Decentralization and Deregulation." In *Regulatory Reform Reconsidered,* ed. Gregory A. Daneke and David J. Lemak, 97–112. Boulder, Colo.: Westview, 1985.

Argyle, Nolan J., and Ryan J. Barilleaux. "Past Failures and Future Prescriptions for Presidential Management Reform." *Presidential Studies Quarterly* 16 (Fall 1986): 716–33.

Arnold, Peri E. *Making the Managerial Presidency: Comprehensive Reorganization Planning 1905–1980*. Princeton, N.J.: Princeton Univ. Press, 1986.

Arnold, R. Douglas. *Congress and the Bureaucracy: A Theory of Influence*. New Haven, Conn.: Yale Univ. Press, 1979.

Aron, Mark G. "Deregulation: The Peaceful Revolution." *Survey of Business* 4 (Summer 1981): 4–13.

Axelrod, Regina S. "Energy Policy: Changing the Rules of the Game." In *Environmental Policy in the 1980's: Reagan's New Agenda,* ed. Norman J. Vig and Michael E. Kraft, 203–25. Washington, D.C.: Congressional Quarterly Press, 1984.

Banks R. L., & Associates, Inc. *Economic Analysis and Regulatory Implications of Motor Carrier Service to Predominantly Small Communities*. Under Contract DOT-OS-50095. June 1976.

Baram, Michael S. "Cost-Benefit Analysis: An Inadequte Basis for Health, Safety, and Environmental Regulatory Decisionmaking." In the Administrative Conference of the United States. In *1979 Recommendations and Reports,* 377–435. Washington, D.C.: Government Printing Office, 1979.

Bardach, Eugene, and Robert A. Kagan. *Going by the Book: The Problem of Regulatory Unreasonableness*. Philadelphia: Temple Univ. Press, 1981.

Bartlett, Robert V. "The Budgetary Process and Environmental Policy." In *Environmental Policy in the 1980's: Reagan's New Agenda*, ed. Norman J. Vig and Michael E. Kraft. 121–41. Washington, D.C.: Congressional Quarterly Press, 1984.

Beck, Nathaniel. "Presidential Influence on the Federal Reserve in the 1970's." *American Journal of Political Science* 3, no. 26 (Aug. 1982): 415–45.

Benze, Maes G., Jr. "Presidential Reorganization as a Tactical Weapon: Putting Politics Back Into Administration." *Presidential Studies Quarterly* 15 (Winter 1985): 145–56.

Berman, Larry. *The Office of Management and Budget and the Presidency, 1921–1979*. Princeton, N.J.: Princeton Univ. Press, 1979.

———. "The Office of Management and Budget That Almost Wasn't." *Political Science Quarterly* 92 (Summer 1977): 281–303.

Bernard, Robert J. "The Truck in Perspective." *I.C.C. Practioner's Journal* 28 (Jan. 1961): 445–60.

Bernstein, Peter. "A Nuclear Fiasco Shakes The Bond Market." *Fortune,* Feb. 22, 1982, 100–18.

Best, James J. "Presidential Cabinet Appointments: 1953–1976." *Presidential Studies Quarterly* 11 (Winter 1981): 62–66.

Bibby, John F., and Roger H. Davidson. *On Capitol Hill: Studies in the Legislative Process*. Hinsdale, Ill.: Dryden Press, 1972.

Bonafede, Dom. "The White House Personnel Office from Roosevelt to Reagan." In *The In-and-Outers; Presidential Appointees and Transient Government in Washington,* ed. G. Calvin Mackenzie, 30–59. Baltimore: John Hopkins Univ. Press, 1987.

———. "White House Staffing: The Nixon-Ford Era." In *The Presidency: Reappraised,* ed. Thomas E. Cronin and Rexford G. Tugwell, 151–73. New York: Praeger, 1977.

Borlaug, Karen L., and Laurence T. Phillips. *Trucking Service in Six Small Michigan Communities.* U.S. Department of Transportation, Office of the Secretary, Office of Transportation Regulation. 1980.

Bowman, Ann O'M. "Hazardous Waste Cleanup and Superfund Implementation in the Southeast." *Policy Studies Journal* 14 (Sept. 1985): 100–10.

———. "Hazardous Waste Management: An Emerging Policy Within an Emerging Federalism." *Publius* 15 (Winter 1985): 131–44.

———. "Intergovernmental and Intersectoral Tensions in Environmental Policy Implementation." *Policy Studies Review* 4 (Nov. 1984): 230–44.

Brauer, Carl. "Tenure, Turnover, and Postgovernment Trends of Presidential Appointees." In *The In-and-Outers: Presidential Appointees and Transient Government in Washington,* ed. G. Calvin Mackensie, 174–94. Baltimore: John Hopkins Univ. Press, 1987.

Breen, Denis A., and Benjamin Allen. *Common Carrier Obligations and the Provisions of Freight Transport Service to Small Communities.* U.S. Department of Transportation. 1979.

Breyer, Stephen. *Regulation and Its Reform.* Cambridge, Mass.: Harvard Univ. Press, 1982.

Brigman, William E. "The Executive Branch and the Independent Regulatory Agencies." *Presidential Studies Quarterly* 11 (Spring 1981): 244–61.

Brown, Anthony E. *The Politics of Airline Deregulation.* Knoxville: Univ. of Tennessee Press, 1987.

Buchanan, Bruce. *The Presidential Experience: What the Office Does to the Man.* Englewood Cliffs, N.J.: Prentice-Hall, 1978.

Burford, Anne M., and John Greenya. *Are You Tough Enough?: An Insider's View of Washington Politics.* New York: McGraw-Hill, 1986.

Burger, Edward J. *Science at the White House: A Political Liability.* Baltimore: John Hopkins Univ. Press, 1980.

Burns, James MacGregor. *Presidential Government: The Crucible of Leadership.* Boston: Houghton Mifflin, 1965.

Campbell, Colin. *Managing the Presidency: Carter, Reagan, and the Search for Executive Harmony.* Pittsburgh: Univ. of Pittsburgh Press, 1986.

Cater, Douglass. *Power in Washington: A Critical Look at Today's Struggle to Govern In the Nation's Capitol.* New York: Random House, 1964.

Chubb, John E. *Interest Groups and the Bureaucracy: The Politics of Energy.* Stanford, Calif: Stanford Univ. Press, 1983.

Cohen, Jeffrey E. "On the Tenure of Appointive Political Executives: The American Cabinet, 1952–1984." *American Journal of Political Science* 30 (Aug. 1986): 507–16.

———. "Presidential Control of Independent Regulatory Commissions Through Appointment: The Case of the ICC." *Administration and Society* 17 (May 1985): 61–71.

Cohen, Richard E. "The Kennedy Staff—Putting the Senator Ahead." *National Journal* 15 (Dec. 1979): 1880–83.

———. "Will Carter be Able to Apply the Brakes to Trucking Regulation?" *National Journal* 9 (May 1979): 746–53.

Cohen, Stephen. "Defusing the Toxic Time Bomb: Federal Hazardous Waste Programs." In *Environmental Policy in the 1980's: Reagan's New Agenda*, ed. Norman J. Vig and Michael E. Kraft, 273–91. Washington, D.C.: Congressional Quarterly Press, 1984.

Cole, Richard L., and David A. Caputo. "Presidential Control of the Senior Executive Service: Assessing the Strategies of the Nixon Years." *American Political Science Review* 73 (June 1979): 399–413.

Conservation Foundation. *State of the Environment: An Assessment at Mid-Decade.* Washington, D.C.: Conservation Foundation, 1984.

Corwin, Edward S. *The President: Office and Powers.* New York: New York Univ. Press, 1957.

Costle, Douglas M. "Environmental Regulation and Regulatory Reform." *Washington Law Review* 57 (July 1982): 409–32.

Cottrell, William B. "Recent Developments: General Administrative Activity." *Nuclear Safety* 23, no. 1 (Jan./Feb. 1982: 97–106.

———. "Recent Developments: General Administrative Activity." *Nuclear Safety* 23, no. 2 (March/April 1982): 224–30.

———. "Recent Developments: General Administrative Activity." *Nuclear Safety* 23, no. 4 (July/Aug. 1982): 474–85.

———. "Recent Developments: General Administrative Activity." *Nuclear Safety* 23, no. 5 (Sept./Oct. 1982): 603–16.

———. "Recent Developments: General Administrative Activity." *Nuclear Safety* 24, no. 4 (July/Aug. 1983): 559–67.

Crandall, Robert W. "The Environment." *Regulation* 6 (Jan./Feb. 1982): 29–32.

Cronin, Thomas E. *The State of the Presidency.* Boston: Little, Brown, 1980.

Dahl, Robert A. *Who Governs?* New Haven, Conn.: Yale Univ. Press, 1961.

Davies, J. Clarence III. "Environmental Institutions and the Reagan Administration." In *Environmental Policy in the 1980's: Reagan's New Agenda,* ed. Norman J. Vig and Michael E. Kraft. 143–60. Washington, D.C.: Congressional Quarterly Press, 1984.

————. *The Politics of Pollution.* New York: Bobbs-Merrill, 1970.

Davis, J. W. *The National Executive Branch.* New York: Free Press, 1970.

DeClerico, Robert E. *The American President.* Englewood Cliffs, N.J.: Prentice-Hall, 1979.

Deering, Christopher J. "Damned If You Do and Damned If You Don't: The Senate's Role in the Appointments Process." In *The In-and-Outers: Presidential Appointees and Transient Government in Washington,* ed. G. Calvin Mackenzie, 100–19. Baltimore: John Hopkins Univ. Press, 1987.

Derthick, Martha, and Paul J. Quirk. *The Politics of Deregulation.* Washington, D.C.: Brookings Institution, 1985.

Destler, I. M. 1977. "National Security Advice to U.S. Presidents: Some Lessons from Thirty Years." *World Politics* 29, no. 2: (Summer) 143–76.

————. "National Security II: The Rise of the Assistant (1961–1981)." In *The Illusion of Presidential Government,* ed. Hugh Heclo and Lester M. Salamon, 263–85. Boulder, Colo.: Westview, 1981.

Dodd, Lawrence C., and Richard L. Schott. *Congress and the Administrative State.* New York: John Wiley, 1979.

Durant, Robert F., Michael R. Fitzgerald, and Larry W. Thomas. "When Government Regulates Itself: The EPA/TVA Air Pollution Control Experience." *Public Administration Review* 43 (May/June 1983): 209–19.

Ebbin, Steven, and Raphael Kasper. *Citizen Groups and the Nuclear Power Controversy.* Boston: MIT Press, 1974.

Edwards, George C., III. *Presidential Influence in Congress.* San Francisco: W. H. Freeman, 1980.

Ehrlichman, John. "How It All Began . . . By a Man Who Was There." *National Journal* (Dec. 13, 1975): 1690–91.

————. *Witness to Power: The Nixon Years.* New York: Simon and Schuster, 1982.

Emmerich, Herbert. *Federal Organization and Administrative Management.* University: Univ. of Alabama Press, 1971.

Erskine, Hazel. "The Polls: Pollution and Its Costs." *Public Opinion Quarterly* 36 (Spring 1972): 120–35.

Evans, Rowland Jr., and Robert D. Novak. *Nixon in the White House: The Frustration of Power.* New York: Random House, 1971.

Falk, Stanley L. "The National Security Council Under Truman, Eisenhower, and Kennedy." *Political Science Quarterly* 79 (1964): 403–34.

Farris, Martin. T. "The Case Against Deregulation in Transportation, Power, and Communications." *I.C.C. Practictioners' Journal* 45 (March/April 1978): 306–32.

Fellmeth, Robert. *The Interstate Commerce Omission: The Public Interest and the ICC.* New York: Grossman, 1970.

Fenno, Richard F. Jr. *The President's Cabinet.* New York: Vintage Books, 1959.

Finer, Herman. *The Presidency: Crisis and Regeneration.* Chicago: Univ. of Chicago Press, 1960.

Fisher, Linda L. "Appointments and Presidential Control: The Importance of Role." Paper presented at the annual meeting of the American Political Science Association, Washington, D.C., August 1986.

Fisher, Louis. 1986. "The Administrative State: What's Next After *Chadha* and *Bowsher*." Paper presented at the annual meeting of the American Political Science Association, Washington, D.C., August 1986.

————. *The Constitution Between Friends: Congress, the President, and the Law.* New York: St. Martin's, 1978.

————. *The Politics of Shared Power: Congress and the Executive.* Washington, D.C.: Congressional Quarterly Press, 1981.

————. *Presidential Spending Power.* Princeton, N.J.: Princeton Univ. Press, 1975.

Fisher, Louis, and Ronald C. Moe. "Presidential Reorganization: Is It Worth the Cost?" *Political Science Quarterly* 96 (Summer 1981): 301–18.

Ford, Gerald R. *A Time To Heal: The Autobiography of Gerald R. Ford.* New York: Harper and Row, 1979.

Fox, Douglas M., ed. "A Mini-Symposium: President Nixon's Proposals for Executive Reorganization." *Public Administration Review* 34 (Sept./Oct. 1974): 487–95.

Freeman, J. Leiper. 1965. *The Political Process: Executive Bureau-Legislative Committee Relations.* New York: Random House, 1965.

Frendreis, John P., and Richard W. Waterman. 1985. "PAC Contributions and Legislative Behavior: Senate Voting on Trucking Deregulation." *Social Science Quarterly* 66 (June 1985): 401–12.

Freudenburg, William R., and Rodney K. Baxter. "Nuclear Reactions: Public Attitudes and Policies Toward Nuclear Power." *Policy Studies Review* 5 (Aug. 1985): 96–110.

Frieden, Bernard J., and Marshall Kaplan. *The Politics of Neglect: Urban Aid From Model Cities To Revenue Sharing.* Cambridge, Mass.: MIT Press, 1975.

Friedlander, Ann F., and Richard Spady. *Equity, Efficiency and Resource Allocation in the Rail and Regulated Trucking Industries.* CTS Report 79–4. March 1979.

Fuchs, Edward Paul. "The Politics of Economic Efficiency: Regulatory Reform During the Carter Presidency." Paper presented at the annual meeting of the Southwest Social Science Association, San Antonio, Texas, March 1986.

————. *Presidents, Management, and Regulation.* Englewood Cliffs, N.J.: Prentice-Hall, 1988.

General Accounting Office. *Federal Employees: Trends in Career and Non-*

career Employee Appointments in the Executive Branch. Washington, D.C.: Government Printing Office, 1987.

Gilinsky, Victor. "Full Ahead for Nuclear Power?" *Technology Review* 85 (March 1982): 10–11; 18.

———. "Nuclear Reactors and Nuclear Bombs." *Chemical and Engineering News* 59 (Jan. 19, 1981): 87–90.

Gilmour, Robert. "Policy Formulation in the Executive Branch: Central Legislative Clearance." In *Case Studies in Public Policy Making,* ed. James Anderson, 80–96. New York: Holt, Rinehart, and Winston, 1976.

Golay, Michael. "How Prometheus Came To Be Bound." *Technology Review* 84 (June/July 1980): 29–39.

Goldsmith, William M. *The Growth of Presidential Power: A Documented History.* Vol. 1, *The Formative Years.* New York: Confucian Press, 1980.

Goodman, Marshall R., and Frederic P. Andes. "The Politics of Regulatory Reform and the Future Direction of Nuclear Energy Policy." *Policy Studies Journal* 5 (Aug. 1985): 111–21.

Goodman, Marshall R., and Margaret T. Wrightson. 1986. "Nuclear Energy and the Politics of Reform." Paper presented at the annual meeting of the Midwest Political Science Association, Chicago, April 1986.

Green, Robert L. "Water Pollution Controls for the Iron and Steel Industry." In *Benefit-Cost Analyses of Social Regulation: Case Studies from the Council on Wage and Price Stability,* ed. James C. Miller III and Bruce Yandle, 131–45. Washington, D.C.: American Enterprise Institute, 1979.

Greenstein, Fred I. *The Hidden-Hand Presidency: Eisenhower As Leader.* New York: Basic Books, 1982.

Haldeman, H. R., and Joseph DiMona. *The Ends of Power.* New York: New York Times Books, 1978.

Hardin, Charles M. *Presidential Power & Accountability: Toward a New Constitution.* Chicago: Univ. of Chicago Press, 1974.

Hargrove, Erwin C., and Michael Nelson. *Presidents, Politics, and Policy.* New York: Knopf, 1984.

Hart, John. *The Presidential Branch.* New York: Pergamon, 1987.

Hays, R. Allen. *The Federal Government and Urban Housing: Ideology and Change in Public Policy.* Albany: State Univ. of New York Press, 1985.

Heclo, Hugh. *A Government of Strangers: Executive Politics in Washington.* Washington, D.C.: Brookings Institution, 1977.

———. "OMB and the Presidency—The Problems of Neutral Competence." *The Public Interest* 38 (Winter 1975): 80–98.

Hedge, David. M., and Donald C. Menzel. "Loosing The Regulatory Ratchet: A Grassroots View of Environmental Deregulation." *Policy Studies Journal* 13, no. 3 (March 1983): 599–606.

Henry, Laurin L. "The Presidency, Executive Staffing, and the Federal Bureaucracy." In *The Presidency,* ed. Aaron Wildavsky, 529–57. Boston: Little, Brown, 1969.

Hess, Stephen. *Organizing the Presidency.* Washington, D.C.: Brookings Institution, 1976.

Hoxie, R. Gordon. "Staffing the Ford and Carter Presidencies." In *Organizing and Staffing the Presidency,* ed. Bradley D. Nash, Milton S. Eisenhower, R. Gordon Hoxie, and William C. Spragens. Washington, D.C.: Center for the Study of the Presidency, 1980.

Ingram, Helen M., and Dean E. Mann. "Preserving the Clean Water Act: The Appearance of Environmental Victory." In *Environmental Policy in the 1980's: Reagan's New Agenda*, ed. Norman J. Vig and Michael E. Kraft, 251–271. Washington, D.C.: Congressional Quarterly Press, 1984.

Ink, Dwight A. "The President as Manager." In *Analyzing the Presidency*, ed. Robert E. DeClerico, 134–45. Guilford, Conn.: Duskin, 1985.

Jones, Charles O. *Clean Air: The Policies and Politics of Pollution Control.* Pittsburgh: Univ. of Pittsburgh Press, 1975.

Joskow, Paul L., and Roger G. Noll. "Regulation in Theory and Practice: An Overview." In *Studies in Public Regulation*, ed. Gary Fromm, 1–65. Cambridge, Mass.: MIT Press, 1981.

Kamerschen, Paul. 1979. "Contract Carriage as a Solution to Service Stability in an Unregulated Motor Carrier Industry." *Transportation Research Forum Proceedings* 20: 159–63.

Katz, James E. "The Uses of Scientific Evidence in Congressional Policymaking: The Clinch River Breeder Reactor." *Science, Technology, and Human Values* 9 (Winter 1984): 51–62.

Katzmann, Robert A. "The Federal Trade Commission." In *The Politics of Regulation*, ed. James Q. Wilson. New York: Basic Books, 1980.

———. *Regulatory Bureaucracy: The Federal Trade Commission and Antitrust Policy.* Cambridge, Mass.: MIT Press, 1980.

Kaufman, Herbert. *The Administrative Behavior of Federal Bureau Chiefs.* Washington, D.C.: Brookings Institution, 1981.

Keefe, William J., and Morris S. Ogul. *The American Legislative Process.* Englewood Cliffs, N.J.: Prentice-Hall, 1981.

Kelman, Steven. *Regulating America, Regulating Sweden: A Comparative Study of Occupational Safety and Health Policy.* Cambridge, Mass: MIT Press, 1981.

Kenski, Henry C., and Margaret Corgan Kenski. "Congress Against the President: The Struggle Over the Environment." In *Environmental Policy in the 1980's: Reagan's New Agenda,* ed. Norman J. Vig and Michael E. Kraft, 97–120. Washington, D.C.: Congressional Quarterly Press, 1984.

Kernell, Samuel. *Going Public: New Strategies of Presidential Leadership.* Washington, D.C.: Congressional Quarterly Press, 1986.

Kessel, John. *The Domestic Presidency: Decision-Making in the White House.* North Scituate, Mass.: Duxbury, 1975.

Kidder, Alice E., and Harold G. Willis. *Shipper/Receiver Transportation Mode Choice.* North Carolina A & T State University under contract DOT-OS-80007. March 1980.

Kimm, Victor J., Arnold M. Kuzmack, and David W. Schnare. "Water-borne Carcinogens: A Regulator's View." In *The Scientific Basis of Health and Safety Regulation*, ed. Robert W. Crandall and Lester B. Lave, 229–49. Washington, D.C.: Brookings Institution, 1981.

King, James D., and James W. Riddlesperger, Jr. 1987. "Senate Confirmation of Appointments to the Cabinet and Executive Office of the President." Paper presented at the annual meeting of the American Political Science Association, Chicago, Aug. 1987.

Kingdon, John W. *Agendas, Alternatives, and Public Policies.* Boston: Little, Brown, 1983.

Koenig, Louis W. *The Chief Executive.* New York: Harcourt Brace Jovanovich.

Kohlmeier, Louis M., Jr. *The Regulators: Watchdog Agencies and the Public Interest.* New York: Harper and Row, 1969.

Kraft, Michael E., and Norman J. Vig. "Epilogue." In *Environmental Policy in the 1980's: Reagan's New Agenda*, ed. Norman J. Vig and Michael E. Kraft, 359–74. Washington, D.C.: Congressional Quarterly Press, 1984.

Kraft, Michael E., Bruce B. Clary, and Richard J. Tobin. "The Impact of New Federalism on State Environmental Policy: The Midwestern Great Lakes States." Paper presented at the annual meeting of the Southwestern Social Science Association, San Antonio, Texas, March 1986.

Krasnow, Erwin G., and Lawrence D. Longley. *The Politics of Broadcast Regulation.* New York: St. Martin's, 1978.

Kristol, Irving. "Some Doubts About De-Regulation." *Wall Street Journal*, Oct. 20, 1975, 14.

Ladd, Everett Carll. "Clearing the Air: Public Opinion and Public Policy on the Environment." *Public Opinion* 5 (Feb./March 1982): 16–20.

Lake, Laura M. "The Environmental Mandate: Activists and the Electorate." *Political Science Quarterly* 98 (Summer 1983): 215–33.

Lanouette, William J. 1981. "Reagan's NRC—Seeking to Streamline the Regulation of Nuclear Energy." *National Journal* 13 (Aug. 1, 1981): 1379–81.

———. 1983. "Reagan's NRC Chairman: Nuclear Power Could Still Be A Viable Option." *National Journal* 15 (July 9, 1983): 1457–58.

Lash, Jonathan, Katherine Gillman, and David Sheridan. *A Season of Spoils: The Reagan Administration's Attack on the Environment.* New York: Pantheon, 1984.

Lefevre, Stephen R. "Trials of Termination: President Carter and the Breeder Reactor Program." *Presidential Studies Quarterly* 15 (Spring 1985): 330–42.

LeLoup, Lance T. *Budgetary Politics*. Brunswick, Ohio: King's Court, 1980.

Lester, James P. "New Federalism and Environmental Policy." *Publius* 16 (Winter 1986): 149–65.

Lester, Richard K. "Is the Nuclear Industry Worth Saving?" *Technology Review* 85 (Oct. 1982): 39–47.

Light, Paul C. "When Worlds Collide: The Political-Career Nexus." In *The In-and-Outers: Presidential Appointees and Transient Government in Washington*, ed. G. Calvin Mackenzie, 156–73. Baltimore: Johns Hopkins Univ. Press, 1987.

Lilley, William, III. "Hostile Committee Chairman, Lobbies, Pledge Fight Against Reorganization Plan." *National Journal* (Oct. 10, 1971): 2072–81.

Lundqvist, Lennart J. *The Hare and the Tortoise: Clean Air Policies in the United States and Sweden*. Ann Arbor: Univ. of Michigan Press, 1980.

Lynn, Laurence E., Jr. *Managing the Public's Business: The Job of the Government Executive*. New York: Basic Books, 1981.

———. "The Reagan Administration and the Renitent Bureaucracy." In *The Reagan Presidency and the Governing of America*, ed. Lester M. Salamon and Michael S. Lund, 339–70. Washington, D.C.: Urban Institute, 1984.

MacAvoy, Paul W., and John W. Snow, eds. *Regulation of Entry and Pricing in Truck Transportation*. Washington, D.C.: American Enterprise Institute, 1977.

Mackenzie, G. Calvin. "'If You Want to Play, You've Got to Pay': Ethics Regulation and the Presidential Appointments System, 1964–1984." In *The In-and-Outers: Presidential Appointees and Transient Government in Washington,* ed. G. Calvin Mackenzie, 77–89. Baltimore: Johns Hopkins Univ. Press, 1987.

———. *The Politics of Presidential Appointments*. New York: Free Press, 1981.

Mallet, Roger J. "Emission Standards for New Motorcycles." In *Cost-Benefit Analysis of Social Regulation: Case Studies From the Council on Wage and Price Stability*, ed. James C. Miller III and Bruce Yandle, 113–130. Washington, D.C.: American Enterprise Institute, 1979.

Mansfield, Harvey C. "Federal Executive Reorganization: Thirty Years of Experience." *Public Administration Review* 29 (July/Aug. 1969): 332–45.

———. "Reorganizing the Federal Executive Branch: The Limits of Institutionalism." *Law and Contemporary Society* 35 (Summer 1970): 461–95.

Marcus, Alfred. "Environmental Protection Agency." In *The Politics of Regulation*, ed. James Q. Wilson, 267–303.

Marshall, Eliot. "Hit List at EPA?" *Science* 219 (March 18, 1983): 1303.

———. "Hit Lists Claim a Victim at EPA." *Science* 220 (April 1, 1983): 38.

Marvich, M. Dennis, and G. Cleveland Thornton. *Trucking Service in Two Small Alabama Communities.* U.S. Department of Transportation, Office of the Secretary, Office of Transportation Regulation. March 1980.

McConnell, Grant. *Private Power and American Democracy.* New York: Vintage Books, 1966.

Melnick, R. Shep. *Regulation and the Courts: The Case of the Clean Air Act.* Washington, D.C.: Brookings Institution, 1983.

Menzel, Donald C. "Redirecting the Implementation of a Law: The Reagan Administration and Coal Surface Mining Regulation." *Public Administration Review* 43 (May/June 1983): 411–20.

Milbrath, Lester W. *Environmentalists: Vanguard for a New Society.* Albany: State Univ. of New York Press, 1984.

Mitchell, Robert Cameron. "Public Opinion and Environmental Politics in the 1970's and 1980's." In *Environmental Policy in the 1980's: Reagan's New Agenda,* ed. Norman J. Vig and Michael E. Kraft, 51–74. Washington, D.C.: Congressional Quarterly Press, 1984.

Mitnick, Barry M. *The Political Economy of Regulation: Creating, Designing, and Removing Regulatory Forms.* New York: Columbia Univ. Press, 1980.

Moe, Ronald C. "The Domestic Council in Perspective." *Bureaucrat* 5 (Oct. 1976): 251–72.

Moe, Terry M. 1985. "Control and Feedback in Economic Regulation: The Case of the NLRB." *American Political Science Review* 79, no. 4 (Dec.): 1094–1116.

———. "Political Control and Professional Autonomy: The Institutional Politics of the NLRB." Paper presented at the annual meeting of the American Political Science Association, Washington, D.C., Aug. 1986.

———. 1985. "The Politicized Presidency." In *The New Direction in American Politics,* ed. John E. Chubb and Paul E. Peterson, 235–71. Washington, D.C.: Brookings Institution, 1985.

———. "Regulatory Performance and Presidential Administration." *American Journal of Political Science* 26 (May 1982): 197–225.

Moore, Thomas Gale. "The Beneficiaries of Trucking Regulation." *Journal of Law and Economics* 21 (Oct. 1978): 327–42.

Mosher, Frederick C. *Democracy and the Public Service.* New York: Oxford Univ. Press, 1982.

Moynihan, Daniel P. *Maximum Feasible Misunderstanding: Community Action in the War on Poverty.* New York: Free Press, 1969.

Nash, Bradley D., Milton S. Eisenhower, R. Gordon Hoxie, and William C. Spragens. *Organizing and Staffing the Presidency.* Washington, D.C.: Center for the Study of the Presidency, 1980.

Nathan, Richard P. *The Administrative Presidency.* New York: John Wiley, 1983.

———. "Institutional Change Under Reagan." In *Perspectives on the Reagan Years,* ed. John L. Palmer, 121–143. Washington, D.C.: Urban Institute, 1986.

———. *The Plot That Failed: Nixon and the Administrative Presidency.* New York: John Wiley, 1975.

———. "Political Administration Is Legitimate." In *The Reagan Presidency and the Governing of America,* ed. Lester M. Salamon and Michael S. Lund, 375–79. Washington, D.C.: Urban Institute, 1984.

National Academy of Public Administration. *A Presidency for the Eighties.* Washington, D.C.: National Academy of Public Administration, 1980.

Neustadt, Richard E. "Presidency and Legislation: The Growth of Central Clearance." *American Political Science Review* 48 (Sept. 1954): 641–71.

———. *Presidential Power: The Politics of Leadership From FDR to Carter.* New York: John Wiley, 1980.

"New ICC Chief." *Wall Street Journal,* June 3, 1977, 1.

Newland, Chester A. "The Reagan Presidency: Limited Government and Political Administration." *Public Administration Review* 43 (Jan./Feb. 1983): 1–21.

Nixon, Richard M. *The Memoirs of Richard Nixon.* New York: Grosset and Dunlop, 1978.

Noll, Roger G. *Reforming Regulation.* Washington, D.C.: Brookings Institution, 1971.

Noll, Roger G., and Bruce M. Owen. *The Political Economy of Deregulation: Interest Groups in the Regulatory Process.* Washington, D.C.: American Enterprise Institute, 1983.

Ogul, Morris S. "Congressional Oversight: Structures and Incentives." In *Congress Reconsidered,* ed. Lawrence C. Dodd and Bruce I. Oppenheimer, 317–31. Washington, D.C.: Congressional Quarterly Press, 1981.

Orvis, Charles G. *Trucking Service to Two Small Kansas Communities.* U. S. Department of Transportation, Office of the Secretary, Office of Transportaion Regulation. 1980.

O'Neal, A. Daniel. "No Clamor for Deregulation: Should There Be?" In *Perspectives on Federal Transportation Policy,* ed. James C. Miller III. Washington, D.C.: American Enterprise Institute, 1975.

Page, Talbot, Robert Harris, and Judith Bruser. "Waterborne Carcinogens: An Economist's View." In *The Scientific Basis of Health and Safety Regulation,* ed. Robert W. Crandall and Lester B. Lave, 197–228. Washington, D.C.: Brookings Institution, 1981.

Patterson, Walter C. *Nuclear Power.* New York: Penguin, 1983.

Perry, Charles R. *Deregulation and the Decline of the Unionized Trucking*

Industry. Philadelphia: Industrial Research Unit, The Wharton School, University of Pennsylvania, 1986.

Pfiffner, James P. "Political Appointees and Career Executives: Managing Change and Continuity." Paper presented at annual meeting of the American Political Science Association, Washington, D.C., August 1986.

———. "Strangers in a Strange Land: Orienting New Presidential Appointees." In *The In-and-Outers: Presidential Appointees and Transient Government in Washington,* ed. G. Calvin Mackenzie, 141–155. Baltimore: Johns Hopkins Univ. Press, 1987.

Phillips, Almarin, *Promoting Competition in Regulated Markets*. Washington, D.C.: Brookings Institution, 1975.

Polsby, Nelson W. *Congress and the Presidency*. Englewood Cliffs, N.J.: Prentice-Hall, 1976.

———. "Presidential Cabinet Making: Lessons for the Political System." *Political Science Quarterly* 93 (Spring 1978): 15–25.

Pressman, Jeffrey L., and Aaron B. Wildavsky. 1973. *Implementation*. Los Angeles: Univ. of California Press.

Pustay, Michael W. *The Impact of Federal Trucking Regulation on Service to Small Communities*. Purdue University under contract DOT-OS-70069. March 1979.

Reagan, Michael D., and John G. Sanzone. *The New Federalism*. New York: Oxford Univ. Press, 1981.

Rechichar, Stephen J., and Michael R. Fitzgerald. *The Consequences of Administrative Decision: TVA's Economic Development Mission and Intragovernmental Regulation*. Knoxville: Bureau of Public Administration, The University of Tennessee, 1983.

Redford, Emmette S., and Marlan Blissett. *Organizing the Executive Branch: The Johnson Presidency*. Chicago: Univ. of Chicago Press, 1981.

Reedy, George E. *The Twilight of the Presidency*. New York: New American Library, 1970.

Reynolds, John, and Leonard Champney. "Streams of Policy Change and the Altered Currents of Nuclear Regulation." Paper presented at the annual meeting of the Midwest Political Science Association, Chicago, April 1986.

Rockman, Bert A. "America's Departments of State: Irregular and Regular Syndromes of Policy Making." *American Political Science Review* 75 (Dec. 1981): 911–27.

Rohr, John A. *To Run a Constitution: The Legitimacy of the Administrative State*. Lawrence: Univ. Press of Kansas, 1986.

Rosenbaum, Walter A. *Environmental Politics and Policy*. Washington, D.C.: Congressional Quarterly Press, 1985.

Rossiter, Clinton. *The American Presidency*. New York: Harcourt, Brace, and World, 1960.

Safire, William. *Before the Fall: An Insider's View of the Pre-Watergate White House*. New York: Doubleday, 1975.

Salamon, Lester M. "The Presidency and Domestic Policy Formulation." In *The Illusion of Presidential Government*, ed. Hugh Heclo and Lester M. Salamon, 177–201. Boulder, Colo.: Westview, 1981.

———. "The Question of Goals." In *Federal Reorganization: What Have We Learned?* ed. Peter Szanton, 58–84. Chatham, N.J.: Chatham House, 1981.

Sanders, Elizabeth. "The Presidency and the Bureaucratic State." In *The Presidency and the Political System*, ed. Michael Nelson, 379–409. Washington, D.C.: Congressional Quarterly Press, 1988.

Schick, Allen. "The Problem of Presidential Budgeting." In *The Illusion of Presidential Government,* ed. Hugh Heclo and Lester M. Salamon, 85–111. Boulder, Colo.: Westview, 1981.

Schlesinger, Arthur M., Jr. *The Imperial Presidency*. Boston: Houghton Mifflin, 1973.

Schorr, Burt, and Andy Pasztor. "Reaganites Make Sure That the Bureaucracy Toes The Line on Policy." *Wall Street Journal,* Feb. 10, 1982, 1, 25.

Schott, Richard L., and Dagmar S. Hamilton. *People, Positions, and Power: The Political Appointments of Lyndon Johnson*. Chicago: Univ. of Chicago Press, 1983.

Seidman, Harold. *Politics, Position, and Power: The Dynamics of Federal Organization*. Oxford: Oxford Univ. Press, 1980.

Seligman, Lester G. "Presidential Leadership: The Inner Circle and Institutionalization." *Journal of Politics* 18 (1956): 410–26.

Shanley, Robert A. "Presidential Executive Orders and Environmental Policy." *Presidential Studies Quarterly* 12 (Summer 1983): 405–16.

Shull, Steven A. "President-Agency Relations in Civil Rights Policy." Paper presented at the annual meeting of the American Political Science Association, Washington, D.C., Aug. 1986.

Sierra Club. *The Sierra Club Foundation 1984–1985 Annual Report*. San Francisco: Sierra Club, 1985.

Silver, E. G. 1984. "Recent Developments: General Administrative Activity." *Nuclear Safety* 25, no. 5 (Sept./Oct.): 720–30.

Smith, V. Kerry (Ed). *Environmental Policy Under Reagan's Executive Order*. Chapel Hill: Univ. of North Carolina Press, 1984.

Snitzler, James R., and Robert J. Byrne. *Interstate Trucking of Fresh and Frozen Fruits and Frozen Poultry Under the Agricultural Exemption*. MRR–24, U. S. Department of Agriculture, Marketing Research Division. March 1958.

———. *Interstate Trucking of Frozen Fruits and Vegetables Under the*

Agricultural Exemption. MRR–316, U.S. Department of Agriculture, Marketing Research Division. March 1959.

Stanfield, Rochelle L. "Nuclear Waste Politics." *National Journal* 18 (Oct. 4, 1986): 2371–73.

———. "Resolving Disputes." *National Journal* 18 (Nov. 15, 1986): 2764–68.

Stewart, Joseph Jr., and Jane S. Cromartie. "Partisan Presidential Change and Regulatory Policy: The Case of the FTC and Deceptive Practices Enforcement, 1938–1974." *Presidential Studies Quarterly* 12 (Fall 1982): 568–73.

Stockman, David A. *The Triumph of Politics: Why the Reagan Revolution Failed*. New York: Harper and Row, 1986.

Stone, Alan. *Regulation and Its Alternatives*. Washington, D.C.: Congressional Quarterly Press, 1982.

Sundquist, James L. *The Decline and Resurgence of Congress*. Washington, D.C.: Brookings Institution, 1981.

Swallow, Wendy. "Has the Freedom of Information Act Worked—Or Has It Worked Too Well?" *National Journal* 13 (Aug. 15, 1981): 1470–73.

Taff, Charles A. 1955. *Commercial Motor Transportation*. Homewood, Ill.: Richard D. Irwin, 1955.

Taylor, Stuart Jr. 1983. "Ex-EPA Aide Says He Drew Up 'Pro and Con' Lists on Personnel." *New York Times*, March 17, 1983: B14.

Thomas, Steve, and John Surrey. "What Makes Nuclear Power Plants Break Down?" *Technology Review* 83 (May/June 1981): 57–66.

Thompson, Frank J., and Michael J. Scicchitano. "State Enforcement of Federal Regulatory Policy: The Lessons of OSHA." *Policy Studies Journal* 13, no. 3 (March 1985): 591–98.

Tobin, Richard J. "Revising the Clean Air Act: Legislative Failure and Administrative Success." In *Environmental Policy in the 1980's: Reagan's New Agenda*, ed. Norman J. Vig and Michael E. Kraft, 227–49. Washington, D.C.: Congressional Quarterly Press, 1984.

Tolchin, Susan J., and Martin Tolchin. *Dismantling America: The Rush to Deregulate*. New York: Oxford Univ. Press, 1983.

Tomkin, Shelley Lynne. "Playing Politics in OMB: Civil Servants Join the Game." *Presidential Studies Quarterly* 15 (Winter 1985): 158–70.

Tribe, Lawrence H. "Policy Science: Analysis or Ideology?" *Philosophy and Public Affairs* 2 (Fall 1972): 66–110.

Vaden, Ted. "Truckers Fear Continued Deregulation Drive." *Congressional Quarterly Weekly Reports* 34 (Nov. 1976): 3249–54.

Vig, Norman J. "The President and the Environment: Revolution or Retreat." In *Environmental Policy in the 1980's: Reagan's New Agenda*, ed. Norman J. Vig and Michael E. Kraft, 77–95. Washington, D.C.: Congressional Quarterly Press, 1984.

Walcott, Charles, and Karen M. Hult. "Organizing the White House:

Structure, Environment, and Organizational Governance." *American Journal of Political Science* 31 (Feb. 1987): 109–25.

Waldmann, Raymond. "The Domestic Council: Innovation in Presidential Government." *Public Administration Review* 36 (May/June 1976): 260–68.

Waldo, Dwight. *The Administrative State*. New York: Ronald Press, 1948.

Walker, David B. *Toward a Functioning Federalism*. Boston: Little, Brown, 1981.

Waterman, Richard W. "The Presidential Conundrum: The Benefits and Risks of the New Techniques of Presidential Leadership." Paper presented at the annual meeting of the Midwest Political Science Association, Chicago, March, 1988.

Waterman, Richard W., and Edward J. Ahern. 1983. "A Re-examination of the Capture Theory: The Cases of the Airline and Trucking Industries." Paper presented at the annual meeting of the Southwest Social Science Association, Houston, Texas, March 1983.

Weidenbaum, Murray L. "Free the Fortune 500." In *Taking Sides: Clashing Views on Controversial Issues,* ed. Theodore D. Goldfard, 72–79. Guilford, Conn.: Dushkin, 1983.

Weingast, Barry R. "Regulation, Reregulation, and Deregulation: The Political Foundations of Agency Clientele Relationships." *Law and Con temporary Society* 44 (Winter 1981): 148–77.

Weingast, Barry R., and Mark J. Moran. "Bureaucratic Discretion or Congressional Control? Regulatory Policymaking by the Federal Trade Commission." *Journal of Political Economy* 91 (Oct. 1983): 765–800.

Welborn, David M. *Governance of Federal Regulatory Agencies*. Knoxville: Univ. of Tennessee Press, 1977.

Williams, Wenmouth Jr. 1976. "Impact of Commissioner Background on FCC Decisions: 1962–1975." *Journal of Broadcasting* 20 (Spring 1976): 239–56.

Wilson, James Q. "The Politics of Regulation." In *The Politics of Regulation,* ed. James Q. Wilson, 357–94. New York: Basic Books, 1980.

Wilson, Woodrow. *Congressional Government: A Study in American Politics*. 1885; rpt. Baltimore: John Hopkins Univ. Press, 1981.

Winter, J. C., and Ivan W. Ulrey. *Supplement to Interstate Trucking of Frozen Fruits and Vegetables Under the Agricultural Exemption*. Supplement to MRR–316, U.S. Department of Agriculture, Marketing Research Division. July 1961.

Wood, B. Dan "Bureaucrats, Principals, and Responsiveness: The Case of the Clean Air Act." *American Political Science Review* 82 (1987): 213–34.

——. "Reagan's Environmental Policy and Federal Clean Air Enforcement Activities." Paper presented at the annual meeting of the Southwest Social Science Association, Dallas, Texas, March 1987.

Yandle, Bruce. 1985. "FTC Activity and Presidential Effects." *Presidential Studies Quarterly* 15 (Winter 1985): 128–35.

Zeckhauser, Richard. "Procedures for Valuing Lives." *Public Policy* 23 (Fall 1975): 419–64.

Congressional Hearings and Reports

House of Representatives

Committee on Appropriations. *HUD-Space-Science-Veterans Appropriations.* 92nd Cong., 2nd. sess., 1972.

Committee on Government Operations. *Overview Hearing on Operations of the Department of Housing and Urban Development.* 92nd Cong., 1st sess., 1971.

Committee on Interstate and Foreign Commerce. *Use of Cost-Benefit Analysis by Regulatory Agencies.* Hearings. 96th Cong., 1st sess., 1979.

Committee on Post Office and Civil Service. *Final Report on Violations and Abuses of Merit Principles in Federal Employment.* Report of the Subcommittee on Manpower and Civil Service. 94th Cong., 2nd sess., 1976.

———. *Impact of Budget Cuts on Federal Statistical Programs.* Hearings. 97th Cong., 2nd sess., 1982.

Committee on Public Works and Transportation. *Examining Current Conditions in the Trucking Industry and the Possible Necessity for Change in the Manner and Scope of Its Regulation.* Hearings before the Subcommittee on Surface Transportation. 96th Cong., 1st and 2nd sess., 1979–80.

———. *Oversight of the Motor Carrier Act of 1980.* Hearings before the Subcommittee on Surface Transportation. 97th Cong., 1st sess., 1981.

———. *Regulation of Carriers Subject to the Interstate Commerce Commission.* Hearings before the Subcommittee on Surface Transportation. 94th Cong., 2nd sess., 1976.

Senate

Committee on Commerce. *Appointments to the Regulatory Agencies.* 94th Cong., 2nd sess., 1976.

———. *National Transportation Policy Report, Senate Report No. 445.* Report of the Special Study Group on Transportation Policies of the United States. 87th Cong., 1st sess., 1961.

———. *Surface Transport Legislation.* Hearings before the Subcommittee on Surface Transportation. 92nd Cong., 2nd sess., 1972.

————. *Nominations — February-March 1973*. Hearings. 93rd Cong., 1st sess., 1973.

Committee on Commerce, Science, and Transportation. *Economic Regulation of the Trucking Industry*. Hearings. 96th Cong., 1st and 2nd sess., 1979–80.

————. *The Impact on Small Communities of Motor Carriage Regulatory Revision*. 95th Cong., 2nd sess., 1978.

————. *Nomination — Secretary of Transportation*. Hearings. 96th Cong., 1st sess., 1979.

————. *Nominations to the Interstate Commerce Commission*. Hearings on the nominations of Marcus Alexis, Darius W. Gaskins, Jr., and Thomas A. Trantum. 96th Cong., 1st sess., 1979.

————. *Oversight of the Motor Carrier Act of 1980*. Hearings. 97th Cong., 1st sess., 1981.

————. *Report Together with Additional and Minority Views on the Senate Committee on Commerce, Science, and Transportation*. 96th Cong., 2nd sess., 1980.

Committee on Environment and Public Works. *American Attitudes toward Clean Air*. Hearings before the Subcommittee on Environmental Pollution. 97th Cong., 2nd sess., 1982.

————. *Fiscal Year 1983 Budget Review*. Hearings. 97th Cong., 2nd sess., 1982.

————. *Implementation of the Toxic Substances Control Act*. Hearings before the Subcommittee on Toxic Substances and Environment. 97th Cong., 2nd sess., 1982.

————. *Nomination of James K. Asselstine*. Hearings. 97th Cong., 2nd sess., 1982.

————. *Nominations of Alan Hill and W. Ernest Minor*. Hearings. 97th Cong., 1st sess., 1981.

————. *Nominations of Anne M. Gorsuch and John W. Hernandez, Jr.* Hearings. 97th Cong., 1st sess., 1981.

————. *Nominations of Frederic A. Eidsness, Jr., and Rita M. Lavelle*. Hearings. 97th Cong., 2nd sess., 1982.

————. *Nominations of John P. Horton and Kathleen M. Bennett*. Hearings. 97th Cong., 1st sess., 1981.

————. *Nominations of Matthew A. Novick and John A. Todhunter*. Hearings. 97th Cong., 1st sess., 1981.

————. *Nominations of Nunzio J. Palladino and Thomas M. Roberts*. Hearings. 97th Cong., 1st sess., 1981.

————. *Reauthorizations*. Hearings before the Subcommitte on Toxic Substances and Environmental Oversight. 97th Cong., 1st sess., 1981.

Committee on Judiciary. *Report on Regulatory Agencies to the President-*

Elect [Landis Report]. Report of Subcommittee on Administrative Practice and Procedure. 86th Cong., 2nd sess., 1960.

Other Government Documents and Reports

Commission on Organization of the Executive Branch of the Government. *The Independent Regulatory Agencies: A Report with Recommendations.* Washington, D.C.: Government Printing Office, 1949.
———. *Legal Services and Procedures.* Washington, D.C.: Government Printing Office, 1955.
Congressional Budget Office. "The Impact of Trucking Deregulation on Small Communities." February 1980.
Council on Environmental Quality. *Environmental Quality 1981.* Washington, D.C.: Government Printing Office, 1982.
———. *Environmental Quality 1982.* Washington, D.C.: Government Printing Office, 1983.
Department of Energy. *1983 Survey of Nuclear Power Plant Construction Costs.* Washington, D.C.: Government Printing Office, 1984.
Department of Housing and Urban Development. *Housing in the Seventies: A Report on the National Policy Review.* Washington, D.C.: Government Printing Office, 1974.
———. *Housing in the Seventies: Working Papers Volumes 1 and 2.* Washington, D.C.: Government Printing Office, 1976.
Department of Transportation. "The Impact of Federal Trucking Regulation on Service to Small Communities." March 15, 1979.
General Accounting Office. *Federal Employees: Trends in Career and Noncareer Employee Appointments in the Executive Branch.* Washington, D.C.: Government Printing Office, 1987.
Interstate Commerce Commission. *Annual Report* [1978]. Washington, D.C.: Government Printing Office, 1979.
———. *Annual Report* [1980]. Washington, D.C.: Government Printing Office, 1981.
———. *Annual Report* [1984]. Washington, D.C.: Government Printing Office. 1985.
———. *Initial Report of the Motor Carrier Task Force.* Washington, D.C.: Government Printing Office, 1979.
Nuclear Regulatory Commission. *Staff Report to the President's Commission on the Accident at Three Mile Island.* Washington, D.C.: Government Printing Office, 1979.
———. *Three Mile Island: A Report to the Commissioners and to the Public.* Vol. 1 and 2. Washington, D.C.: Government Printing Office, 1980.

Office of Management and Budget. "Prepared Written Statement of James C. Miller III, Director, Office of Management and Budget, before the Subcommittee on Intergovernmental Relations, Committee on Governmental Affairs, United States Senate, on Executive Regulatory Oversight." Jan. 28, 1986.

———. *Regulatory Program of the United States Govrnment, April 1, 1987–March 31, 1988.* Washington, D.C.: Government Printing Office, 1987.

Office of Technology Assessment. *Nuclear Power in an Age of Uncertainty.* Washington, D.C.: Government Printing Office, 1984.

Papers Relating to the President's Departmental Reorganization Program: A Reference Compilation. Washington, D.C.: Government Printing Office, 1972.

President's Commission on the Accident at Three Mile Island. *The Need for Change—The Legacy of TMI.* Washington, D.C.: Government Printing Office, 1979.

President's Private Sector Survey on Cost Control. *Report on the Department of Energy, the Federal Energy Regulatory Commission, and the Nuclear Regulatory Commission.* Washington, D.C.: Government Printing Office, 1983.

———. *Report on the Environmental Protection Agency, the Small Business Administration, and the Federal Emergency Management Agency.* Washington, D.C: Government Printing Office, 1983.

President's Summit Conference on Inflation. *The Conference on Inflation.* Washington, D.C.: Government Printing Office, 1974.

———. *The Economists' Conference on Inflation.* Vol. 1. Washington, D.C.: Government Printing Office, 1974.

President's Task Force on Model Cities. *Model Cities: A Step toward the New Federalism.* Washington, D.C.: Government Printing Office, 1970.

Public Papers of the Presidents: Ronald Reagan, 1981. Washington, D.C.: Government Printing Office, 1982.

Index

Stone, Alan, 76, 209
Sullivan, William, 123–24
superfund, 110, 119, 174
super-secretaries, 65–66, 74, 127, 181
Sundquist, James, 196, 199
Swallow, Wendy, 225
Szanton, Peter, 204

Taff, Charles, 212
Taft, William Howard, 35
"take care" clause (of the Constitution), 16–17
Taney, Roger, 33
Taylor, Stuart, 218
Teamsters, 86, 88, 98, 101, 103, 187
Tennessee Valley Authority (TVA), 110–11
Tenure of Office Act, 34
Thomas, Larry, 216
Thomas, Lee, 136
Thompson, Frank, 198
Thornburgh, Richard, 153
Thornton, G. Cleveland, 211
Three Mile Island (TMI), 144, 148, 151, 153, 156–57
Tobin, Richard, 127, 219–20, 222
Todhunter, John, 138
Tolchin, Martin, 165, 216, 223, 226–27
Tolchin, Susan, 165, 216, 223, 226–27
Tomkin, Shelly, 204
Tower, John, 31
Tozzi, Jim, 131
Train, Russell, 113, 117
Train v. New York, 71
Trantum, Thomas, 90–91, 97, 104
Tribe, Lawrence, 205
Truman, Harry, 6, 28, 46
Tugwell, Rexford, 197

Udall, Morris, 147
Ulrey, Ivan, 211
Urban Affairs Council, 54, 205–6
U.S. Department of Agriculture, 61, 64, 80
U.S. Department of Commerce, 85
U.S. Department of Defense, 48, 66

U.S. Department of Energy, 90, 146, 155, 160–61, 165, 226
U.S. Department of Health, Education, and Welfare (HEW), 52, 58, 60–61, 69, 108, 176
U.S. Department of Housing and Urban Development (HUD), 11; analysis of administrative presidency strategy and, 170, 172, 176, 177; Nixon and HUD, 51–74, 104, 115
U.S. Department of the Interior, 52, 56, 61, 81, 108, 127, 173
U.S. Department of Justice, 96, 113, 117, 123, 174
U.S. Department of State, 57
U.S. Department of Transportation, 52, 56, 61, 64, 80, 85–87, 91, 96, 104, 212
U.S. Department of Treasury, 61
U.S. v. Lovett, 203

Vaden, Ted, 213
Vietnam, 6, 29, 52
Vig, Norman, 217–18, 221–22, 225
Volpe, John, 52, 55–56, 58, 62

Walcott, Charles, 5, 196
Waldo, Dwight, 196
Walker, David, 44, 139, 205, 219, 223
War Powers Act of 1973, 19
Washington, George, 7, 34
Watergate scandals, 6, 12, 22, 66, 68, 70–71, 73, 176–77
Waterman, Richard, 196, 200–1, 212, 214
Watkins, Goldie, 224
Watt, James, 127
Weidenbaum, Murray, 215
Weinberger, Caspar, 60, 65, 207
Weiner v. U.S., 203
Weingast, Barry, 199
Welborn, David, 44, 83, 204, 212
White House Personnel Office (WHPO), 59

Presidential Influence and the Administrative State was designed by Sheila Hart, composed by Lithocraft, Inc., printed by Cushing-Malloy, Inc., and bound by John H. Dekker & Sons, Inc. The book is set in Sabon. Text stock is 60–lb. Glatfelter Natural Antique.